TOTAL DESTRUCTION
OF THE
TAMIL TIGERS

Some of Paul Moorcraft's other books on military topics

A Short Thousand Years: The End of Rhodesia's Rebellion (1979)

Contact 2: The Struggle for Peace (1981)

Africa's Superpower (1982)

African Nemesis: War and Revolution in Southern Africa, 1945-2010 (1994)

Axis of Evil: The War on Terror (with Gwyn Winfield and John Chisholm) (2005)

The New Wars of the West (with Gwyn Winfield and John Chisholm) (2006)

Inside the Danger Zones: Travels to Arresting Places (2010)

Shooting the Messenger: The Politics of War Reporting (with Phil Taylor) (2011)

The Rhodesian War: A Military History (with Peter McLaughlin) (2011)

Mugabe's War Machine (2011)

TOTAL DESTRUCTION
OF THE
TAMIL TIGERS

The Rare Victory of Sri Lanka's Long War

PAUL MOORCRAFT

Pen & Sword
MILITARY

First published in Great Britain in 2012 by
PEN & SWORD MILITARY
an imprint of
Pen & Sword Books Ltd
47 Church Street
Barnsley
South Yorkshire
S70 2AS

ISBN 978 1 78159 153 6 Hardback
ISBN 978 1 78159 304 2 Paperback

A CIP catalogue record for this book is
available from the British Library

Typeset in Times New Roman
by CHIC GRAPHICS

Printed and bound in England
by CPI Group (UK) Ltd, Croydon, CR0 4YY

Pen & Sword Books Ltd incorporates the imprints of
Pen & Sword Aviation, Pen & Sword Family History, Pen & Sword Maritime,
Pen & Sword Military, Pen & Sword Discovery, Wharncliffe Local History,
Wharncliffe True Crime, Wharncliffe Transport, Pen & Sword Select,
Pen & Sword Military Classics, Leo Cooper, Remember When,
The Praetorian Press, Seaforth Publishing and Frontline Publishing

For a complete list of Pen & Sword titles please contact
PEN & SWORD BOOKS LIMITED
47 Church Street, Barnsley, South Yorkshire, S70 2AS, England
E-mail: enquiries@pen-and-sword.co.uk
Website: www.pen-and-sword.co.uk

Contents

AFTER THE SHOOTING WAR

About the Author

Professor Paul Moorcraft has worked extensively in Asia as a foreign correspondent, lecturer and author. He covered wars and political conflicts in Cambodia, Vietnam, Nepal, Pakistan and Afghanistan, as well as reporting on large countries such as China and producing TV documentaries in small ones, for example the Maldives. In Sri Lanka he travelled throughout the war zones in the north and east of the island. He has interviewed many of the senior political and military leaders on both sides of the war, as well as foreign diplomats, members of non-government organizations and journalists.

The former editor of a range of specialist security and foreign policy magazines, Professor Moorcraft also worked for Western TV networks as a freelance producer/war correspondent. He has also lectured full-time in journalism, politics and international relations at ten major universities in the US, Britain, Southern Africa and Australasia He was a Distinguished Radford Visiting Professor in Journalism at Baylor University, Texas. He has worked in 30 war zones in Africa, the Middle East and the Balkans, often with irregular forces, most recently in Afghanistan, Iraq, Palestine/Israel, and in the various regional conflicts in Sudan. He headed a 50-strong British observer mission in Sudan for the national elections in 2010, as well as reporting on the 2011 referendum in the now Republic of South Sudan.

Dr Paul Moorcraft is a former senior instructor at the Royal Military Academy, Sandhurst, and the UK Joint Services Command and Staff College. He worked in Corporate Communications in the Ministry of Defence in Whitehall. In 2003 he was recalled to government service in Whitehall and Iraq.

He is the author of a wide range of books on military history, politics, travel and crime, as well as being an award-winning novelist. Paul Moorcraft is a regular contributor to British, US and South African newspapers (with frequent columns across the political spectrum from the *Washington Times* to the UK *Guardian* as well as writing for 35 years for his home-town newspaper, the Cardiff-based *Western Mail,* and temporary home, Johannesburg, for *Business Day* for the last five years). He also toils as a broadcaster and pundit on BBC TV and radio (for BBC Radio Wales for 35 years) and more recently Sky and Al-Jazeera. He has produced a number of TV news documentaries for Britain's Channel Four News.

His co-authored study, with Professor Phil Taylor, *Shooting the Messenger: The Politics of War Reporting*, was published in 2008; the updated paperback in 2011. Dr Moorcraft also co-authored the much-acclaimed *The Rhodesian War: A Military History* in 2008 (paperback 2011). This was followed by *Mugabe's War Machine* in 2011. His autobiographical *Inside the Danger Zones: Travels to Arresting Places* came out in 2010.

Dr Moorcraft is the director of the Centre for Foreign Policy Analysis, London, as well as being a Visiting Professor at Cardiff University's School of Journalism, Media and Cultural Studies.

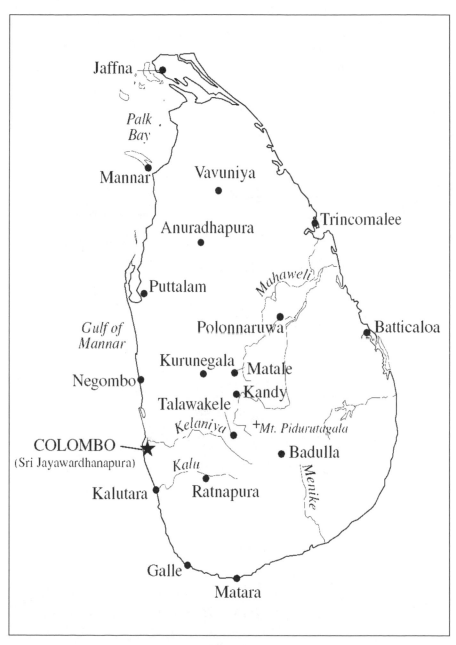

Map 1

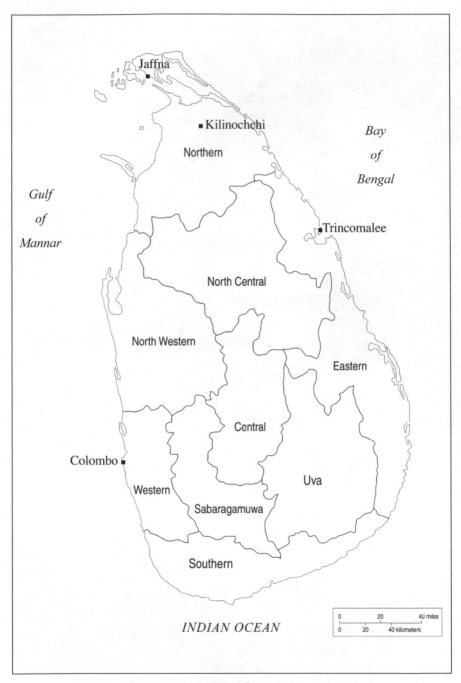

Jaffna

■Kilinochehi

Northern

Bay

of

Bengal

Gulf

of

Mannar

■Trincomalee

North Central

North Western

Eastern

Central

Colombo ■

Uva

Western

Sabaragamuwa

Southern

| 0 | 20 | 40 miles |
| 0 | 20 | 40 kilometers |

INDIAN OCEAN

Map 2

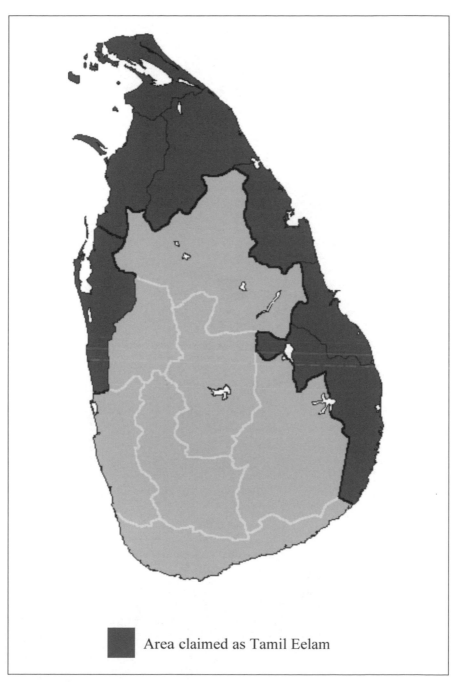

Area claimed as Tamil Eelam

Map 3

Map 4

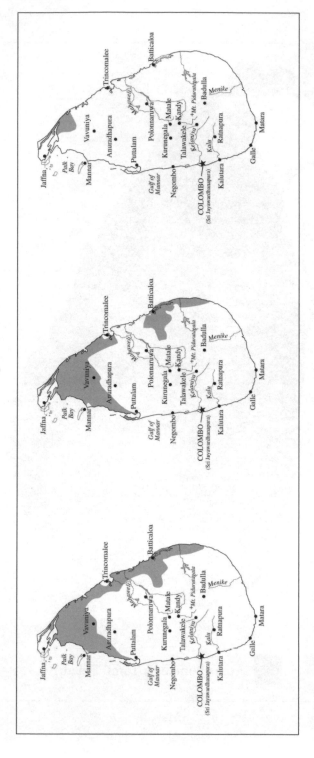

Losing ground. Shaded areas denote:

1. Tiger control in November 2005

2. February 2007

3. January 2009

Abbreviations

APC	Armoured Personnel Carrier
CCHA	Consultative Committee on Humanitarian Assistance
CFA	Ceasefire Agreement
CID	Criminal Investigations Department
COIN	Counter-Insurgency
DMI	Director of Military Intelligence
DMK	*Dravida Munnetra Kazhagam* (Dravidian Progress Foundation)
HE	His Excellency, very common term for the Sri Lankan President
ICRC	International Committee of the Red Cross
IDP	Internally Displaced Person
IED	Improvised Explosive Device
IISS	International Institute of Strategic Studies (London)
IPC	Inshore Patrol Craft
IPKF	Indian Peacekeeping Force
JVP	*Janatha Vimukthi Peramuna* (People's Liberation Front)
LLRC	Lessons Learnt and Reconciliation Commission
LRP	Long Range Patrol
LTTE	Liberation Tigers of Tamil Eelam
MBRL	Multi-Barrel Rocket Launcher
PLOTE	People's Liberation Organization of Tamil Eelam
P-TOMS	Post-Tsunami Operational Management Structure
RABS	Rapid Action Boat Squadron
RAW	Research and Analysis Wing (Indian intelligence)
RPG	Rocket-Propelled Grenade
SAS	Special Air Service (UK)
SBS	Special Boat Squadron (Sri Lankan Navy)
SBS	Special Boat Service (Royal Navy)

Secretary (the)	Universal term in military circles for Gotabaya Rajapaksa, the Permanent Secretary at the Ministry of Defence
SF	Special Forces
SIOT	Special Infantry Operational Team
SIS	State Intelligence Service
SLFP	Sri Lanka Freedom Party
SLMM	Sri Lanka Monitoring Mission
SLN	Sri Lankan Navy
STF	Special Task Force
TID	Terrorism Investigation Department
TNA	Tamil National Alliance
TRO	Tamil Rehabilitation Organization
TULF	Tamil United Liberation Front
UAV	Unmanned Aerial Vehicle
UNP	United National Party
UPFA	United People's Freedom Alliance

Brief Timeline

1948	Ceylon gains independence from Britain
1956	Sinhala made sole official language. Over 100 Tamils killed in protests
1971	Sinhalese Marxist JVP uprising
1972	Ceylon changes name to Sri Lanka. Buddhism became primary religion
1976	LTTE formed
1983	Thirteen soldiers killed in LTTE ambush. Sparks anti-Tamil riots in Colombo and elsewhere. Start of what Tigers called Eelam War I (1983–87)
1987	Deployment of Indian troops
1988–90	Second JVP uprising
1990	Indian troops leave, fighting between LTTE and army escalates (Eelam War II 1990–95). Thousands of Muslims expelled from north by LTTE
1991	Assassination by LTTE of Rajiv Gandhi
1993	LTTE kills President Premadasa
1995–2002	Eelam War III
2002	Beginning of long but uneasy ceasefire
2004	Split in LTTE – Colonel Karuna defects. December, tsunami kills 30,000
2005	Prime Minister Mahinda Rajapaksa wins presidential race
2006	Fighting resumes in the east. Peace talks in Geneva fail. Start of Eelam War IV. Fighting intensifies; hundreds of Tamils rounded up in Colombo in June
2008	Ceasefire officially abrogated. Launch of massive northern offensive
2009	January. Army captures LTTE capital of Kilinochchi. Heavy fighting as LTTE pushed into the Cage. May, Prabhakaran killed
2010	Rajapaksa wins presidential and parliamentary elections by a landslide

Introduction

Why the Sri Lankan War is Important

In the first months of 2009 the Sri Lankan government forces destroyed the Tamil Tigers, who had fought an insurgency for twenty-six years. The outright military victory brought peace to the island. Arguably, it was the first time since the end of the Second World War that a large-scale indigenous insurgency had been defeated by force of arms. Elsewhere, negotiations, in the end, had usually prevailed.

Sri Lanka and Ireland are islands of roughly the same size. The Sri Lankan government's victory was as if the British Army had killed thousands of Irish Republican Army members in a mere few months to end completely the conflict in Northern Ireland. Instead, years of complex negotiations, aided (or impeded) by international diplomacy from the Republic of Ireland and the US, and a willingness by the Provisional IRA to negotiate a settlement, created an eventual political deal. The Northern Ireland conflict was modern Europe's longest insurgency and it splutters on, even though just a few dozen active hardliners still see violence as an option.

In Sri Lanka, the Tigers wanted to create 'Tamil Eelam', an independent state on the island. Since their final defeat Sri Lanka has not had to suffer any significant post-conflict insurgent violence (or 'terrorism') – no bombings at all; so far. This is unusual. If the peace is truly permanent, the conflict may well teach other nations how to end wars and bring peace.

Historians might argue that Sri Lanka's military victory is not unique. In Malaya, the British colonial forces set a rare template in successful (and sometimes brutal) counter-insurgency (COIN). But Malaya was exceptional in many ways, not least in that the British had set an imminent date to quit the colony, unlike the French in Algeria. The colonial authorities were also fighting an insurgency emerging out of a minority within the majority Malay population. The Americans tried to replicate the Malayan experience in Vietnam, but failed not least because they could not duplicate the 'hearts and minds' policy, a phrase that originated in the Malayan insurgency.

Historians could also point to the crushing of Islamist rebellions in, say, Egypt or Syria in the period before the Arab Spring. Yes, a number of insurgencies have been vanquished. There is no equivalent in the modern world, however, for the complete defeat of large-scale insurgency, often in semi-conventional warfare, which had lasted decades.

The Sri Lankans did try the conventional diplomatic route – ceasefires and international mediation, for example via India and later Norway – and endless peace negotiations in a variety of foreign capitals. In the end, in 2005–06, the government decided that talks had led to a strategic cul de sac. The Colombo government decided to win their long war, by a mixture of political will, military reform, and a highly focused war council. This decision was assisted by strategic and tactical errors on the part of the LTTE. The Sri Lankan administration also skilfully engaged with international and regional powerbrokers, especially India and China, and reached an understanding with the United States. This allowed the government to sidestep pressure from the United Nations and other western powers.

The massive military campaign in early 2009 provoked a barrage of international criticism, because of the deaths of thousands of civilians trapped in the final envelopment by Sri Lankan forces. Caught between swamp, lagoon, sea and the advancing pincer movement of the army, the Tigers fought to the last, although they expected international pressure to secure the evacuation of their leadership. The denouement of the Tigers has been dubbed 'the Cage'.

The fate and the numbers of civilians caught in the death throes of the Tigers are still the subject of much international diplomatic and media controversy. So is the fact that the Sri Lankan forces managed to exclude nearly all international journalists from the Cage and indeed much of the war. They also censored local Sri Lankan correspondents. Militaries in the best western democracies did note – quietly – that a strong correlation might have existed between the absence of media and the presence of a clear military victory. The (inaccurate) legacy of the Vietnam myth – the US lost because of TV pictures – is still pervasive in even the most politically correct of North Atlantic Treaty Organization (NATO) armies.

Sri Lanka's lengthy conflict was savage – a war psychosis infected the whole population of the beautiful if benighted island. Tens of thousands were killed on both sides in this complex struggle. Now the country is rebuilding not only its economy, especially tourism, but above all its ethnic social cohesion. Some outsiders predict that the war has not finished, and the Tamil diaspora around the world encourages this revanchism. Yet the new optimism of the dominant Sinhalese and the apparent acceptance of the Tamil minority who live on the island suggest that, as in Northern Ireland, the vast majority of the war-weary population want to get on with their own family lives and careers.

This book considers the origins of the war and the four main phases of the fighting. It analyzes also the structures of the main combatants, their equipment and their tactics. International negotiations are examined, as well as the foreign military support for both sides. The final military surge, the trapped civilians and the international outcry are considered in some detail. At times the media war, especially on the internet, seemed almost as intense as the actual fighting. As the Arab Spring has suggested, international TV networks, the internet and especially social media *may* sometimes catalyze as well as merely cover major conflicts.

The book concludes with an overall assessment of the war and asks whether the Sri Lankan experience has relevance for other current and future conflicts. This analysis is not a moral tract. Rather, it is intended to be an objective military assessment of what works in war and peace.

My background is that I have spent much of the past forty years concerned with insurgency and counter-insurgency: as a theoretician in various universities and in the British Ministry of Defence in Whitehall, and as a senior instructor at the Royal Military Academy, Sandhurst, and later at the Joint Services Command and Staff College; and as a close observer in the field, often in the front line, either in UK government service or, more often, as a freelance correspondent for TV, radio and print, in over thirty war zones in the Balkans, Asia, the Middle and Near East, and Africa, where I often worked alongside insurgents. I have written a wide range of books on military conflicts covering Afghanistan to Zimbabwe.

In Sri Lanka, I walked as much of the final battlefield, 'the Cage', as possible, sometimes on foot very slowly in minefields as they were being cleared, and by a variety of military vehicles, planes and helicopters around numerous other battle sites. I managed to secure access to all levels of political leadership in the government, from the President to the top brass and non-commissioned officers in the army, navy, air force and police, as well as senior bureaucrats and intelligence officials. On the other side, I managed to secure an interview with 'K P' (Kumaran Pathmanathan), the most senior surviving Tiger leader, despite his close, though comfortable, house arrest in Colombo. I also visited hardcore Tigers still in prison. I spoke to Tamils in the diaspora and also interviewed foreign diplomats and workers from non-government aid organizations and the media.

I have generally avoided detailed references in order to simplify the narrative, though some of the relevant sourcing is disclosed in the bibliographic endnotes. Some of the sources have not been given partly because they wished to remain anonymous. I have also shifted away from academic practice by simplifying some of the nomenclature, especially of place names. For example, instead of giving both Tamil and Sinhalese names, I have usually opted for the names better known in English – the use of any name is not intended to show favour to one side. Indeed, I have tried to be as objective as I can be about a highly charged and vicious war. No doubt I have made factual mistakes and errors of interpretation, for which I apologize in advance. I trust that any infelicities can be rectified in future editions.

Above all, I have tried to provide an accessible narrative account of the war in the hope that it can reach a more general audience, not just Sri Lankan or military specialists. Interpreting history by simplifying wars – as I have done in many other books – can bring opprobrium as well as praise to an author. I have simply done my best.

Paul Moorcraft
Surrey Hills, England
30 June 2012.

Chapter 1

The Background to the War

Sun, sand and sea ... and monsoons

Despite romantic imperial connotations as the 'pearl of the Indian Ocean', the island has suffered from millennia of religious, ethnic, caste and class conflict. Peace has intruded as well, mainly under colonial rule, though historians are forbidden to mention that because of union rules and PC regulations. Sri Lanka has had many names, often reflecting whoever was in charge of most or just some of the island or sometimes merely because of the linguistic quirks of travellers and mapmakers. Early explorers all attested to the island's physical charms, however. As Portugal's national poet, Luís Vaz de Camões, noted (in translation):

> *Ceylon lifts her spicy breast,*
> *And waves her woods above the watery waste*

This is an apt summary of an island of mountains, forests, lagoons and sea. The land mass is 65,610 square kilometres (25,332 square miles); the coastline comprises 1,056 miles which was handy for all the seaborne invaders. In Sanskrit the country was known as 'Tambapanni' because of the copper-coloured beaches. Later, visiting Greeks and Romans called it 'Taprobane', although Ptolemy's famous second-century AD map inscribes it as 'Taprobanam'. Arab sailors called it 'Serendib', a corruption of the Sanskrit 'Sinhaladvipa'. The Portuguese settled on 'Celao', which had begun as 'Si-lan' (a Chinese version) and was transformed by medieval travellers such as Marco Polo into 'Seylan'. The English version – 'Ceylon' – was the modern compromise. The Sinhalese had long called their land 'Lanka' and the country was officially renamed in 1972 as 'Sri Lanka' (the prefix means 'holy' or 'beautiful'). The state became formally (in English) the 'Democratic Socialist Republic of Sri Lanka' in 1978.

Despite its travails, foreigners were irresistibly drawn to the country. Arthur C. Clarke lived there because he was sucked in: he believed that parts of the island had an extra-strong gravitational pull. The science-fiction writer mapped out much of the future in a place where Clarke felt at home for nearly fifty years. Sri Lankans may well find Clarke's views on gravity-plus persuasive, because they are deeply superstitious and often obsessed by astrology. More conventional modern visitors, 'tourists' if you must, would notice first the apparently homicidal driving, especially the trishaws. From their drivers' windscreens dangle a variety of charms – Jesus, Buddha, Ganesh and the odd guru. They need all the divine insurance they can get. Tourists would also be told: 'In areas of "human-elephant conflict" do not venture out after dark.' While Clarke pontificated on black holes, many guidebooks of the last decades simply left blank large parts of the country, especially the north, especially at night. That was the permanent but unmentionable elephant in the room – the war.

The island has endured many unconventional visitors and not just war tourists, though most used to come in search of booty. Early explorers relied upon trade winds – aptly named for the ancient seafarers often had to wait a long time to catch winds back to Greece, China or Arabia. They came for spices and gems, but their becalmed ships often forced them to mingle with the local cultures and especially the women. If the topography allowed for easy naval incursions, the climate also influenced military campaigns inland. The low mountains were dumping grounds for the monsoon rains. Sri Lanka is unusual in that it has *two* monsoon seasons, coming from different directions at different times. The modern capital, Colombo, and the southwest get soaked from April to October. The east coast is drenched from November to January. The monsoons mark out what seasons the country has. Because it is so close to the equator, the temperatures are high throughout the year, with an average of 27C (80F), though often the humidity makes it feel much hotter. Understanding the sometimes steep, often wooded/jungle topography and the difficulties of soldiering in humidity, heat then torrential monsoon rains, makes it clear why sometimes the terrain and climate stalled the fighting in the long civil war. It is also a relatively crowded island: the size of Scotland but with four times the population (around 20 million).

The rulers: from the Stone Age to 1948

An indigenous Stone Age culture can be traced back to 10,000BC; a few hundreds of this Veddha people, related *inter alia* to the indigenous tribes of Australia, have survived, just, until today. The first Sinhalese arrived in the country in the sixth century BC – probably from northern India.

Buddhism, later to become a powerful religious influence in the country, came in the mid-third century BC. A great civilization grew up around the cities of Anuradhapura (a kingdom from 200 BC to AD 1000) and Polonnaruwa (1070 to 1200). In the fourteenth century a south Indian dynasty established a Tamil kingdom in Sri Lanka's northern areas, closest to the Indian mainland.

The previous three sentences are extracted from a Central Intelligence Agency summary of the country's history. This might be suitably neutral and even anthropologically correct, but it would not be sufficient for a history overpopulated with foundation myths. In shorthand, the lion people (*sinha* is a lion) vied for supremacy with the tigers, the symbol of the early Tamil settlers; it was also a supposed ethnic clash between Dravidians and Aryans, which later played into the hands of those who portrayed the Sinhalese majority as proto-fascists.

Few (sane) Western historians, without an incisive knowledge of the country's early history, and a detailed command of the relevant languages, would attempt a definitive conclusion about the historical precedents for Sinhalese and Tamil claims. Both sides can display a fanatical fervour (and *fantastical* fervour, for example regarding medieval flying machines or the power of holy relics) when it comes to establishing who came first and with what religious sanction. It is somewhat like the antagonists in the Balkan wars of the 1990s – few could discuss any military campaign there without reference to events of hundreds of years before, and often with the aid of maps, perhaps dating to the division of the Roman Empire. Yet much of the Balkan ethnic hostility had been whipped up by partisan politicians and media dating from the 1980s. Likewise, much of the Sri Lankan fratricide could be traced to events which followed independence in 1948, especially regarding language rights.

Relying totally on the CIA summary would be inadequate. Tamil military leaders were powerful as far back as 200 BC, and a successful Tamil invasion took place from AD 432; although Year One of the Buddhist era in Sri Lanka is 543 BC. The first entries in the *Mahavamsa* ('Great History') date from this time, and the arrival of the Sinhalese led by Prince Vijaya. The first Sinhalese royals traced their lineage to a union between a handsome lion and an amorous princess.

In the modern period, a crucial date was 1505, the arrival of the Portuguese who soon occupied parts of the coastal areas. Nevertheless, indigenous kingdoms, especially the polity centred on Kandy, resisted this encroachment. After 1656 the Dutch defeated the Portuguese on land and at sea, and foreigners secured a tighter grip of the island, though Kandy, hidden in deep jungle, continued to rule itself, along with some strange customs. In 1660 a young sailor from London named Robert Knox was held in Kandy for nineteen years. He recounted his often favourable impressions of the kingdom in a journal. An exception was his description of occasional deaths by elephant: executions by trampling or goring. His journal was filched in part by Daniel Defoe as the basis for *Robinson Crusoe*.

In 1796, the British — concerned about revolutionary France's ambitions — wrested the island from the Dutch. As a bonus, the coveted natural harbour at Trincomalee became a Royal Navy staging post. In 1802 Ceylon was declared a British Crown Colony. In 1815 the last king of Kandy was deposed and exiled, though guerrilla wars spluttered on. The last rumblings of resistance were inspired by a (false) rumour in 1848 that women were to be taxed according to the size of their breasts – which perhaps indicated some of the less lofty preoccupations of the British colonizers.

On a more positive note, the British did their usual civilizing thing – not least building roads and railways. In comparison with India, Ceylon was far more intensively colonized as witnessed by the dramatic transformation of the landscape that occurred with the establishment of the plantation economy. The central highlands were changed from forest to farm. Tens of thousands of Tamils were imported from south India to work on first the coffee and then the far more successful tea plantations. The 'new Tamils' did not integrate well with the existing minority Tamil population, not least because the incomers soon almost equalled the numbers of indigenous Tamils.

In 1915, the centenary of the abdication of the last independent king of Kandy, fired up by overzealous Buddhist nationalism, Sinhalese mobs attacked Muslim traders in the southwest. From then on, the Muslims were usually caught between the more aggressive demands of the larger Tamil minority and the dominant Sinhalese majority.[1] Despite the ethnic tensions, the various subject peoples of the Crown could see an advantage in allying to end colonial rule, though Tamils felt that the future division of power should be 50:50 between the Sinhalese and the various minorities. The Ceylon National Congress was formed after the Great War; it was made up of all the main communities, although the Tamils were later to break away.

The British introduced a universal franchise in 1931 (including women) and, following the Indian model, rapid moves were made towards self-governance. The Sinhalese often accused the British of divide and rule by favouring the Tamil minority, especially in the civil service. Nevertheless, both sides, along with other minorities such as the Muslims, often worked together towards the goal of political independence. Many on both sides agitated for the equal use of both vernacular languages, Tamil and Sinhala, to replace English as the dominant medium of government, courts and higher education. The indigenous languages with their distinct alphabets were mutually unintelligible, although more Tamils tended to speak Sinhalese (and English) as well as their own tongue, not least for commercial reasons.

When Japan made rapid military advances in the Second World War, and as India itself looked increasingly vulnerable, Ceylon's strategic position made it 'the Clapham Junction of the Indian Ocean'; it became the location of Lord Louis Mountbatten's South-East Asia Theatre Command. Trincomalee was a vital naval sanctuary, even though it was bombed by the Japanese. The wartime demand for rubber and the presence of so many Allied service personnel helped to boost the local economy. The military also waged an incessant campaign to eradicate malaria. As part of their anglicization process, the British left a lasting legacy of loyalty to good secondary schools. The Spartan standards of the English public schools were faithfully reproduced. When a new British headmaster turned up at Trinity College, Kandy, he found 1,000 boys waiting to be caned as an opening duty. Well into the twenty-first century the ruling elites in the Sinhalese community formed classic school-based 'old-boy' networks within the political parties, the bureaucracy and especially the armed forces. They practised, for life, their own form of *omerta*.

As the war-weary British scuttled from the Raj, and looked on almost helplessly at the blood-soaked partition of the former jewel of Empire into India and Pakistan, the Ceylonese achieved their own national freedom in 1948. Soon after independence the leaders of the indigenous Tamils colluded with the Sinhalese-dominated government to send 'home' to India around half-a-million Tamils, many of whom had been in Sri Lanka for a generation or more. The Buddhist Sinhalese constituted perhaps 70 per cent of the population; the Hindu Tamils (both local and remnants of those more recently arrived from India) made up perhaps 20 plus per cent. Muslims were small in number but influential; they came from as far as Malaya or Indonesia or were descendants of much earlier Arab traders. Many spoke Tamil. In addition the population comprised mixed-race descendants of the Christian Dutch and Portuguese, sometimes called Burghers. Portuguese names proliferate in the modern Sri Lankan society; the legacy is particularly noticeable at graduation ceremonies. Many other smaller communities had thrived, not least the British settlers, as well as Jews and small groups of distinct African communities, who had arrived as slaves, first of the Portuguese.

At independence Sri Lanka was a Rubik's Cube of religion, race and languages, though caste was also a rigid social denominator. Regional identities were also significant – elites emerged in Colombo and Kandy for example, frequently based on class and education (often at British universities) as well as historical or even royal lineages. Then party-political cleavages were added to the mix. Ceylon escaped the massacres of the independence of the Raj; ethnic tragedies were merely delayed, however.

The first years of independence

The first prime minister of independent Ceylon, D. S. Senanayake, a former agriculture minister in the colonial days, was keen to develop and improve on the celebrated irrigation systems of the independent kingdoms. This was related to his overall Sinhalese nationalist agenda, another part of which was to prevent the 'New Tamil' plantation workers voting for Tamil parties which could oppose his United National Party (UNP). The prime minister urged his Indian counterpart, Pandit Jawaharlal Nehru, to accept them as Indian nationals who should return home.

Sri Lankan politics has tended to be dynastic. Senanayake senior was replaced – briefly – by his son, Dudley; and then a former general took over the ruling UNP. S. W. R. D. Bandaranaike's Freedom Party displaced the UNP. Bandaranaike championed the language issue – that Sinhala alone should replace English. Many in the new leadership had been educated at Oxbridge but now nationalism demanded not pin-striped suits but white cloth draped from the waist with a loose long-sleeved white shirt. This was Sri Lanka's version of Chairman Mao's buttoned-up tunic. In 1956 Bandaranaike's 'Sinhala Only Act' prompted Tamil riots. This Act was a catalyst of the war that was to come.

Ethnic rioting and a rapid decline in economic conditions after the nationalization of key industries, such as transport and ports, created a crisis of confidence. Tamils living in Colombo and other areas were driven out and sought refuge in ancestral lands in the north and east. Many Sinhalese moved south. This was the beginning of what later became known as 'ethnic cleansing'. Bandaranaike tried to end the chaos by offering to do a deal with the Tamils. A Buddhist monk took exception to this: he walked up to the prime minster and emptied a revolver into him at point-blank range. This set a pattern for a long series of political assassinations by all sides in the Sri Lankan imbroglio.

After a brief caretaker government, the dynastic ping-pong continued. Dudley Senanayake came back for three months. Then Mrs Sirimavo Bandaranaike, the assassinated prime minister's widow, won power on a wave of sympathy, re-confirming the tradition of family rule. Not only was she the world's first female premier, but she did not even hold a seat in parliament (she soon secured one in the Senate). While politicians swapped seats on the gravy train, ethnic tensions continued to simmer. Mrs Bandaranaike ensured that half-a-million 'New Tamils' were deported to India, with 300,000 allowed to stay. While her gender milestone played well as a beacon of the international non-aligned movement, her domestic record was poor. Some members of the armed forces and police plotted to step in to sort out the political mess, a common international fashion of the 1960s. The plot failed but it was to have a long-lasting impact on the relationship between the military and politicians.

The failed coup

In 1961, in the Tamil-dominated areas, the Mahatma Gandhi-influenced *satyagraha* movement had grown. This was non-violent opposition to the government's language policy. Army units were stationed in Jaffna and, under the Public Security Act, a state of emergency was declared. A number of Tamil leaders were arrested under the emergency regulations. Even after the Tamil non-violent agitation abated, the state of emergency was maintained. One advantage to the government was that the volunteer elements of the armed forces could legally remain mobilized and thus be utilized against not only ethnic Tamil disturbances but also trade union-led strikes. In November 1961 port workers struck in Colombo. Other industrial action followed and trade union leaders called for a national general strike in January 1962. The armed forces and police made contingencies to maintain essential services. Leftist leaders suggested that the government was about to install military rule. Extra media censorship was introduced.

The military conspiracy must be understood in the paranoia of the time. A coup was indeed planned for 27 January 1962. The reasons for the conspiracy – a small but well-planned one – were varied. Some of the middle-ranking police and military men considered Mrs Bandaranaike unfit to rule, especially in a country which was too left-leaning (for them) and threatened by strikes and ethnic disturbances. It was to be a very British coup in many ways, in that a 'gentlemanly' code of behaviour was stressed, although the model suggested at the time was the military coup in Pakistan in 1958.

The Sri Lankan coup has been variously defined: firstly as a 'Buddhist' coup, because 'not a drop of blood was to be shed'. It could be more accurately defined as a 'Christian coup' because the overwhelming number of people eventually charged were Protestants and Catholics drawn from the Sinhalese, Tamil and Burgher communities. Only three were Buddhists. The officer corps was dominated by Christians with large minorities of Tamils and Burghers. Mrs Bandaranaike had rapidly promoted Sinhalese officers. The Christian elite, which had dominated under British rule, felt that its position was being eroded; religion more than race played a role in the conspiracy. Nevertheless, the 'Colonels' coup' is also an apt description because many of the conspirators were of colonel or lieutenant colonel rank or equivalent. None of the three service chiefs or the head of police was involved. It would be misleading to over-emphasize the religious element because other factors, including concern about the left-wing nature of the government, were at play.

The *putsch* was intended to be bloodless, swift and precise. Codenamed Operation HOLDFAST, the plan was to seize strategic positions in and around Colombo, capture the Radio Ceylon building (there was no television then), detain senior politicians and especially the prime minister, and to get her to announce a 'voluntary' transfer of power. (In many ways, albeit on an inevitably smaller scale, this coup attempt prefigured the successful army-police coup against the democratically elected Maldivian president, Mohamed Nasheed, in February 2012.)

The first part of Operation HOLDFAST was the establishment of a military dictatorship. The second phase was 'indirect democracy' where a council of ex-prime minsters would assist the governor-general in ruling the country. The third phase was a parliamentary election based on a new constitution guaranteeing equality to all races and religions. In short, some of the coup planners were trying to pre-empt a Sinhalese-Buddhist oligarchic regime. Great attention was paid to good treatment of those to be arrested. The plotters fretted about no harm coming to Mrs Bandaranaike and her son and two 'beautiful' daughters. The Bandaranaikes were to be sent off to comfortable exile in England, and the plotters had even spent time worrying about how the eldest daughter could gain access to Oxford. Some of the passwords prepared for the plot smacked of an Ealing comedy (for example, 'Dowbiggin', named after the 'father of British colonial police').

It was not to be. At the last minute the prime minister changed her itinerary for entirely incidental reasons. She did not suspect a coup, but the plotters thought she had been warned. Then followed a comedy of errors when some of the plotters started the coup and others confessed to the authorities. Thirty-one people were arrested and others were sent on leave or early retirement. The court case was entitled 'the Queen vs Liyange'. A part of the indictment was that the plotters had 'conspired to wage war against the Queen'. Douglas Liyange was a senior civil servant, but he was not the coup mastermind. A much more prominent planning role had been taken by a former deputy inspector-general of the police, Sydney de Zoysa. The Bandaranaike government had a particular distaste for de Zoysa, however, and did not want his name to go on the top of the charge-sheet and thus win fame in a landmark case involving the name of the British sovereign.

Officially, the suspects were treated well, being housed in a two-storey building within Temple Trees, the prime ministerial compound. Mrs Bandaranaike was given a good press – she was said to have paid careful attention to the detainees' welfare, even, it was said, checking the toilets herself to see that all was in order. In reality, some of the suspects were poorly treated, and one died in detention. Twenty-four were charged in court and, after a protracted trial, eleven were found guilty. But the drama was continued when the case was referred to the Privy Council in London. The appeal by the eleven was upheld on a technicality and they were discharged.

The legacy of the failed coup was an enduring one. Mrs Bandaranaike's suspicions of the military and its threat to civilian rule seemed confirmed. More Sinhalese Buddhists were rapidly promoted in the military, but the role of the armed forces was downgraded. Some units were merged or disbanded, especially those suspected of backing Operation HOLDFAST, including those led by officers recently trained at the Royal Military Academy, Sandhurst. Funding for military hardware was slashed, especially in the navy which lost its blue-water capability. Inter-service cooperation, especially in the form of joint operations, was suspended. The military was ill-equipped for what was to come, starting with the 1971 Janatha Vimukthi Peramuna (JVP) insurrection. In the future, the armed forces could be strengthened, as they would have to be for the Tamil insurgency, only if they were completely controlled by the civilian leadership.

The much more powerful armed forces of the period following 2005/6 were to be unified, yes, but subservient to very close and co-ordinated civil-military direction under the administration of Mahinda Rajapaksa. A major factor in the breakdown of the relationship between a prime architect of victory in 2009, General Sarath Fonseka, and the government was the suspicion of a possible coup. In the annex to his resignation letter, General

Fonseka accused the president of doubting the loyalty of the army and being paranoid about a coup. Until Fonseka, who chose to challenge President Rajapaksa in the polls, senior defence chiefs tended to avoid direct involvement with politics, partly because of the legacy of the aborted coup in 1962.

Politics as normal

Once fears of military rule had died down after 1962, civilian politics returned to its usual dynastic revolving doors. Dudley Senanayake came back to power in 1965 and — like his father — tried to improve agriculture. After five years Mrs Bandaranaike came again through the same revolving door; she decided to name the country Sri Lanka and declare a republic (within the Commonwealth). Buddhism was declared the state religion and Sinhala was designated the official language. Her nationalization of the plantations and allegations of her corruption led to electoral defeat and later expulsion from parliament.

Tamil discontent mounted, as it did among left-wing Sinhalese, divided inevitably among various pro-Russian and pro-Chinese factions. Ultra-leftists formed the JVP. During an attempted national insurrection in 1971 over 10,000 JVP rebels, mainly young men, were arrested and some were killed or 'made to disappear'. A handful of police stations were completely overrun and over sixty policemen and soldiers were killed. This was the height of the Cold War so East, West and non-aligned rushed to help. China condemned the JVP as 'Guevarists' and sent loans to Colombo. The US supplied weapons. The Indians provided men and equipment as back-up. The bloodshed in Ceylon was not, however, a media event. The press pack focused on the mass killing in East Pakistan and the slide into another Pakistan-Indian war.

The government tried to win over JVP left-wing dissidence (some of it encompassing Tamils as well as Muslims) by bringing Sinhalese youth into the new nationalist Buddhist narrative of the 1972 republican constitution. Many of the conventions to protect minorities in the first constitution were jettisoned. (The policy did not work: a second bloodier JVP rebellion broke out in 1987–89.) The revolt had created a precedent for Tamil rebellion (and sometimes Tamil agitators shared prison cells with JVP revolutionaries); the 1972 constitution had seemed to Tamils a confirmation of second-class status. Even worse for Tamils, who had traditionally prized higher education, was the new university admission system, which discriminated against them.

Mrs Bandaranaike doubled her domestic troubles by nationalizing all remaining private agriculture and tea estates, practically the only economic areas that were prospering. In 1977 Junius Richard (J. R.) Jayawardene led the United National Party back in to power to try to clean up the mess left by the fatally doctrinaire socialism of his predecessor. His model was not China but Singapore. Jayawardene also tried to address the language crisis. Tamil and English were promoted to the status of 'national' languages although this was still one notch down from Sinhalese, the 'official' language. He also advocated proportional representation to guarantee parliamentary seats to the minority parties. He established too a French-style presidential system which could create chaos if president and premier of different (usually squabbling) parties had to co-habit.

The island's economy began to improve – tourists and foreign investments flowed in. After years of dynastic political infighting and corruption, it seemed as though Sri Lanka could allow itself some fresh optimism. Then the looming war of secession began in earnest.

Chapter 2

The Rise of the Tigers

The causes of the Sri Lankan civil war have many parallels with the Palestinian v Israeli cycle of violence. Two peoples and two nationalisms fired up by different languages, religions and ancient histories contended for the same small piece of sanctified land. During the colonial period many of the Tamils, often educated in English-speaking mission schools, prospered in the British administration. At the same time many Hindu Tamils reacted against anglicization and established their own schools, temples and societies. Increasingly, Tamils thought of themselves as a separate and distinct community. The long political debate about parliamentary representation in the colonial period and then in the early days of independence galvanized the notions of separate identity. This was enhanced by the occasional pogroms suffered in Sinhalese-dominated areas. In addition, state-sponsored colonization schemes in favour of the Sinhalese changed the regional demographic balance, especially in the Eastern province considered by many Tamils to be part of their homeland. In the 1970s Tamil-language films, books and magazines from the cultural core in India's Tamil Nadu state were discouraged then banned. Foreign exchange allowances for Tamils to study in India were also curbed. The government argued that many of these moves were inspired by economic self-sufficiency as part of the socialist agenda, but the result was that Tamils felt they were being cut off from their cultural roots and left isolated.

Although the government believed that its university reforms were founded partly on positive discrimination to help geographically isolated Sinhalese, again the Tamils argued that it was a further apartheid-like move against them, especially in their favoured educational careers in medicine and engineering. Tamils found themselves more and more excluded from the bureaucracy. The middle-class Tamils' fluency in English was no longer an advantage when Sinhala became the official language. Around 75 per cent of the population were fluent in Sinhala, and the remaining 25 per cent were proficient in Tamil; many in the middle classes were competent in both and often in English as well.

Citizenship was also an issue. Many of the so-called 'New' or 'Estate' Tamils were shipped home. Large numbers of the 600,000 to be repatriated remained, but they were effectively unable to vote, travel abroad or be active in civil society. (It was not until 2003 that these stateless Tamils in the 'hill country' were given full citizenship.)

Facing such inequalities, the concept of regional self-government on a federalist model became popular. The Federal Party, an offshoot from the All Ceylon Tamil Congress Party, advocated autonomy. Some Tamils joined Sinhalese-dominated national parties, while others began to move in the opposite direction – the advocacy of a totally independent Tamil state. Anton Balasingham, of mixed Hindu-Catholic parentage, became the dominant theoretician of independence. A former journalist who worked as a translator for the British High Commission in Colombo, he moved to England, where a substantial Tamil diaspora was based. He helped to develop a new founding myth for militant separatism based on the first-millennium Chola empire; the tiger was the symbol of the Chola state.

The Tamil United Liberation Front (TULF) was forged from the more radical Tamil groups. It adopted the Vaddukoddai Resolution (named after the village where they met) which demanded a Tamil independent state – 'Tamil Eelam'. In the 1977 general election it won eighteen seats in the north and east. In 1983 Tamils in parliament and in the civil service were required to take an oath of allegiance to the unified state of Sri Lanka. Tamils openly supporting a separate state were effectively barred from public office.

The die had been cast much earlier, however, when many of the radical groups had assumed the necessity of armed struggle. Initially, around thirty groups claimed to represent the revolutionary cause, though only five – *inter alia* the Tamil Eelam Liberation Organization and the Eelam Revolutionary Organization of Students – could persuasively boast any effective structure and ideology. Soon they were to be swallowed up – by persuasion or brute force – by one dominant independence movement: the Liberation Tigers of Tamil Eelam – the LTTE (founded in 1976) – led by Velupillai Prabhakaran.[2]

The Colombo government did try to appease some Tamil demands, especially in education, but it was too little too late. A full-scale war loomed. The Tigers became probably the most disciplined, deadly and effective insurgency of its era. The LTTE was to wage a war lasting twenty-six years – from 1983 to 2009.

Chapter 3

Outbreak of the War

The initial violence, especially in the Jaffna peninsula, was akin to gang warfare. It was more a tropical version of 1920s Chicago rather than Vietnam's Tet offensive. Bank robberies funded assassinations, *hartals* (strikes), and sabotage of government installations. The Tigers targeted moderate Tamils who were condemned for advocating a dialogue with the Colombo government. The first significant assassination was Alfred Duraiappah, the mayor of Jaffna, on 27 July 1975, allegedly by the hand of the LTTE leader himself. At dawn, as the mayor was on his way to a temple, Prabakharan fired a volley of homemade bullets from a rusty old revolver. The state would not exact its retribution for thirty-four years – as the Tiger leader became the most notorious man in the country and also a modern-day Scarlet Pimpernel. He was also held personally responsible for the murder of a Tamil MP in 1977. The Tigers killed leaders of rival Tamil groups as ferociously as they targeted Sinhalese police and army personnel.

By the mid-1980s they were the dominant insurgent force in the peninsula. The small and relatively untrained government armed forces reacted clumsily or over-reacted brutally and were soon, in Tamil eyes, transformed into an army of occupation. After two policemen were killed, Sinhalese policemen were accused, in June 1981, of torching the illustrious Jaffna library, a strikingly elegant building containing rare Tamil manuscripts. Tamils saw this as cultural genocide. Two years later government troops were blamed for damaging the partially restored building and the new collection of archives that was being assembled.

Some of the police violence was not instinctively aimed at Tamils. Both the small army and police force were nowhere near as disciplined as they later became. For example, if a policeman were killed in the south, his comrades took it as their right to bash a few Sinhalese heads, and worse, in retaliation. Sometimes, the army and police and even the respectable members of the air force would indulge in punch-ups and very occasionally wreck messes and police stations. One example of ill-discipline was the so-called Rajarata Mutiny. A soldier was killed during the 18 May 1983 polling in Jaffna. A scratch unit, including, literally, cooks and clerks, rioted in the local market and rampaged against local Tamils. Later, four of the sergeants were sentenced to be discharged from the army; over sixty soldiers deserted in protest. The unit was reformed and some of the officers were punished. Amid the growing lawlessness in the north the armed forces and police needed to show extra discipline not less.

The Tamil TULF party had tried periods of mourning and fasts. The angry 'boys' in the militant groups, however, wanted no more of Gandhi-style *satyagraha*. Strikes had worked for a while perhaps, but soon Guevara was to replace the Mahatma. In July 1983 Prabhakaran led a deadly ambush, triggered by a landmine, on an army patrol outside the town of Thirunelveli. The troops had arrived in Jaffna the previous day. The LTTE claimed their attack was revenge for the assault of three Tamil women at an army camp (although Prabhakaran later admitted that it was a retaliation for the death of his close comrade, Charles Anthony). One officer and twelve soldiers were killed. The response was immediate. In Jaffna many Tamils were dragged from their homes and beaten; over forty were killed. The army admitted that its troops had 'gone berserk'. The reaction was even more tragic in Colombo when the thirteen military fatalities were flown to be buried at the Borella cemetery. After a delay in the funeral arrangements, a restive crowd pelted the police with stones. Angry mobs of Sinhalese roamed the city with clubs and, worse, tyres and petrol, to anticipate the awful Soweto-style burning necklace deployed in the anti-apartheid unrest. Tamil shops were looted and burned. Innocent Tamils were murdered in their homes, although sometimes Sinhalese neighbours took extraordinary risks to hide and protect them.

Gangs, including — according to Tamil and foreign witnesses — members of the security forces, checked for ID cards and tested people held at roadblocks with difficult-to-pronounce Sinhalese words. When homes were searched Tamils later claimed that some of the attackers carried voter registration lists, seen as evidence of official involvement. The government put the death toll at around 300, though Tamils claimed up to ten times that number. Thousands were wounded and raped, and numerous homes and shops were looted and burned. Even Tamils in prisons were murdered by their Sinhalese cellmates.

The 1983 attacks in Colombo, known to the Tamils as 'Black July', sparked the civil war. To many Tamils, it was their *Kristallnacht*. Some

Tamils fled north by any transport, some escaped in ships provided by India, while others stayed in the south and tried hard to assimilate, not least by removing the *pottu,* the small dot that Hindus wear on their forehead. Many of the well-educated and wealthy families sought refuge abroad, however, in India, Canada, England and Australia. Some made large fortunes. With memories of their homeland seared by Black July, they donated enormous sums to the international financial network which funded the Tigers' savage campaign against the Sinhalese and Muslim population in their home country. The flight of so many refugees to India stirred up the Tamil Nadu state government as well as the politicians in the political Centre. Black July and the arson of Tamil culture at the Jaffna library were potent propaganda tools to prompt military intervention. India had shown its military muscle in confronting China in the 1962 border war, and had nurtured the independence of Bangladesh after its war with Pakistan in 1971. India had levered East Bengal from its parent state; could the same happen for Tamil Eelam? As Indian military intelligence had trained and now started arming Tamil separatists from Sri Lanka (while suppressing any copycat separatism in Tamil Nadu), Colombo feared that its internal conflict could soon be internationalized by the intervention of the regional superpower.

The Indians continued to train Sri Lankan Tamil militants for three years after the 1983 clashes. Around 5,000 young Tigers and their local rivals underwent basic training, especially in jungle warfare, as well as sabotage tactics. The age-old smuggling runs from southern India to the Jaffna peninsula brought in relatively modern small arms. Occasional groups of Tamils had already been sent to Lebanon to be trained by the Palestine Liberation Organization. Most returned home early but some of the radical Islamist suicide tactics were taken on board, soon to be developed in dramatic fashion at home in Sri Lanka.

The Sri Lankan armed forces tried to respond to the new militancy, but they were little more than a ceremonial army, partly because civilian governments feared a repetition of the aborted coup of 1962.The 11,000-strong army had some experience of hard policing and soft counter-insurgency during the first JVP uprising and had not hesitated to quell a Sinhalese revolt. There were few qualms now about bashing Tamil rebels, but the almost entirely Sinhalese army was ill-equipped to counter the young men trained by the vastly superior Indian army. The Tigers were disciplined, well-motivated and determined to protect not just their ancestral homeland but also their families. The government army was poorly led, partly because the politicization of appointments meant that good officers were kept back by placemen. Poor pay, deficient training, old and ill-co-ordinated equipment procurement and totally inadequate logistics (troops often had to hitch-hike or catch buses to the front) all boded ill for Colombo's first attempts at COIN on the cheap and on a wide front.

Chapter 4

Eelam War I (1983–87)

From 1984/5 until the intervention of the Indian troops in 1987, newly trained Tamil rebels faced the largely ineffective regular forces of the state. This has been called 'Eelam War I'. Both sides accused the other of atrocities. The Tigers indulged in spectaculars – the massacres of Sinhalese civilians at Kent and Dollar farms in 1984; the government was blamed for the Kumudini boat massacre when twenty-three Tamils were killed. The Tigers tightened their grip – removing local opposition by killing Tamils and Sinhalese, military and civilians, any who opposed their vision of Tamil Eelam. The Colombo government did attempt to talk to the Tigers but the war continued. Government troops tried to eliminate LTTE rebels in their heartland around Jaffna, but by 1987 the fighting was beginning to move from isolated insurgency to more large-scale operations on both sides. In May–June 1987 the government's Operation LIBERATION tried to control the peninsula via conventional warfare. This operation was led by more competent officers, including the then Major Gotabaya Rajapaksa, later to play a dominant role in the final stages of the war. This operation almost netted Prabhakaran who escaped by the skin of his teeth from advancing troops at Velvettiturai.

On 6 July 1987, just after nightfall, a truck packed full of explosives battered its way through the gates of a school in the village of Nelliady, on the Jaffna peninsula. It was a temporary army base. The driver was Vallipuram Vasanthan, a dedicated Tiger. His suicide bomb killed eighteen soldiers and wounded twenty-one. Tigers on the perimeter shot dozens more, reaching a tally of forty soldiers killed by the morning. The truck driver, better known by his nom de guerre of 'Captain Miller', was the first of the 'Black Tigers', the elite and soon to-be-infamous suicide squad of the LTTE. The lessons of the PLO were being applied in earnest. In Beirut in October 1983, a Palestinian 'martyr' had killed 241 US troops guarding the International airport. That truck bomb prompted the rapid exit of US Marines from Lebanon. Captain Miller's iconic bomb attack could not have the same effect on a government fighting on its own territory.

The government offensive had pushed back the Tigers to the south into the jungles of the Vanni area, and then on through to Jaffna, where the guerrillas were penned into the area surrounding Jaffna town itself. Colombo hoped to finish off the Tigers, but the possibility of extensive urban fighting and the inevitable death of many Tamil civilians provoked outrage in India and especially in Tamil Nadu. Rajiv Gandhi's government started to air-drop food and medicine to the besieged fighters in June 1987. Sri Lanka's sovereignty was publicly breached.

The central Indian government as well as the state authority in Tamil Nadu played ambiguous and often contradictory roles in the Sri Lankan war. New Delhi had constant ambitions to project its power as the regional hegemon, and worried also about the contagion effect of separatism on its own actual and potential insurgencies throughout the country, including Tamil Nadu with its 60 million Tamils. Ethnic kinship in that state played a major role in pan-Indian policy. The Indian intelligence agency, the Research and Analysis Wing (RAW), tended to see a sinister rival, Pakistan's ISI (the Inter-Service Intelligence) agency, behind many of these threats. Previously, Indian intelligence had been criticized by its political bosses for failures in the conflicts with Pakistan and China, and so a reformed RAW was set up and modelled on the CIA to deal with external intelligence. Sri Lanka was of special interest besides the Tamil factor. Indian intelligence had been concerned by perceived Sri Lankan support for Pakistan in the 1971 conflict over Bangladesh. Pakistani ships had been allowed to refuel at Sri Lankan ports, despite complaints from New Delhi. A few years later RAW had trained various Sri Lankan Tamil groups to contain and control the Eelam movement by divide and rule. That was all very covert.

The Jaffna airdrop, however, was a very open intervention. The Sri Lankan army wanted to finish the job as they felt the LTTE was on the ropes. New Delhi had decided that a Tiger defeat was not in its interest. The Sri Lankan navy blocked Indian civilian ships from resupplying the Tigers. And so the airlift (with An-32 cargo planes, guarded by Indian Mirage fighter aircraft) was the immediate answer.

President Jayawardene was extremely reluctant to engage in open conflict with the giant neighbour. The military offensive was halted, and negotiations ensued. Jayawardene and Rajiv Gandhi signed the Indo-Sri Lankan peace accord on 29 July 1987. Gandhi had flown into Colombo to fix the deal, a brave move as his intelligence told him anti-Indian hysteria was mounting. Gandhi had to duck when a member of the Sri Lankan naval honour guard tried to strike his head with a rifle butt. And an Indian naval flotilla stood ready to evacuate the High Commission staff from Colombo. Under pressure from New Delhi, Colombo made a number of concessions to Tamil demands. The Tamil language was to be given official status and some power would be devolved to the northern and eastern provinces which could later merge, after a referendum. The Indians promised not to aid any of the Tamil insurgents and would ensure peace by sending in their own troops – the Indian Peacekeeping Force (IPKF) – to temporarily police the Tamil provinces. The Gandhi-Jayawardene pact also contained secret clauses, including the promise that the LTTE would be funded by New Delhi to stop their extortion rackets/taxation of Tamils and frequently criminal overseas fundraising.

The Tamil fighters were excluded from the top-level talks. So the LTTE was wary of the deal but initially went along with the ensuing ceasefire. Some of the minor rivals to the Tigers did disarm, but the LTTE kept its powder dry.

Chapter 5

Big Brother Steps In: The Indian 'Peacekeepers'

Then followed the tragedy of an insurgency alongside an insurgency. The Indians decided to demobilize forcefully and disarm the Tigers. The IPKF was overconfident of its role as the local superpower – its highly trained and very large regular army would have little trouble disarming a bunch of rag-tag jungle fighters, many of whom they had trained and worked with in the past. Or so the Indian top brass thought. Instead, the Tigers put up a remarkable demonstration of skilled armed resistance. Three years of heavy fighting followed. The Indian nemesis was that they would leave with their tails between their legs.

Some senior Sri Lankan officers were quietly satisfied that their big brother was being outwitted by the Tigers (although the Indian army's performance did improve markedly towards the end of their involvement). But more important was *the* lesson the Sri Lankan military hierarchy learned – if the Tigers were on the verge of defeat again, Colombo would not allow foreign intervention to save the necks of Prabhakaran and the LTTE leadership.

Meanwhile, much of Sinhalese public opinion was outraged by what they saw as foreign occupation troops on their island. IPKF was translated as Innocent People Killing Force. It was fertile ground for a resurrection of the JVP. Following an almost successful assassination attempt on President Jayawardene, murder, mayhem and enforced general strikes went on for two years. Embarrassingly, at the onset of the revolt, the Indian air force had to airlift Sri Lankan troops from the north to deal with the southern revolt. Eventually the JVP leader, Rohana Wijeweera, was captured in a hill station near Kandy. He was caught shaving off his trademark beard, while living with his family and posing as a tea planter. He was taken to Colombo in November 1989 and, after interrogation, was 'encouraged' to issue on film an order to his followers to stop fighting. Shortly afterwards, he was shot in the Colombo Golf Club's grounds 'while attempting to escape'. He was killed by an army sergeant, an ironic end for a man who worshipped the career of Che Guevara.

By early 1990 the JVP leadership and membership had been crushed – perhaps 7,000 JVP members were 'removed'. In addition, local feuds took advantage of the chaos. Death by burning tyre around the necks and the medieval barbarity of severed heads stuck on poles were often noted. Colombo was widely criticized for ex-judicial methods, although in the chaos of concurrent wars, with an array of uniformed combatants and civilian militias, the truth was frequently blurred, deliberately and otherwise. A noted critic of the Sri Lankan government, Gordon Weiss, observed, 'The stories of what happened to tens of thousands of Sinhalese youths in the second JVP uprising tell of a bloodlust more easily attributed to the rampages of the Mongols or the pillages of the Norsemen.'[3]

In the north, the Indians also came in for a beating, both in the field and in international opinion where Indian troops were accused of human rights abuses. The thirty-two months of combat, not peacekeeping, caused the deaths of nearly 1,200 Indian soldiers and perhaps as many as 5,000 Sri Lankans, though estimates of the latter vary widely. The Colombo government wanted the Indians out, especially once the southern Sinhalese revolt had been tamed. Colombo was even accused (accurately) by foreign intelligence agencies of arming their arch enemies, the Tigers, in order to hasten an Indian exit. Rajiv Gandhi refused, but his defeat in the December 1989 election meant a new government could order its troops home. The last left on 24 March 1990.

The intervention was a major humiliation for a power which had one of the world's largest armies. It was more an attempt at power projection, the first major overseas expedition, rather than merely a peacekeeping action. India was angry with Colombo about far more than the treatment of the local Tamils. Pakistan, the eternal enemy, had been too active in Sri Lankan affairs, not least with arms and training. And New Delhi, then at odds with Washington, worried that the US Navy might cast avaricious glances at Trincomalee. It was time to make sure that Colombo knew who was boss; that was the essential intended political message of the intervention.

After their military humiliation, senior Indian officers reflected on the 'lessons learned', to use the hackneyed military phrase. Their verdict was brutally frank: 'an unnecessarily messy and ill-conducted campaign'.[4] It is often said that amateurs talk about tactics while professionals talk logistics. In the Indian Operation PAWAN, the official name for the intervention, poor planning and support were ubiquitous. The politicians blamed their armed forces, the military leaders squabbled and then blamed poor intelligence. At every level from strategic incompetence of the political leadership to the ineptness of the poor bloody infantry on patrols, Indian military specialists started regularly quoting Norman Dixon's celebrated book on the psychology of military incompetence.[5]

The Indian political leadership did not provide a clear objective and exit strategy, the classic Clausewitzian dictum. Initially, it was thought that the Indian forces would have to take on the Sri Lankan army, then it became a matter of 'policing' the Tamil disarmament and demobilization. It all went horribly wrong. As two senior Indian officers noted:

> The IPKF should have been Sri Lanka's saviour in its dark hour. Instead it ended up being hated by the very people it went in to save. Hated and condemned. It suffered too. Suffered terribly in an alien terrain, fighting an enemy which had the full support of the people … fighting a war which was not its [own]. It killed thousands, lost thousands. And came home under a cloud so dark and heavy that it has cast a permanent shadow over the fourth-largest army in the world. Totally unprepared and ill-equipped, that was the IPKF.[6]

Some Indian critics alleged that it was India's Vietnam, though that parallel could withstand little careful analysis. Not least that the two countries were separated by only thirty-five kilometres, and Indian peacekeepers included many Tamils, as infantry and police, who shared the language and culture. India had overwhelming strength and firepower and many cultural advantages, but the deployment was a disaster from the start. Some of the best-trained counter-insurgency troops were sent to the Indo-Pakistan border, New Delhi's first priority. The units that went were understrength and under-trained. Just as Dr John Reid, the British Secretary of State for Defence, foolishly promised that his troops would not fire a shot when they were deployed to Helmand in 2006, so too the Indian planners expected no fighting and did not include ammunition replenishment.

Even when the Indians eventually had enough bullets, the guns were deficient. The Indian army had introduced the SLR (self-loading rifle) as a result of the debacle in their war with China in 1962. That may have made sense in the open mountainous terrain, but in the much closer confines of urban and jungle warfare, the short and much lighter, fully automatic AK-47s and American M-16s made for much easier and lighter handling.

Lighter, smaller ammunition meant that far more rounds could be carried by the guerrillas. In short, the Indians found that the Tigers could produce a much greater volume of fire than the same number of Indian infantrymen. The Indian webbing was antiquated – based on a pre-Second World War British design. And the large Indian infantry backpacks were of pre-1914 design. Some Indian officers liked to say they were more British than the British Army, but this was taking military legacy too far.

Indian generals criticized their own men for poor fire discipline, deficient fire and movement tactics, a lack of initiative at company (and below) level, a habit of avoiding landmines by sticking to roads and nervously patrolling in ambush-prone large groups instead of spreading out into small groups of three to five men each. Even when the Indians secured a tactical advantage in the field, their marksmanship was usually poor. Their fieldcraft, in sharp contrast with the Tigers who were defending a terrain they knew well, was dangerously below par. Their counter-ambush skills were often non-existent. Indian field communications were inadequate, especially contrasted with their opponents. The list of weaknesses could fill a whole chapter of this book. It was lucky that the Indians – over 80,000 strong at the start, later to more than double – had the numbers and air supremacy. In the latter case, it was here that the parallel with Vietnam could stand up. Indian strategists also compared it with the British achievement of launching a successful expedition to the Falklands Islands, 'across 13,000 km of cold and hostile ocean, a three-week one-way sailing time for warships at average speed, and not just across a 35 km strip of sea'.[7]

Of course the Indian media were blamed too, especially for running stories about the alleged softness of Tamil soldiers towards the Tigers, and of Tamil Nadu police arranging the transit of wounded Tigers to Indian hospitals, so that they could return and fight Indian troops. The military also blamed their leaders – the Indians did not construct an effective and unified war council in New Delhi, but nor did the three armed services restrain their turf warfare to form an effective joint operational command in Sri Lanka. Colombo's military leadership took very careful note of Indian mistakes, especially the lack of unity of command. The Sri Lankan army started planning for the next round of their fight with the Tigers, who were now much stronger. The Tamil insurgents believed they had just humbled a superpower. Beating the much weaker Sri Lankan forces should be easy, they thought. The vision of Tamil Eelam shimmered ever closer.

The Indian military also chose to focus on the failure of intelligence, especially RAW. As in many failed campaigns, the military blamed poor intelligence, and the intelligence officers accused the military of not listening properly. One disastrous manifestation of the poor relationship was the heliborne assault on a Tiger HQ in the Jaffna University campus in the opening stages of Operation PAWAN. RAW said the army was 'gung ho' and went in without consulting them. The Indian paratroopers were easy targets for the sharpshooting Tiger cadres.

A year later, RAW tried to rehabilitate its tattered reputation. In November 1988, around 200 members of the PLOTE (the People's Liberation Organization of Tamil Eelam) invaded the Maldives in a quirky coup attempt. The Maldives was run by one of the most enduring Asian dictators, Abdul Gayoom, but few outsiders cared about his tyranny. Honeymooning visitors came to explore each other, not the island's political foibles. Gayoom appealed to India for help. This time the Indians managed an airborne operation over 2,000 kilometres. Indian paratroopers restored Gayoom's dictatorship in a few hours. Speed, accuracy and precise intelligence made all the difference.

RAW could not rest on its minor Maldivian laurels. The Indian spooks must have thought, 'What could be worse than the Sri Lankan cock-up?' The answer came at 10.20 pm on 21 May 1991. Rajiv Gandhi was campaigning in Tamil Nadu, perhaps feeling confident that he had done his bit for the Tamil cause. He was on the southern leg of his campaign to be re-elected. He was visiting the town of Sriperumbudur, about twenty kilometres from Chennai, to meet some of the party faithful in an open-air gathering. The police had carefully co-ordinated with party activists to screen those who were allowed to get close to the Indian leader. Two policemen had metal detectors, but the female officers, who were tasked with searching women, did not. They missed the female with a suicide vest full of ball bearings. A bespectacled young woman, wearing a green and orange *salwar kameez,* had mingled with the official guests. As she edged her way forward to greet Rajiv Gandhi, one of his female party organizers pushed her aside, but Gandhi waved her to come forward. The bespectacled Tamil woman was ushered into his presence by members of his own Congress Party. She placed her sandalwood garland around his neck and then bent before him as if to touch his feet; it was common in India for the young to touch elders' feet as a mark of respect. The charismatic statesman, his shoulders garlanded with yellow marigolds and the sandalwood gift, paused to recognize the gesture of the small woman at his feet. Still kneeling before Gandhi, she detonated the charge, killing the Indian leader and sixteen others as well as blowing off her own head. Amid the fire and smoke, surviving policemen tried to find his body, recognizable by his distinctive Lotto shoes. The assassin was Dhanu, her nom de guerre in the Tamil Tigers. Their supremo, Prabhakaran, had felt personally betrayed by Gandhi. The assassination of a leader of the world's largest democracy demonstrated the reach of the Tigers. This was a dramatic example of the so-called 'propaganda of the dead', a term used in the West by the IRA and throughout the Middle East by Islamic radicals.[8]

Previous Indian military support for the Tigers had suckled a Frankenstein monster as far as New Delhi's interests were now concerned. Divide and rule in Sri Lanka was not supposed to inspire the death of their own political leader. RAW once more got it in the neck for its lack of intelligence. But it was also to be a dramatic own goal for the Tiger leadership. Partly as a result of the Gandhi assassination, the LTTE was declared a terrorist organization in 1997 in the USA and in the UK in 2001, making fundraising for the Tigers illegal in these countries. More importantly, India was later to prove far less likely to exert its leverage over Colombo.

The Tigers moved into the areas evacuated by the Indians and established administrative structures. A tentative ceasefire held while politics was supposed to be given a chance. The Tigers, flushed with their perceived defeat of the Indians — which Prabhakaran had dubbed 'a satanic force' — assumed a new confidence. The few surviving rival Tamil militant groups were finally purged or absorbed. Only the Tigers would be allowed to pursue Tamil Eelam. The government's forces had extinguished the dying embers of the JVP revolt. Both sides were ready to resume hostilities when the government launched an offensive to retake Jaffna. This second phase of the conflict, Eelam War II, was to be marked by unprecedented brutality.

Chapter 6

Eelam War II (1990–95)

In 1990 the Tigers felt they had defeated the regional superpower, India, ironically with the help of the enfeebled Colombo government. The mood of the insurgents perhaps paralleled the Afghan Jihadists after the defeat of the Russians who quit Afghanistan in 1989. Al-Qaeda came to believe that yet another superpower could be toppled, this time the US. Certainly in 1990 the much stronger LTTE felt ready to take on the Sri Lankan army. Prabhakaran was to achieve a great deal in the second round of fighting, both abroad and at home, on land and sea. The LTTE indulged in ethnic cleansing of Muslims and Sinhalese and isolated and defeated a long series of army garrisons and police camps. And the Sea Tigers began openly confronting and sometimes getting the better of the navy.

Hostilities recommenced on 11 June 1990 in Batticaloa when a Muslim youth who was also an LTTE supporter was arrested by police over an altercation with a Sinhalese man. The Batticaloa police station was surrounded by LTTE cadres. Other police camps and stations in the region were also besieged. Soon army camps were similarly attacked. As the police stations fell to the LTTE, police officers were taken captive and many later killed in cold blood. Over 600 police were to be slaughtered. Then police stations in the north were taken over by the LTTE, including Jaffna. The policemen in the Batticaloa region had been ordered to avoid confronting the LTTE. Some police officers wanted to fight, but the Premadasa government was anxious to avoid another major round of civil war, although no doubt it did not believe that the insurgents would slaughter so many police officers who had surrendered. In the Kalmunai Division 324 officers, under Acting Superintendent Ivan Botheju, were surrounded by overwhelming numbers of LTTE cadres. He pleaded for reinforcements. A senior police officer was sent with specific orders from President Premadasa to give up their weapons. None of the surrendering policemen was ever heard of again, although Tamil sources later indicated that they were ordered to lie down on the ground in a long line, with their hands tied, and then machine gunned. Their bodies were heaped up, soaked with petrol and set on fire. Their charred remains were buried secretly. The massacre of the policemen was one of the worst atrocities of the whole war.

Not surprisingly, police morale plummeted, but soon the army's morale was ground down as well. The large army base at Kilinochchi was attacked on 14 June 1990, as the army abandoned a number of other northern camps. The Kaluwanchikudi army base, twenty kilometres south of Batticaloa, was besieged. It was reinforced by some of the policemen from the next-door police station. Sixty-one army and police fought off 300 LTTE cadres for four days until the army's Rapid Deployment Force was able to rescue them. Another camp, Kokavil, which had been vacated by the Indian peacekeepers, was manned by forty-eight soldiers from the 3rd Sinha (Volunteer) Battalion. After running out of food and water, and with most of his men wounded, the lieutenant in charge was ordered to withdraw on foot. No helicopter resupply was possible because of the close encirclement. The young commanding officer refused, saying that his wounded men were in no condition to break out. After a month with just a few supplies dropped by air, the LTTE brought in their armoured bulldozers for a final assault; only a cook and two soldiers escaped alive. Most of the camps in the north were run by volunteer forces and then in small numbers because the regulars had been kept busy in the south by the JVP rebellion. One major siege was defended by a headmaster in civilian life. These actions were common throughout the north and east, with the LTTE usually coming out on top.

The LTTE purged their territory of most government outposts. The insurgents also ordered all Muslims living in Jaffna to quit the peninsula. At least 30,000 were driven out at just three hours' notice. Some Muslims were killed by the LTTE, including 142 in a mosque in Kattankudi. This was pure ethnic cleansing, although the term would not come in to common parlance until a few years later, during the Balkan atrocities.

One of the centrepieces of the fighting was the siege of the iconic military base in Jaffna fort. It was the largest military fort in the country, built originally by the Portuguese after 1618 and then renovated by the Dutch. British military forces garrisoned the fortification until 1948. In 1990 the old colonial fort was held by 172 men, mostly police, a very small number to defend such lengthy ramparts. No land route was possible and a Chinese-built Harbin Y-12, guarded by two SIAI Aermacchi SF-260TPs, provided intermittent air drops. The seriously under-armed Aermacchis also strafed the perimeter of the fort at night. The fall of Jaffna fort would be a humiliation too far, decided the Sri Lankan high command. The fort had to be relieved even if the rescue cost more in lives than the 172 men actually inside the fort. Two of the most famous fighting officers in the Sri Lankan army were to be involved in the rescue – Gotabaya Rajapaksa and Sarath Fonseka, both then colonels. In a combined operation the army ventured a rare amphibious night landing to capture Kayts Island and then troops jumped to the nearby Mandativu Island. Over eighty LTTE cadres were killed, with very minimal army casualties. Large caches of weapons were captured, a rare success story for the army. Across the lagoon, the LTTE troops around the fort melted away. But the successful troops on the nearby islands did not take advantage of this as a result of excessive caution in the high command. Helicopters did manage to take in supplies and extract some of the wounded in the fort. Eventually, an opposed amphibious operation was launched in dinghies across the three kilometres of the lagoon. One flank was led by Colonel Gotabaya Rajapaksa and the other by Sarath Fonseka, later to be army commander. Casualties were high – over ninety men were killed from Rajapaksa's battalion alone. A similar number were killed in Fonseka's unit. The relieving troops managed to fight their way into the fort, but other goals, such as the capture of Jaffna itself, were not achieved. In October 1990 the fort was evacuated but the two island garrisons were held.

Mankulam camp was also threatened. It lay in the centre of the Vanni with the strategic Elephant Pass camp twenty-eight kilometres to the north. Mankulam, held by 200 men, was reliant on air drops. Helicopters were then sent in under heavy fire to remove some of the army bodies which were often in a state of decomposition. The removal and burial of bodies were considered vital to maintain some army morale. But the force of the rotor blades on the open doors of the choppers would strip away some of the flesh (not in body bags) which would sometimes land on the choppers' windscreens.[9] When the bodies were landed, their condition presumably did little for morale of the air force personnel involved.

The troops in Mankulam were ordered to make a breakout on foot to the south to a base at Vavuniya, thirty kilometres away. Just under 150 members of the 200-strong garrison made it through the heavy rains and jungle to the base. Some of the stragglers were rescued by Bell 212 choppers only after they were ordered to drop their weapons and advance towards the chopper with hands up and displaying their ID cards. The LTTE could easily have disguised themselves in army uniforms.

The fall of Mankulam was followed by another blow to the army. One of the most popular officers in the army, Brigadier Lucky Wijeratne, who was area commander of Trincomalee district, did not live up to his nickname. He was blown up by a massive landmine. A few months later the charismatic deputy defence minister, Ranjan Wijeratne, was killed in another massive bomb blast a few metres from his home in the centre of Colombo. The LTTE seemed capable of striking anywhere.

The army was completely overstretched. Its frontline forces were ferried from one defeat to another, trying to hold one besieged garrison after another. If the army did recapture one area, it had to be withdrawn to fight elsewhere and then the LTTE would seep back in. It was a futile 'whack-a-mole' reactive strategy, which Colonel Rajapaksa railed against. In frustration he left the army. He said of this period:

> A lot of good officers left because they thought the war being conducted was an exercise in futility. The LTTE would be cleared from one place only to return the moment the army withdrew. There was no driving factor to remain because nothing worthwhile was happening.[10]

The newly married Colonel was encouraged by his wife to leave the army and then move to the US to work in the IT industry. Gotabaya Rajapaksa, however, was to spend much time musing about the military failures before returning to Sri Lanka to take up the role of Permanent Secretary at the Ministry of Defence, and with a burning mission to right the wrongs of the previous decade.

Meanwhile, the war went from bad to worse for the government. At sea, the Tigers were beginning to attack rather than evade the navy and used much faster and better armed boats as well as suicide craft. In the air, Colombo was struggling to buy and then later arrange pilot training for ground-attack aircraft. On land, the LTTE was about to inflict another iconic defeat to match the army's forced withdrawal from Jaffna fort.

By April 1991 the LTTE's intense mortar attacks on the chopper landing site at Elephant Pass made air force pilots unwilling to take any more risks, especially after the guerrillas also began to deploy anti-aircraft weapons. By June the base was under close siege by 3,000 insurgents and could be supplied only by air drops. Water was delivered by dropping ice blocks, and food supplies usually ended up in the adjacent lagoon where soldiers had to fish them out. The base was defended by over 600 troops of the Sinha Regiment led by Major Sanath Karunaratne. On 10 July 1991 the LTTE moved in for the kill with heavy mortars and RPGs. After three days the LTTE pushed into the inner defences of the camp with an armoured bulldozer with cadres streaming behind. In the close-quarter combat an infantryman, Gamini Kularatne, clambered up the steel ladder of the bulldozer and lobbed two grenades through the open hatch. Kularatne was killed, but the bulldozer's destruction forced the LTTE to withdraw by midnight.

Operation BALAVEGAYA was launched to save the Elephant Pass base. In the biggest amphibious assault so far, the army landed on a beach to the east of the camp. About forty-five dinghies were assembled for the initial landing. Twelve soldiers were deployed in each dinghy and, no matter how heavy the incoming fire, no boat could turn back unless more than six men were hit. Eight of the first fifteen dinghies, which were to establish the beachhead, made it to the shore under very heavy fire. Other dinghies and barges with armoured wheeled vehicles landed once the beach was secure. The distance from the beach to the camp was less than eighteen kilometres but it took almost three weeks for the two infantry battalions to fight their way there, sometimes crawling, and scooping out depressions in the sandy soil with their helmets in order to create some cover. The insurgents copied the Viet Cong and hid in one-man foxholes only to pop up behind the slowly advancing infantry.

After nearly three weeks of hard going, the relieving force reached the Elephant Pass base on 3 August, although the fighting went on until 9 August, when the LTTE made an orderly withdrawal. The guerrillas conceded that 573 Tigers had been killed (Colombo claimed around a thousand). The army admitted that it had lost 212 soldiers, but the LTTE claimed it had killed over 400. Later, more independent estimates put the overall mortality figure as 2,000. The Sri Lankan President admitted that it was the 'mother of all battles', a phrase made popular at the time by Saddam Hussein.

The Elephant Pass base was of immense strategic importance as the isthmus was the road and rail gateway to the Jaffna peninsula. The base had been considered practically impregnable, but the LTTE had almost taken it. Normally, the attack-defence ratio is reckoned to be 3:1, but a maximum of 5,000 insurgents had almost defeated around 10,000 defending forces. No mean feat. The LTTE, however, was finally to conquer the base eight years later, only to lose it again, also eight years after that, in the final offensives of the war. The government claimed the 1991 battle as a great victory; such exuberance about winning one defensive battle by a larger conventional force against guerrillas without air power was an indication of the low standards set by Colombo.

When Lieutenant General Cecil Waidyaratne became commander of the army on 16 November 1991 he was depressed by what he found. As he confided later in his unpublished memoirs, 'I had to face a situation where terrorists had the upper hand within the north and the east and Army morale was low.'[11] The army needed a whole range of new equipment from tracked vehicles to radios and flakjackets. It had become an aimless war fought by a demoralized army that was far too small and often poorly led. The LTTE, however, was fighting a successful protracted revolutionary war and winning on the international propaganda front, not least by playing up real and fabricated army and police atrocities.

The new army commander set about reforming his degraded forces. At the strategic level the debate about clearing the east first versus the north first was an argument that was to run for another fifteen years. At the tactical level, the army needed many layers of improvement in training. Reading the complaints of senior commanders suggested a poorly disciplined force. From troops and officers running from combat, often in different directions, to failure to set up sentries, to grouping together in open terrain or the obverse, of 'hugging' armour in closed terrain. The LTTE excelled at night fighting, whereas the army's sentries, when posted, were often fatigued. Frequently the insurgents could pass through or around large detachments of troops to penetrate the army's rear. Surprise counter-attacks from the rear were often the LTTE's major weapon.

Despite attempted reforms, it got worse for the army. The LTTE decided to launch a retribution offensive to mark the anniversary of the 'Black July' 1983 pogrom. The guerrillas hit the Janakapura base and its nearby satellite camps. Twenty three soldiers were killed and nearly thirty were reported missing. A vast store of arms and ammunition was seized. And to add insult to injury the cadres flattened the main camp using the army's own bulldozers.

In November 1993 the sprawling Pooneryn camp was attacked. The base was on a thin promontory that almost reached Jaffna town, with sea to the west and the Jaffna lagoon to the east. Hundreds of cadres infiltrated from the lagoon using foam floats with plastic bags to keep their weapons dry. The camp held 1,000 troops but twice as many were needed to secure such a large two-by-six-kilometre perimeter. The surprise attack was very successful: 500 soldiers were killed, lots of equipment was taken. Most embarrassingly the cadres drove away two T-55 tanks. Why they simply drove them off instead of deploying them in battle is unknown. The camp was not overrun because some of the defenders managed to regroup around the main HQ. About half the garrison survived to defend the last strongpoint, which was supported by air drops, although the small perimeter meant that once again much of the bounty from the sky ended up with the insurgents. Reinforcements arrived after four days of heavy fighting, although it took another week to clear the camp of the LTTE. The army had lost over 500 men and claimed a similar number of LTTE killed. The fact that the garrison was not completely lost was deemed a minor triumph, but the accompanying LTTE onslaught on nearby naval detachments was also humiliating for Colombo. Five inshore patrol craft that were supposed to patrol the Jaffna lagoon were destroyed and 105 naval personnel lost their lives, the biggest loss in a single engagement of the whole war.

It was the conventional wisdom of foreign experts throughout most of the war that the LTTE could not be defeated, but by 1994 it looked as though the government could actually *lose* the war to the insurgents. In the elections of August 1994 a new government led by Chandrika Kumaratunga came to power under the banner of People's Alliance, albeit led by the Freedom Party. Colombo lifted the restriction of some goods to the north. Peace talks were held and a ceasefire began in January 1995. Colombo was desperate for the ceasefire to hold, even hushing up armed attacks on army camps. For its part the LTTE complained of restrictions on Tamil fishing rights and that the army was still stopping food and other supplies getting through their checkpoints. Nevertheless, Colombo did offer extensive political devolution – even though hardliners in parliament may not have swallowed any real end to the unitary state. The LTTE also remained determined to forge an independent Eelam.

The ceasefire was brief. The LTTE could look back at major achievements. The insurgents had built up finances and weaponry from the ever-expanding network of front organization abroad. The cadres had often dominated in battle against the state's sea and land forces. They had assassinated a range of senior officers and defence officials. But arguably the two main political assassinations would prove counter-productive in the longer term. The killing of Rajiv Gandhi in 1991 soured Indian support even in Tamil Nadu. And the assassination of President Premadasa at a May Day rally in Colombo in 1993 was a gift to the Sri Lankan hardliners who refused any deal on devolution. Premadasa was probably the most accommodating leader the LTTE was likely to face – his killing was another strategic error. The war resumed. The Tigers fought for Eelam and the government called it 'war for peace'.

Chapter 7

Eelam War III (1995–2002)

On 19 April 1995 four suicide frogmen from the Sea Tigers planted large C-4 explosive charges under four strike craft moored together in Trincomalee harbour. Two ships were obliterated. Twelve naval personnel were killed and the bodies of the four frogmen were also found. Just over a week later the LTTE brought down two air force planes with surface-to-air missiles. This panicked the air force which did not have effective countermeasures. It also meant that the isolated army garrisons could not be supplied by air.

Despite its military weakness, the government decided to retake Jaffna. In early July 1995 the army built up its numbers in the peninsula, accompanied by heavy aerial bombing. The air force had previously dropped leaflets telling civilians to seek shelter in places of worship. Jets bombed St Peter and St Paul's Church at Navali to the north of Jaffna. At the time the International Committee of the Red Cross reported sixty-five civilians killed and 150 wounded.[12] The government blamed the LTTE but eventually backtracked. After seven weeks of intense fighting, dubbed Operation RIVIRESA, the government controlled Jaffna town for the first time in almost a decade. Many civilians had died as well as perhaps 2,500 combatants on both sides. The national flag was raised in Jaffna fort once more, however. As it retreated, the LTTE forced hundreds of thousands to leave the Jaffna area, often with just a few hours' notice. Though some were allowed to drift back over the following months, many stayed in the Vanni area to the south, under Tiger control. In later stages of Operation RIVIRESA, the army expanded its control of the peninsula, for example retaking the Point Pedro-Velvettiturai area with the loss of just ten soldiers. Prabhakaran's home town fell with very little LTTE resistance.

The LTTE hit back in July 1996 with its 'Unceasing Waves' offensive which, on 18 July 1996, overwhelmed the well-armed and well-provisioned government base at Mullaitivu. Two of the most senior officers were absent from the camp and the defence was conducted like 'a disorganized rabble', according to one army source. The base was to be reinforced by 100 men from the 1st Special Forces Battalion, but the camp fell before they got there, overrun in a seven-hour night battle. The ensuing battle was waged between the victorious LTTE and the SF men, backed by Mi-24s. The Sea Tigers also fought a battle to cordon off the beach to prevent 450 troops landing as reinforcements. Suicide boats disrupted the landing; eventually all the navy could do was rescue some survivors from the battle at the main camp. In the ferocious fighting as many as 1,200 army personnel were killed, 200 after surrendering, according to Colombo. A redemptive attack after the Jaffna defeat was to be expected, especially as so many LTTE cadres had retreated from the north and were assembling in the area.

The following month the army launched a counter-attack forcing many thousands of civilians to flee the fighting. Kilinochchi was taken by the army by the end of August 1996. The loss of the town, the main administrative centre for the LTTE, was perhaps some compensation for the military disaster at Mullaitivu.

The LTTE expanded its operations by urban warfare. In January 1996 suicide bomb attacks at the Central Bank in Colombo killed ninety and injured over 1,000. In October 1997 the LTTE bombed the World Trade Centre. In January 1998 a truck bomb damaged Kandy's Temple of the Tooth, one of the holiest of Buddhist shrines and the most precious symbol of Sinhalese pride. In response the LTTE was outlawed and Colombo worked hard abroad to get the insurgents rated as a terrorist organization, with mixed results on the movement's overseas fundraising.

In September 1998 the LTTE launched 'Unceasing Waves II', led by Commander Karuna Amman. Under his bold leadership, Kilinochchi fell in horrific hand-to-hand fighting, although at the same time the army recovered the town of Mankulam. The strategic aim of Colombo was to try to clear the A9 highway linking central Sri Lanka with the Jaffna peninsula. The soldiers nicknamed the route 'the highway of death'. The army would advance and then lose ground in LTTE counter-attacks in a constant flow of mutual attrition. In 'Unceasing Waves III' in 1999 the LTTE retook nearly all the crucial Vanni region, threatening the main base at Elephant Pass and the garrison in Jaffna. In December 1999 the LTTE almost managed to assassinate President Chandrika Kumaratunga. Amid other injuries she lost an eye, but continued in her presidential campaign and was re-elected to a second term of office. The President, the daughter of two former prime ministers, had also witnessed the assassination in 1988 of her husband, Vijaya, the film star-turned politician. That hit was done by the JVP. The family exemplified both the dynastic nature of Sri Lankan politics as well as its violence. President Kumaratunga showed immense personal courage but, on the strategic front, her army was at its lowest ebb.

Prabhakaran's annual speech of 26 November 1999 was suitably triumphalist:

> Our massive campaign in the Vanni codenamed 'Unceasing Waves 3' has effectively demonstrated to the world the extraordinary growth and development of the Tiger fighting forces in the art of modern warfare. The speed of our strikes, the ability of rapid deployment, the unified command, the high discipline, the spectacular offensive tactics and the tremendous courage displayed by our fighting forces formations have astounded the world military experts.

From December 1999 the LTTE started attacking the extensive lines around Elephant Pass. The insurgents came from three fronts, including the sea, infiltrating at night and sometimes wearing Sri Lankan army uniforms and speaking Sinhala. The army gradually withdrew to the central complex, often after suffering 80 per cent fatalities in their units. The LTTE's artillery strikes were deadly accurate. Finally, the cadres managed to capture the wells that supplied water to the divisional HQ. A rescue party of 800 inexperienced men, from the 9th Gajaba Battalion plus some troops from the 1st Sinha Battalion, was encircled by the guerrillas. After less than two days of fighting the relieving forces, now down to 100 men, needed rescue themselves.

Inside the ever-diminishing defence perimeter of the Elephant Pass base confusion and demoralization reigned. Soldiers were shooting themselves in the foot in the hope of a casevac by air and senior officers were also reporting sick. By mid-April, the decision was made to withdraw and to destroy all the equipment that could not be carried. A small group of officers, however, decided to lead a small night convoy to withdraw the artillery north to the government lines in Jaffna. The LTTE, however, seized the guns.

On 20 April 2000 the Tigers stormed the remains of the Elephant Pass military complex. Over 5,000 troops had been deployed in this vital southern bastion of the government's position in the Jaffna peninsula. Many had been killed in the four months of fighting around the base. The army had ordered a retreat through enemy territory. Despite some armoured cover, the troops were pummelled by mortars and ambushes; 300 soldiers were killed and 500 wounded. The survivors who staggered through to friendly lines were traumatized. A middle-ranking officer who escaped said simply, 'It was the worst experience of my life.'

The LTTE advanced north on land and across the Jaffna lagoon. Some of their most able leaders, Commander Theepan and Commander Sornam, were heading the attacks. The army was in disarray: the LTTE recorded small units of female cadres chasing away army units ten times their size. The 34,000 troops in the Jaffna garrison were now threatened. Its fall would have ended the war in favour of the LTTE. In May, Major General Sarath Fonseka, one of the most able Sri Lankan commanders, reluctantly drew up a plan for a fighting retreat from Jaffna. He secretly outlined four diminishing defence lines. But, if they all fell, the surviving troops faced either massacre or an escape by air or sea for which the logistics did not exist. In desperation, Colombo even put out feelers for Indian military support. After the peacekeeping fiasco the New Delhi government politely declined to intervene again.

Despite mammoth logistic challenges the army resupplied Jaffna and managed to hang on. With their backs literally to the sea, a number of leading officers fought bravely in the front lines alongside their men. In addition, multi-barrel rocket launchers had just arrived from Pakistan to provide extra firepower. The seemingly invincible LTTE were pushed back and the army even clawed back some lost ground.

Mid-2000 was perhaps the high point of Tiger success and the lowest level of army control. The insurgents claimed complete control in 70 per cent of the designated independent homeland. The Tigers switched back and forth from land battles to terror tactics with spectaculars, 'propaganda by deed'. In July 2001, in probably the most dramatic insurgent attack of the whole war, twenty LTTE cadres hit the poorly defended Colombo international airport area destroying a range of air force frontline planes as well as civilian aircraft. The military was humiliated and the economy was stabbed in the heart as tourists stayed away and investors turned their backs.

Chapter 8

The Long Ceasefire

The al-Qaeda assault on 9/11 dramatically undermined international support for the LTTE as the US launched its universal war on terror. The insurgents did not want Washington to fully endorse Colombo. The LTTE was aligned with a whole range of international terror groups including Jihadists in Pakistan. The Tigers had also immersed themselves in the arms and terror networks embedded in Eritrea. Even the hard core around Prabhakaran knew that a strategic reassessment was needed. The government in Colombo faced a shattered economy and an electorate that could see no gains for the 'war for peace' rationale. On 9 December 2001 the United National Front party, led by Ranil Wickremasinghe, won on a platform of peace and a negotiated settlement.

The LTTE responded by announcing a ceasefire. Despite strong military opposition to the ceasefire, the government reciprocated and agreed to lift the long-running embargo of non-military goods to LTTE areas. One of the reasons for hostility in the intelligence leadership to a ceasefire was because a secret and long-planned strike on Prabhakaran was about to be put into action. Amid the sensitive negotiations for a peace deal, with Norway in the lead, military intelligence rushed to complete the mission. On 20 December a special forces team was in place in the Vanni jungle. For once, it knew for certain where the elusive Tiger leader was. The assassination team was due to strike on Christmas Eve. The team leaders were just ready to press the start button when they were countermanded, despite fierce intelligence arguments that Prabhakaran's death would end the war. But the new government feared the collapse of the ceasefire negotiations. The death squad was not disbanded – it was pulled back.

The special forces operatives were stood down temporarily in a safe house in Colombo. In one of the biggest intelligence own goals of the war, the house was raided by Special Branch police from Kandy. The highly secret operation was exposed. It was not a case of overzealous detectives; a senior minister in the new government had got wind of the audacious raid.

The heads of military and national intelligence were overridden when the police arrested the operatives and jailed them in Kandy. They were released after two weeks and, as a scapegoat, a middle-ranking police officer was suspended, temporarily. It didn't end there: the intelligence leadership was accused of using the safe house as a base to assassinate the prime minister. Once again the Tiger leader was unscathed.

And, once again, Norway played an active role behind the scenes in bringing the two combatants to the peace table. On 22 February 2002 a permanent ceasefire agreement (CFA) was announced. Along with other Nordic countries, Norway would monitor the ceasefire via a formal mission: the Sri Lanka Monitoring Mission (SLMM). Roads were re-opened, especially the A9 highway, and traffic started moving between north and south albeit after paying a tax to the LTTE. Foreign aid and NGOs began to flow in, and many Sri Lankans risked optimism for the first time in many years.

Optimism did not reach the more cynical hearts in the intelligence leadership. Still nursing the recent grievance about the Keystone Kops raid on their most secret operation, they also harboured deeper suspicions about foreign intervention. Constant meddling from New Delhi was bad enough, but the military and intelligence leadership had long personal and professional connections with the Indians, whom they understood. The moral entrepreneurship of a 'humanitarian great power' such as Norway was harder for them to stomach. The fairly recent secessionist history of Norway (it broke away from Sweden in 1905) was just one of the reasons that inclined them to support the LTTE, some in Colombo believed. The pious manners and attempts to drive rather than finesse policy were other irritants. The hard men were also tired of listening to the alleged triumphs of the 1993 Oslo accords to 'settle' the Arab-Israeli imbroglio. The 'pre-eminent global peacemakers' were mere trouble-makers who would help Prabhakaran secure his own two-state solution. And meanwhile Norway's intercession would introduce more doses of what Colombo felt was NGO colonialism.

When the ceasefire was formalized, it meant that the LTTE was recognized as an equal legal party with the Colombo government, the views of other Tamils were ignored, and the LTTE was given effective control over all Sri Lankans in its zones of control. British conservative newspapers dubbed it 'the greatest giveaway in history'. Colombo had ceded sovereignty and territory and got very little in return, except a temporary and often disrupted peace.[13]

A series of six direct talks followed in Thailand, Norway, Germany and Switzerland. The government shifted towards a federal solution, and the LTTE appeared to edge away from its demand for a separate state. Both sides exchanged prisoners of war. International conflict resolution experts even opined that Kosovo might be a model for a future Tamil Eelam.

The flavour of the administration of the ceasefire was not Balkan, however, but very Nordic. One of the lead figures was Norway's special envoy to Sri Lanka, Erik Solheim, a lanky politician from the left of Norwegian politics. Oslo set up a troika of Solheim, Kjertsi Tromsdal, from the Norwegian foreign ministry, and Vidar Helgesen, the deputy foreign minister. This diplomatic threesome conducted shuttle diplomacy between the government in Colombo and Anton Balasingham, the main LTTE negotiator based in London. Once the ceasefire agreement was announced, the SLMM – the monitoring mission – was created with staff from the five Nordic countries, Denmark, Finland, Iceland, Norway and Sweden. Norway would usually take the lead of the sixty-five monitors, comprising ex-military and police personnel as well as academics and technical specialists. The monitors were dutiful but often found the high temperatures oppressive and the cultural complexities challenging. They commented in their journals and memoirs about the functional anarchy of the madcap driving and the concerns about driving into cows, sacred to the Hindus, as well as the dangers of collisions with elephants at night.[14] Colombo also established a Peace Secretariat to work with the external mission; one of its main complaints was the Nordic mission's lack of enforcement mechanisms – the peace accord did not include any means of sanctions against the LTTE for its endless infringements.[15]

This was perhaps the time that a federal solution might have brought a just and lasting peace. *Perhaps*. If international players and foreign events had combined to bring a ceasefire, domestic factors conspired against peace. Both the LTTE and the government were to be divided internally.

The prime enemy of the two main Sinhalese parties was each other, with the LTTE usually coming a poor second. The 2001 elections had created for the first time a prime minister and a president from different parties. Prime Minister Wickremasinghe's UNP party favoured a federal solution, but the hardline elements in President Kumaratunge's party as well as nationalist allies regarded the LTTE's ceasefire as a manoeuvre to rebuild for war. Tamil moderates still faced grisly denouements. The LTTE continued to recruit, including child soldiers – 'baby brigades' as the army called them. The cadres expanded their sphere of influence farther south, and set up more bases around key sites, especially the Trincomalee naval base. In the north, fairly clear demarcation lines existed between government and LTTE territory; this was not true of the more mixed east, which allowed the cadres to indulge in creeping expansion.

Equally the LTTE enlarged its international networks especially for arms procurement. The end of the Cold War had opened up vast opportunities for weapons, drugs and people smuggling especially in central Asia and eastern Europe. A white-collar 'clean-skin' operation headed by K. P. (Kumaran Pathmanathan) maintained offices in cities such as Bangkok, Paris, Kuala Lumpur and Johannesburg. The front offices operated legal businesses to launder the dirty goods – heroin and arms. Behind the fronts, for example in Hindu temples throughout the diaspora in Britain and Canada, financial command and control centres extorted money via protection rackets on Tamil exiles, and then, via their legal businesses, a whole range of frauds, but especially credit card crime.

Prabhakaran had his own fiefdom with its own customs posts. The LTTE president negotiated with Nordic leaders and foreign warlords who visited his provisional capital in Kilinochchi. Thousands of older fighting cadres were demobilized to return to their families and the idealistic sons and daughters of the diaspora came back home to enjoy the fledgling Eelam. But the Tigers' media campaign maintained their martial drumbeat Prabhakaran's annual Great Heroes Day speech on 27 November used to be broadcast on the Voice of Tigers radio station. By 2005 the speech came via the LTTE TV service, and then via satellite throughout the diaspora. The internet was skilfully deployed by the Tigers' numerous websites. The 'LTTE' office in London was called Eelam House, copying the former ex-colonial examples of Australia House and Canada House.

The cult of martyrdom was enhanced in LTTE-controlled areas. Instead of the traditional Hindu custom of cremation, the LTTE built lavishly maintained cemeteries for families to mourn the heroes of the struggle. Flags fluttered and a temple-like aura was created. The ceremonies at these burial areas, as well as videos of suicide missions, were used as propaganda abroad to stir the diaspora into paying for the new statelet. In short, some of the hard-line suspicions in Colombo that the LTTE was talking peace but preparing for the next round of war were justified.

The government was criticized by the military and especially the intelligence wings for appeasement. Naval officers were pressurized into cutting back on patrols against the Sea Tigers and were told to keep quiet about their fears about the LTTE encirclement of Trincomalee. The concerns of military intelligence were also ignored, especially about the alleged bias of the SLMM mission which had a free run in government areas but only limited access to Tiger territory, that often amounted to little more than meetings in Kilinochchi. The military felt that the far more numerous LTTE breaches of the peace agreement were being ignored by the government and the international community.

In April 2003, the peace negotiations publicly stalled as the LTTE argued *inter alia* that they were not getting proper economic dividends from the ceasefire. The insurgents later issued their own peace proposals based on an Interim Self-Governing Authority. This maximalist move was interpreted by many southern politicians as a step too far on the road to Tamil independence. The LTTE's ill-timed diplomacy weakened its putative partner for peace in Colombo, the UNP government. The Sinhalese opposition parties continued to parade the numerous infractions of the ceasefire by the LTTE.

The regular murders of Tamil opponents by the Tigers riled not only Colombo. In March 2004 Prabhakaran's vice-like grip on the LTTE was broken. Colonel Karuna, the nom de guerre of Vinayagamoorthy Muralitharan, led around 5,000 to 6,000 cadres in the east. A senior commander since 1987, he had seen a lot of combat and how the leadership worked and decided he had had enough of Prabhakaran's murderous rule. Disputes about strategy, weapons allocations and, finally, money led to Prabhakaran summoning Karuna to his command bunker in the north. Karuna suspected that it would be a one-way journey. Karuna summarized his feelings at the time:

> My problem with Prabhakaran was mainly because of his rigid attitude … He wanted Eelam or nothing … Then there was another problem within the LTTE. Since Prabhakaran came from Jaffna, the leadership and all important posts within the organization were always given to the Northern Tamils. Although most of the fighters came from the East, we never got our due … When I raised these issues … I realized they would like to get rid of me … But I read the signs early and decided to break away.[16]

Karuna was already in touch with military intelligence and was wooed away, initially to stay in the comfort of the Colombo Hilton. Karuna's defection did not add much to the army's strength, though the two main insurgent factions did clash intermittently in the early stages of the split. What the fissure did achieve, however, was to hand over a wealth of intelligence on Tiger operations both at home and abroad. It was 'pure gold', according to the chief of National Intelligence.

Some of Karuna's ablest lieutenants were put in a safe house, eighteen kilometres outside Colombo, where they were drugged by the cook and then shot by an LTTE assassin. Despite military intelligence's respect for Karuna as a game-changing asset, his position was ambiguous to some of the so-called 'appeasers' in the government, who worried that support of Karuna might sour the peace deal. Karuna was sent off temporarily, via Nepal, to India for his own safety. (Later, when the Rajapaksas came to power, Karuna was courted, especially by Gotabaya Rajapaksa, who always felt that the LTTE should be encouraged to defect and not be punished. After a short stint in an English jail — for breaking immigration rules — Karuna and some of his supporters were persuaded to return to provincial and national politics. It was a gesture to democratic politics, but it was also a subtle divide and rule strategy to widen the existing rifts between the eastern and northern Tamils.)

The ceasefire staggered on despite the political splits in the LTTE and in Colombo, where the frictions between military intelligence and the government were leaked to the media by ministers. By 2005 the international monitoring mission had tallied up 300 infractions by the government, but ten times that number by the LTTE. Both sides accused the other, accurately, of covert operations in each other's territories. The LTTE blamed the Karuna breakaway on Colombo, not its own brutal relationship with many Tamils in the east.

The Karuna defection coincided with the election, on 6 April 2004, of Mahinda Rajapaksa as prime minister. He headed the United People's Freedom Alliance, which was elected on a tougher policy towards the Tigers. Like all successful Sri Lankan politicians, Prime Minister Rajapaksa came from a political dynasty, which hailed not from the bourgeoisie in Colombo but from humbler stock in the south, Hambantota. His trademark reddish-brown shawl was the colour of korakan, a rough grain that was the staple diet of poor farmers. His sarong and tunic were always immaculately white, signifying Buddhist purity and spirituality, but his bejewelled fingers and hearty laugh perhaps signalled more earthy interests. The barrel-chested rugby fan, with the suspiciously jet-black hair, liked to portray himself as a man of the people, and this came across in his rough-and-ready English when he engaged with foreign visitors.

Prabhakaran had played central stage for two decades, but Mahinda Rajapaksa was to displace him as the most forceful Sri Lankan politician of his generation. In November 2005 he was to become president. Once more, the Tigers were architects of their own downfall. In the 2005 presidential elections they largely prevented Tamils from voting for the pro-peace party, thus ensuring a narrow margin of victory for Rajapaksa's war platform. Rajapaksa's core Freedom Party had allied with the now ultra-nationalist party, the JVP, as well as the new National Heritage Party, inspired by a hardline Buddhist desire to end what it saw as a Hindu threat. The Alliance group consolidated its position in 2004–5 with a promise to the military that it would finally crush the Tigers. If the LTTE had not indulged in its electoral intimidation it would not have had to face the biggest threat to its existence.

Then nature intervened — again. In May 2003 the country had suffered its worst-ever floods which had left 200 people dead, and destroyed thousands of homes. Much worse was to come. On Boxing Day, 26 December 2004, the island was hit by the Indian Ocean tsunami. Over 300,000 people were wiped out in the region; American soldier-statesman Colin Powell compared the impact with a Hiroshima-sized nuclear explosion. Others described it as Asia's 9/11. More than 30,000 Sri Lankans were killed and many more made homeless. The destruction hit the LTTE hard, especially its naval bases. Military analysts in Colombo estimated that over 2,000 cadres had been killed, although publicly on TamilNet the organization hugely downplayed its losses in men and boats. The tsunami effects that were conceded did boost sympathy, and of course huge funds from the diaspora. One of the main fronts, the Tamil Rehabilitation Organization, raised nearly $500 million, according to its own accounts – in just one month. The government and the LTTE did manage initially to set up the so-called P-TOMS (Post-Tsunami Operational Management Structure) which led to inevitable squabbles (and then law suits) about local funds and $3 billion foreign aid money not reaching the north and east. The JVP left the government over the controversy. The natural disaster did achieve a minor miracle – a marked decrease in violence as Sri Lankans tried to rebuild their lives.

Nonetheless, the Machiavellian policies of the LTTE chieftain ensured that the foreign aid pouring in also allowed ample scope for smuggling in weapons, including the nucleus of his air power. Militarily insignificant, it was a PR disaster strategically. From Washington's perspective, in the aftermath of al-Qaeda's fascination with suicide aircraft, the fact that an organization publicly committed to martyrdom should become the world's first terrorist air force was bound to set off alarm bells. It might have been a domestic propaganda coup, but it was a clear act of military overreach in the international context. A similar own goal was the assassination by an LTTE sniper of Lakshman Kadirgamar, a foreign minister and a Tamil who was highly respected by foreign diplomats for his courage, skill and wit.[17] The killing of a diplomat who had been in the running to become Secretary General of the Commonwealth complemented the increasing international marginalization of the Tigers.

In the November 2005 presidential elections Prime Minister Rajapaksa won on his platform of a more robust approach to the LTTE. Prabhakaran declared that he would renew the struggle in 2006 if the government did not take rapid moves to a full peace. The stage was set for the next round of conflict – Eelam War IV. This would not be a replay of the push-me-pull-me struggle of the fighting before 2002, however. Rajapaksa represented a government which was utterly determined to wage all-out war for victory, if necessary. A parallel was the meat-grinder strategy of the Soviet Union in the last stages of the battles on the eastern front in the Second World War. This would be a fight to the finish, not to be sidetracked by foreign intervention, not from India and certainly not from the Nordic countries.

Before narrating the events of the final round of the war, it would be useful to consider in detail the nature of the two combatants so as to understand what Marxists might call the correlation of forces. What were their chief strengths and weaknesses, their main strategies and tactics?

THE MAIN COMBATANTS

Chapter 9

The Sri Lankan Government Forces

Background

The regular Ceylon Defence Force (CDF) was founded in 1910 although a reserve volunteer force had existed since 1881. The CDF came under the command of the British Army. It was mainly British officered and the other ranks were Ceylonese. An exception was the Ceylon Planters Rifle Corps, which was made up of Europeans. This rifle corps took part in the South African war of 1899–1902, as did the Ceylon Mounted Infantry. During the Great War many Ceylonese of all races volunteered to join the British Army fighting in France. Ceylonese units served in Egypt and in the Gallipoli campaign. During the Second World War the regular units came under the control of Britain's South East Asia Command, headed by Lord Louis Mountbatten. The island was fortified extensively in anticipation of a Japanese invasion. In April 1942, for example, Japanese bombers, escorted by Zero fighters, mounted a large-scale surprise attack on Colombo and on a nearby Royal Air Force base, knocking out eight Hurricanes. Ceylon's colonial forces deployed to occasional exotic garrison duties in the Seychelles, and also in the Cocos islands (where it had to put down a small Trotskyite mutiny among its own ranks; three soldiers were court-martialled and hanged, making them the only 'Commonwealth' soldiers executed by the British during the war). By 1945 the CDF numbered around 20,000.

After the war the CDF, in one case supported by British Royal Marines, countered left-wing strikes. On independence, technically the colonial force was disbanded but it was reconstituted into a new regular and reserve force structure. The formal foundation of the post-independence army dates from 9 October 1949 (now celebrated annually as army day; the navy and air force celebrate different foundation days). In contrast with the rapid mobilization of 1939–45, the CDF was reduced to around half its previous size. A defence agreement of 1947 offered the new colony British protection in the event it was attacked by a foreign state. British military advisers were provided and in effect a British brigadier commanded the fledgling army. Promising young Ceylonese officers were sent to the Royal Military Academy, Sandhurst, and more senior officers were trained at the British Staff College at Camberley. Some officers were sent to accompany the British Army of the Rhine for cold weather, and Cold War, experience. The emphasis on foreign military training was to continue as a hallmark of staff-officer education into the twenty-first century, though Britain was to give way to the US, China, India and Pakistan. Likewise, insignia, rank structure and officer ethos were long influenced by the British Army, though the dictates of ethnic war transformed some of the rules and standards taught at Sandhurst and Camberley. Ironically, Sri Lanka much later offered to instruct NATO armies in jungle-warfare skills.

Army
The Ceylonese army, now under an indigenous commander, led its first major operation (Operation MONTY) to stop the influx of illegal South Indian immigrants smuggled into the country. The army co-ordinated with what was then the Royal Ceylon Navy. The army was busy in support of the police throughout the 1950s during strikes and domestic riots. Trade union and left-wing parties were active in much commercial disruption, most notably the 1961 Colombo port strike which caused major food shortages. Against this background of left-wing agitation a number of officers planned the 1962 coup. It was squashed just a few hours before it was due to be enacted. Fear of military intervention undermined political confidence in the forces for decades. The immediate result was the reduction of the military. In 1972 the three main services were renamed to reflect the republican status. From 1983 the main focus of the army was COIN against the Tamil insurgencies, although the two JVP Sinhalese insurrections (1971 and the late 1980s) also demanded extensive military operations. Few armies have had to fight a series of civil wars for over three decades. The ruling politicians were forced to learn to love their armed services and pump men and money into them – just to survive.

Like many developing countries Sri Lanka contributed to UN peacekeeping operations, in the early 1960s in the Congo and then, after 2004, a series of missions in Haiti. The average Haitian deployment was around 1,000 personnel. In 2007 over 100 members of the mission, including three officers, were accused of sexual misconduct including child abuse (though the latter related to women under eighteen paid for sex). The UN investigation found all the accused Sri Lankan military personnel guilty of the charges, although in Colombo nationalist politicians talked of an international conspiracy, related to criticisms from NGOs involved in the Tamil insurgency at home. Colombo promised an official inquiry and prompt punishment while replacing the offending regiment with 750 troops from the Gemunu Hewa Regiment. In 2010–11, small deployments were also sent to Chad, the Central African Republic, Sudan, and Western Sahara, while maintaining its major mission in Haiti. In November 2010 a mechanized infantry company (around 150 troops) was sent to join UN forces in Lebanon.

Structure and size

The army's organization is based on the British Army model. And, like the Indian army, it has maintained in particular the regimental system inherited at independence. The infantry battalion, the basic unit in field operations, would typically include five companies of four platoons each. Platoons usually had three squads (sections) of ten soldiers each. In 1986 a new commando regiment was formed. Support for the infantry was standard – armoured regiments, field artillery regiments, plus signals and engineering support etc. In addition to commando forces, of interest were the special forces and a rocket artillery regiment.

Official and unofficial Sri Lankan figures and ORBATs (orders of battle) tend to differ from the standard Western data provided, for example, by the International Institute for Strategic Studies (IISS).[18] The IISS put the current strength of the army at 117,000 comprising 78,000 regulars and 39,000 recalled reservists. That is a big army for a small country (with a population of just over 20 million), but not in the context of a long war. The army was certainly much larger, however, during the intense fighting in 2006–09. My interviews with a range of officers at or above the rank of brigadier all confirmed that the immediate post-war strength was around 230,000. Many senior officers insisted that the army should not be reduced, despite the potential post-war peace dividend, although they accepted, grudgingly, that natural wastage would reduce their ranks. When the same officers were asked their guesstimate of the size of the British Army, they all opined that it was much larger than theirs. They were stunned to discover that it was just over 100,000 and being reduced to 80,000. They then stopped complaining about possible reductions in the Sri Lankan army. The 1983 strength was roughly 12,000 regulars. Aggressive recruitment followed the outbreak of the Tamil war.

Today's high figure of about 200,000 includes nearly 3,000 women. In 1979 the Army Women's Corps was formed as an unarmed, non-combatant support unit. Inspiration and early training came from the British Women's Royal Army Corps. Women in the British Army – except medical, dental and veterinary officers and chaplains (who belonged to the same corps as the men) and nurses (who were members of the Queen Alexandra's Royal Army Nursing Corps) – were in the WRAC from 1949 to 1992.[19] Initially the Sri Lankan equivalent was similar to its British parent. Enlistment involved a five-year service commitment, (the same as men) and recruits were not allowed to marry in this period. They did basic training and drill, but not weapons and battle training. Females, however, were paid at the same level as the men, but were generally limited to communications, clerical and nursing duties. The long war prompted the expansion of the Women's Corps; two women reached the rank of major general. By 2011 the Women's Corps comprised one regular and four volunteer regiments.

Since Sri Lanka forces were all-volunteer services – that is, there had been no conscription – all personnel had *volunteered* for regular or reserve service. Conscription had been regularly debated and since the 1985 legislation the government has had the legal power to enforce national military service. Economic pressures, patriotism, religious nationalism and local, familial or caste traditions had managed to fill the ranks, however. Recruitment was in theory nationwide, though this did not apply in the northern and eastern provinces during the war (some Tamils, however, joined pro-government militias as well as the regular forces). After the war, plans were announced to form a 'Tamil regiment' to promote integration in the army. (Another exception was the Rifle Corps which recruited from a specific area.)

The Sri Lanka Army Volunteer Force (SLAVF) was the main volunteer reserve of the army. It was the collective name for the reserve units as well as the National Guard. The SLAVF was made up of part-time officers and soldiers, who were paid the same as the regular forces when on active duty. This was in contrast to the Regular Army Reserve, which comprised people who had a mobilization obligation for a number of years after their former full-time service in the regular army had been completed.

Operational command varied according to the tempo of the COIN war. The Army General Staff had been based at the Army HQ. Troops were deployed to protect the capital – which suffered a series of major terrorist attacks. Troops to defend the capital were based at Panagoda cantonment, the headquarters of a number of regiments, as well as a major arsenal and military hospital. The majority of infantry troops were deployed into the northern and eastern provinces during the war; they were placed under six commands known as Security Forces Headquarters: in Jaffna (SFHQ-J); Wanni (SFHQ-W); East (SFHQ-E), Kilinochchi (SFHQ-KLN); Mullaitivu (SFHQ-MLT) and South (SFHQ-S).

For officer training Sri Lanka largely adopted the British model. The local equivalent of Sandhurst was the Sri Lanka Military Academy (SLMA) based in Diyatalawa, where the young officer cadets trained for ninety weeks, much longer than their UK equivalents. Following the British model (set up in the UK in 1997) middle-ranking officers from all three services were educated at the Defence Services Command and Staff College. Just outside Colombo, the Kotelawala Defence University was established in 1981, as a tri-service college for young cadets (aged eighteen to twenty-two) to pursue a three-year course. Foreign senior-officer training migrated from the UK to more friendly, or generous, allies in Pakistan, China, Malaysia, the US and more recently the Philippines. More covert was the COIN training received from the Israelis, who have had a close intelligence and procurement relationship with Sri Lanka since the mid-1980s. In the early period the Israelis assisted with instruction in FIBUA (Fighting In Built-Up Areas).

Army's weapons

The army's equipment was initially British Second World War surplus, although some post-war armoured fighting vehicles such as the Saladins, Saracens and Ferrets were also added to the inventory. By the 1970s the USSR, Yugoslavia and China had displaced Britain; Chinese support was the most consistent. Modern counter-insurgency demanded modern military hardware, including heavy machine guns, rocket-propelled grenade launchers, 106mm recoilless rifles and 60mm and 81mm mortars as well as up-to-date sniper rifles and night-vision equipment. Armoured mobility was also needed. The old Saladins and Ferrets and the like were too vulnerable to anti-tank weapons let alone mines. China provided an array of tracked and wheeled armoured personnel carriers (APCs) including the Type 85 amphibious variant. From Moscow came forty-five of the BTR-80 APCs to replace the trusty old BTR-152s. After 1985 South Africa provided Buffels which had proved very effective in apartheid's bush wars, especially against land mines. Sri Lanka then developed its own variants, the Unibuffel (300 were locally manufactured) and the Unicorn. The Soviet Union provided nearly 300 infantry fighting vehicles (variants of the BMP). The Czechs shipped in around eighty T-55 medium battle tanks, while China matched the supply of tanks (Type 59s). The army also used Chinese Type

63 amphibious tanks. Sri Lanka claimed it had sixty-two MTBs (Main Battle Tanks).[20] Much of the imported kit was obsolete or obsolescent, but it was refitted and often proved useful in combat.

Artillery came largely from China, especially 122mm, 130mm and 152mm howitzers introduced from the mid-1990s. From 2000 the deadly offspring of the 'Stalin Organs', 122mm multi-barrel rocket launchers, were deployed. Colombo acquired around thirty RM-71s from Czechoslovakia and a handful of BM-21s from Russia. Rocket artillery may not be very accurate but it can have a devastating effect, physically and morally, at the receiving end. The army was also well equipped with the standard array of mortars, from 60mm light mortars to 120mm towed versions — all courtesy of Beijing. It also used fairly sophisticated radar counter-battery equipment, the US-designed AN/TPQ-36 Firefinder at first. But the American system was old and the Sri Lankans had problems with spare parts. Then the Chinese stepped in with better equipment. When I asked the army commander, Lieutenant General Jagath Jayasuriya, what he regarded as his most useful bit of kit, he did not hesitate: 'Artillery locating radars. We could locate friend and foe. That was the most important. We had five of them [systems]. With interlocking systems, we had total coverage. From 2008, it was in position.'[21] Most of the army casualties had been from LTTE mortars and artillery.

A senior artillery expert in the army, Brigadier A. P. C. Napagoda, summarized the 2006–09 campaign thus:

> From the battle of Marvil Aru to the final battle at the Nandikadal lagoon the artillery brigade employed a sufficient number of light field medium guns, MBRL [multi-barrel rocket launchers] and locative radars ... which facilitated the creation of high gun density over any given area.[22]

The Sri Lankans patched together local and imported signals systems. Perhaps the most important was the provision of live feeds from unmanned drones to the army HQ and divisional HQs. The other primary means of communication were radio and CDMA (code division multiple access technology); the latter allowed commanders at all levels secure and interactive full 'duplex' communication. VHF and UHF jammers were deployed to disrupt enemy networks. The army also used locally manufactured manpack bomb jammers to nullify LTTE improvised explosive devices.

Sri Lanka acquired a wide range of infantry weapons. The Beretta M9s and Glock 17s were frequently used handguns. The communist-sourced AK-47 assault rifles were very common, and, from the West, Heckler and Koch G3s, FNs and American M16s. Machine guns were varied too: ranging from the classic British Sterling to German MP5s and also Israeli Uzis. The vintage FN MAG gun was a traditional and reliable workhorse. The Chinese versions of the Russian RPD (Type 56 LMG) were also in evidence. Grenade launchers arrived from South Africa and Germany as well as the M-203 from the US. Many of the RPGs (man-portable rocket launchers) came from China and anti-tank missiles were sourced from Pakistan.

Army tactics

On land and sea the government forces fought conventional war unconventionally, sometimes aping and mastering the asymmetric tactics of the insurgents. Above all they used small-group long-range tactics by special forces to destabilize the enemy rear. The Commando regiments were set up in 1980, but the most effective troops were the special forces (SF) set up in 1985.

The special forces comprised around 5,000 troops in five regiments. They trained originally with the Israelis, mainly in urban warfare, but soon the Sri Lankan SF became arguably the best jungle fighters in the world. They fought in eight-man teams, although sometimes two teams of eight would combine, especially in an emergency or for logistical purposes. For example, one surveillance team might overlap with a team establishing a forward-supply cache (usually of ammunition, water and medicine) and then join forces if they met hostile elements. The SF did not use helicopters for insertions, partly because of the jungle terrain and partly because of stealth. They would walk in and often penetrate up to forty to fifty kilometres behind the lines. The air force was used only five times in emergency casevacs, usually by Mi-24 choppers. Nor did the SBS or navy work directly with the army SF. The SF commander told me: 'We did no landings by sea – ground penetration was safer for us.'[23] Paradrops were not considered, not least because of the Indian army debacle in Jaffna.

The long-range patrols (LRPs) could last up to a month. They would act as spotters for air and artillery strikes. They would also disrupt LTTE movement not least by targeting their leaders and communications. The SF were also used defensively to plug successful LTTE counter-attacks or to staunch the occasional LTTE spectacular. For example, on 29 September 2008, the LTTE elite Black Tigers hit an air force base in the rear of army operations. Two Tiger aircraft also bombed the base. SF squadrons were rushed in to halt further LTTE exploitation of the surprise attack.

Interestingly, the special forces did not utilize captured insurgents, partly because many Tigers took suicide pills rather than surrender. Even when they were captured, the SF were extremely reluctant to accept any 'turned' insurgents. Despite the widespread and effective use of so-called 'turned terrorists' in the Rhodesian Selous Scouts, itself based upon British 'pseudo-gang' techniques applied in Malaya and Kenya, the Sri Lankan SF deployed only a handful of Tamil-speaking former Tigers and then very reluctantly and very occasionally. According to SF sources, there was only one example of a pseudo using his insurgent knowledge and the Tamil language to enable SF troops to disengage from a position where they were vastly outnumbered.

The army's massive recruitment drive – attracting 3,000–5,000 men per month in the last two years of the war – allowed for attack and defence in depth. Combined services provided two or three infantry lines to prevent the previous LTTE tactic of outflanking or penetrating the lines, and then attacking from the rear. This would imply an unimaginative linear type of mentality. In fact, the ethos of the SF and commando long-range patrols were applied throughout the infantry in the focus on small-unit initiative. Special Infantry Operations Training (SIOT) – the initial courses were forty-four days – allowed the small units to carry out complex operations in often difficult terrain. The insurgents knew their own territory and so the army sought infantrymen who had been born and bred in the villages and who might also possess the same familiarity with jungles and endurance as the guerrillas they encountered. The small group approach from the SF down to the ordinary infantry created flexibility and often area dominance. Ability, not least from NCOs, was rewarded; promotion of good NCOs to officers was also encouraged. Mission command was to be seen at most levels, certainly best practice in COIN.

A close observer of the war, Dr David Kilcullen, an acknowledged authority on COIN, commented on the final stages:

> The Tigers chose to confront the government in a symmetrical way, in terms of open warfare. In response, the Sri Lankan army destroyed them with a combination of conventional and counter-guerrilla tactics that denied the Tigers a comparative advantage while the tempo of operations prevented the Tigers from regrouping.[24]

The basic approach of the LTTE was to combine guerrilla warfare, positional defence and IEDs to slow down and inflict heavy casualties by indirect fire – artillery and mortars. The LTTE erected numerous ditches and bunds which were often heavily, and randomly, mined. Army sappers had to devise all sort of means of dealing with these fortifications, including the use of improvised Bangalore 'torpedoes'. An independent bridging squadron was also formed as part of the combat engineering effort. On a smaller scale, the infantry used spring-loaded ladders to deal with bunds. Engineers modified tractors to compensate for the lack of roads, especially during heavy monsoons and flooding. Often rations had to be airdropped. The much larger army required a massive logistical back-up.

One engineering challenge was met by installing steel mesh in the Iranamadu and Udayar Kattu reservoirs to protect against underwater Tiger infiltrators. Water was also a challenge for the Army Medical Corps. Near drowning, an unexpected type of casualty, was encountered when the LTTE blasted the bund around the Kalmadukulam Tank (reservoir). Frontline medics had to deal with 60 per cent of casualties from mortar and artillery blasts and 40 per cent from gunshot wounds. They also had to treat tropical diseases, especially Hepatitis A. Post-traumatic stress disorders also took their toll.

In short, tactical flexibility plus the massive numerical superiority (as well as air supremacy) allowed the army to dominate and then overwhelm the Tigers towards the end of the campaign.

The Navy
As befits an island in the middle of crucial sea lanes, naval defence has always been a major security issue. In 1937 the Ceylon Naval Volunteer Force (CNVF) was set up. The Second World War meant a rapid absorption into the Royal Navy. In 1950 a small nucleus of officers and men forged the Royal Ceylon Navy, to change its name, as with the other services, when the country became a republic. Initial naval expansion depended upon purchase of ex-British and Canadian ships. The navy suffered perhaps even more than the army from the fallout from the 1962 coup conspiracy. Ships were sold off and manpower reduced, as was training in the UK. The navy was therefore ill-prepared for the first JVP insurrection and the beginning of the Tamil revolt. The immediate stopgap was the gift of initially one of the more advanced Shershen-class torpedo boats from the USSR and purchase of the unsophisticated Chinese Shanghai-11-class fast gunboats for coastal patrols and port protection. New bases were built primarily to

interdict smuggling operations from southern India. The navy also developed a land component for base defence, becoming known later as Naval Patrolmen and capable of offensive operations. The navy also replicated the British SBS – the Special Boat Service. As the LTTE war expanded – and the Tigers relied on extensive overseas procurement – Sri Lanka developed a blue-water strategy capable of sinking large ships, even just outside the territorial waters of Australia.

The naval HQ was based in Colombo; this controlled six naval command areas. After the war some of the coastal defence was transferred to a newly formed Coast Guard.

The 2012 fleet consisted of over fifty combat, support ships and inshore craft, sourced from China, India, Israel and, more recently, from indigenous build.

The IISS put the size of the navy as 9,000 personnel, both active and reserve, but this appeared to be an underestimate. Probably the more accurate figure was 48,000, of whom approximately 15,000 were dedicated to land deployment. Women served in regular and reserve roles. Initially women were limited to the medical branch but the tempo of war led to females serving in all branches. A female doctor reached the rank of commodore in 2007.

The navy's weapons

The navy boasted about 150 vessels, but the core consisted of around fifty combat and support ships. In addition, the navy rapidly manufactured 200 small inshore patrol craft. The majority of the larger vessels came from China, India and Israel, though the Sri Lankans began building their own bigger ships. The largest warships were five offshore patrol vessels, with the SLNS *Jayasagara* built in Sri Lanka (and commissioned in 1983). All the blue-water vessels could operate naval helicopters (but insufficient funding and air force opposition prevented any such deployment). The offshore patrol ships played a vital role in interdicting and finally sinking the major Tiger supply and storage ships. In 2001 two Israeli Saar 4-class fast missile boats were procured. Dubbed the Nandimithra class by the Sri Lankan Navy (SLN), they carried Gabriel 11 anti-ship missiles as well as a range of guns which augmented the conventional warfighting capability.

The workhorse of the navy – involved in regular coastal combat – was the fast attack flotilla. It was formed in the early 1980s with Israeli Dvora-class boats to counter LTTE gun-running in the Palk Strait between India and Sri Lanka. Two Dvoras were purchased in 1984 and another four in

1986. Around twenty-five metres long, and displacing about forty-seven tons, able to reach 45 knots and bristling with rapid-fire guns, they were able to deter the 'swarming' wolf-pack tactics of the Sea Tigers – a major element in asymmetric naval warfare. Small fibreglass Sea Tiger suicide craft would attack naval and civilian convoys. The fast-attack flotilla also patrolled the many creeks and landing points in LTTE territory to disrupt smaller boats securing resupply from the larger blue-water Tiger ships. The flotilla was made up of a variety of fast-attack craft types: four heavier Israeli Super Dvora (Mark 11) were delivered in 1995–96. The navy also used the Israeli Shaldag-class design to construct its own Colombo class. Ten other fast-attack craft originated in China.

Compared with their counterparts in other navies, the SLN fast-attack craft were much more heavily armed. They started with two or three machine guns but became more heavily armed to counter the arsenals fitted on Sea Tiger craft. Eventually, the fast attack craft had Typhoon 25–30mm stabilized cannon as the main armament. They were connected to day-and-night, all-weather, long-range electro-optic systems. The recent Colombo class was equipped with an Elop MSIS optronic director and the Typhoon GFCS boasted its own weapons control system. They also sported fancy surface search radar systems. In addition they carried weapons such as the Oerlikon 20mm cannon, automatic grenade launchers and PKM general purpose machine guns. This sounds over-armed but heavy firepower was required to protect the crews from suicide Sea Tigers trying to ram them or explode themselves close by. The fast-attack craft typically had eighteen crew members and operated in group patrols, usually, but not always, at night. The Tigers fought very hard and would not retreat; occasionally the flotilla had to withdraw from engagements. A fast-attack captain said, 'Flak jackets were no good, except for bits of shrapnel; the heavy calibre [Tiger] guns would tear people in half.'[25]

Inshore patrol craft were much smaller (fourteen metres long). They were used for harbour defence and amphibious operations. In addition, the seven-metre-long Arrow class were heavily armed speedboats manufactured in Sri Lanka and used by the SBS and its variant, the Rapid Action Boat Squadron (RABS). The SBS, formed in 2005, comprised around 600 men. Those who passed the tough training for the SBS but who were not good enough for the final selection phase could join the RABS, which numbered around 400 men.

To support larger amphibious operations the SLN had a tank landing ship and other utility craft. The Yuhai-class ship could transport two tanks and

250 troops. There were also smaller Chinese-made landing craft. The SLN had several auxiliary vessels for personnel transport and replenishment.

During the war the navy had no dedicated air assets or UAVs. Afterwards, the embryonic fleet air arm based on the offshore patrol ships started experimenting with HAL Chetak (the Indian revamp of the venerable French Alouette III) and HH-65 Dolphin choppers, used extensively by the US Coast Guard in short range air-sea rescue roles.

Most of the naval assets and SBS units were based during the war at Trincomalee, one of the best and most attractive harbours in the world. It was attacked consistently during the war, from and under the sea, and from cadres who had infiltrated the nearby wooded hinterland. Any British visitor to the base would be struck by its colonial heritage: the streets and junctions are named after Oxford Street and Piccadilly Circus. Monkeys clamber over verandahs of Seymour Cottage in Drummond Hill Road. It is very orderly, very Royal Navy, including the smart waiters in the mess/wardroom serving up a perfectly chilled gin and tonic in the sticky heat.

Maritime tactics

It is very rare for an insurgency's naval forces to reach parity and even on occasions outmatch the conventional COIN power's force. The naval war was long, active and intense: it involved the biggest tonnage of ships sunk since the Falklands war of 1982. To defend the 679 nautical miles of coastline the navy grew to nearly 50,000 (including 15,000 Naval Patrolmen for land-based security), almost the same size as the Indian navy. But for most of the war the Sea Tigers proved more flexible and destructive especially with their swarming tactics mixing suicide and attack boats. They sank a Dvora fast attack craft in August 1995 and another in March 1996. The Tigers filmed their sea victories for their propaganda outlets. They destroyed a further six of other classes of fast attack craft. After the ceasefire ended in 2005, the Sea Tigers sent out larger and more craft, mixing suicide craft among the wolf pack. The Black Tiger suicide crews and boats were difficult to detect, with their low profiles and 35–40 knot speed.

Just as the army developed the small-group concept, the navy advanced its own small boat variant. They tried to 'out guerrilla' the guerrillas. The navy copied the Sea Tigers' asymmetric swarm but on a much larger scale. Hundreds of small inshore patrol craft were built from fibreglass; the smallest was the twenty-three-foot Arrow. Large fourteen-metre and seventeen-metre variants were also built. The larger boats had double-barrelled 23mm guns and a 44mm automatic grenade launcher (the latter acquired from Singapore). The fast-attack craft had more endurance, reach and firepower, but they were unstable in heavy seas and often needed to be augmented by the small boats to defeat swarms. The inshore patrol craft (IPCs) were based in strategically important locations ready for rapid-reaction forays against surprise assaults by the Sea Tigers. Although much of the fighting was at night, the navy had to maintain twenty-four-hour surveillance. Several squadrons could unite to form an anti-swarm of sometimes up to fifty or sixty boats. Echoing infantry tactics on land, they used an arrowhead formation to expand the arc of fire. Or they would attack in three adjacent columns in single file to mask their numbers and increase the element of surprise.

The SBS operated in four- or eight-man teams, deploying in Arrow boats or rubber inflatable boats for covert insertions. The SBS provided vital surveillance but also took part in land-strike missions. SBS basic training was for one year, with the majority dropping out before the end. Their training was said to be augmented by Indian Marine Commandos, as well as US special forces, including SEALs. The RABS manned the large number of anti-swarming boats, a tough and dangerous role.

The navy's lacklustre performance was much improved after 2006. It contributed immensely to the government's war effort by coastal interdiction of arms supplies to the Tigers, then it went further by adopting an extended blue-water strategy by sinking eight 'Pigeon' ships, the LTTE floating warehouses. Crucially, it also provided the umbilical supply line to the garrison in Jaffna. Towards the end of the war it prevented escape by sea of the surviving Tiger leadership, as well as engaging in humanitarian missions for civilians fleeing the fighting.

The keys to LTTE logistics were the unflagged merchant ships which would loiter 1,600 kilometres from the island, and then advance to 150 or so kilometres off the coast to liaise with LTTE fishing trawlers, escorted by armed Sea Tiger boats. The navy initially attacked the logistic trawler fleet, sinking eleven in the first year of renewed fighting. With the help of Indian and, sometimes, US intelligence, the navy sought out the LTTE Pigeon ships. The navy deployed its most up-to-date offshore patrol vessels, the *Sayura* (ex-Indian navy, re-commissioned in 2000) and *Samudura* (formerly the USS *Courageous*, transferred from the US Coast Guard in 2004); it quickly converted old merchant ships and rust-bucket tankers as replenishment vessels. The long-range fleet sank the first floating warehouse on 17 September 2006, 1,350 nautical miles from Sri Lanka. A further three were sunk in early 2007. Then audaciously the navy extended itself 1,620 nautical miles southeast, close to the Australian territory of the Cocos Islands off the coast of Indonesia, to destroy three ships in September 2007 and a fourth in early October.

Vice Admiral D. W. A. S. Dissanaayake, the naval commander, was sitting in his splendid office in Naval HQ in Colombo, with a fine view of the sea and the lighthouse built by the British. He was a poet and songwriter in his spare time. 'We are not a big navy – we don't have frigates. We improvised,' he said. 'But we went nearly all the way to Australian waters and sank the last four vessels.'

The Pigeon ships did not possess heavy-calibre weapons but they would open up with machine guns, mortars and RPGs when challenged by the navy. The Vice Admiral explained how – after initial resistance – the LTTE seamen did not offer to surrender. They either swallowed their cyanide tablets or simply drowned. On both sides in the naval war, there were few stories of capture at sea or rescue of survivors. Little or no quarter was given in littoral or deepwater combat. Because the LTTE vessels were rogue ships, naval officers claimed the right to protect themselves when they came under attack from the Pigeons. The loss of their supplies of weapons, ammunition and medicines was a major logistical defeat for the Tigers.

The Vice Admiral was equally voluble about the navy's logistical achievements, especially the supply to Jaffna. The city was an icon to both sides in the war. The Tigers occupied it in 1986 and the Indian forces managed to briefly and precariously occupy it in 1987; it returned to rebel control from 1989 to 1995. The army regained the city in 1995. Thereafter its long siege was as symbolic to the Colombo government as Leningrad (now St Petersburg) was to the Soviets in the Second World War. It had to be held at all costs.

The navy escorted a converted cruise ship they dubbed the *Jetliner* to resupply the city. It took five to six hours to pass LTTE controlled coastline on the dangerous journey from Trincomalee up the northeast coast to Jaffna. The western route is not navigable, except by very small boats or hovercraft. The *Jetliner*, heavily armed itself with machine guns, was typically escorted by over twenty ships and boats, to deter Sea Tiger raids. Beechcraft aircraft and UAVs tracked the convoy. It left early in the morning and, once in Jaffna, had to organize a very quick turnaround, thirty minutes, so as to traverse the LTTE coast before dark on the return journey. Over forty tons of cargo and approximately 3,000 troops were transported once or twice a week. The whole of the navy and indeed most of the top brass in defence HQ would be on alert until the convoy sneaked past the dangers of LTTE artillery and sea attack. Jaffna was also supplied by air but only the navy could provide the heavy lift of sufficient men and equipment to keep the city in government hands.

'If the ship had gone down, we would have lost the war,' the navy commander admitted.[26]

The navy was also proud of its actions during the final phases of the war. The Vice Admiral insisted the navy did not use any naval gunnery to attack the LTTE remnants in the Cage, but it did take extensive risks from last-ditch suicide boats to rescue thousands of civilians from the beaches as they tried to flee Tiger punishment squads and the Sri Lankan army envelopment.

The navy endured heavy fighting — some sea battles lasted fourteen hours — and many early reverses in ships sunk. The navy leadership was also targeted by Black Tiger squads. On 16 November 1992 the head of the navy, Vice Admiral W. W. E. C. Fernando, was killed in Colombo by a suicide bomber on a motorcycle who drove into the Admiral's staff car. In October 2007 a truck bomber killed an assembly of 107 off-duty sailors, one of the most deadly suicide attacks of the war. In all, the navy lost over a thousand of its personnel in the conflict. Nevertheless, it finally achieved sea dominance because of its small-boat concept in defeating the Sea Tiger swarms, and the major interdiction of LTTE supplies. It was a four-dimensional war – a land, air and sea and underwater fight. The navy did not develop a sophisticated anti-mine warfare capability, however. The Tigers used frogmen with mines and semi-submersibles to destroy navy ships. The Tigers were trying to develop submarine warfare; various crude prototypes were captured by the army in the last stages of the war.

Air Force
The air force was the junior service, founded in 1951 as the Royal Ceylon Air Force. Unsurprisingly, much of the ethos and style of the service were based on Britain's Royal Air Force, which provided the early training aircraft. When the British closed their bases in Ceylon in 1956, the two main RAF bases were taken over by the Ceylonese. In its early years the air force was engaged largely in immigration patrols. During the Tiger insurgency the air force moved from transport and patrol duties to active counter-insurgency operations.

Initial combat aircraft came from the UK — de Havilland Vampire jets, although they were never deployed. They were replaced with twelve BAC Jet Provost T51 aircraft, but they were also put in storage (to be rapidly mobilized for the first JVP rebellion in 1971). The first helicopter in the inventory was the Westland Dragonfly HR 5, later augmented by US and Indian choppers.[27]

The first active-duty demand for the air force was the JVP insurrection, especially to relieve sieges of isolated army and police outposts; an air force base at Ekala was also attacked by the Sinhalese insurgents. The left-leaning Bandaranaike administration turned to the Soviet Union for emergency aid; Moscow responded quickly with helicopters and fixed-wing aircraft, including MiG-17Fs. This was the time when the rival superpowers competed for the non-aligned vote, so Washington felt obliged to match the Russians by sending six Bell 47G helicopters, which were deployed after only five days of pilot training.

After the defeat of the 1971 rebellion, funds dried up for the air force, which enterprisingly turned to running a commercial business to fly foreign tourists around the island's many beauty spots. But the outbreak of the Tiger insurgency compelled the air force to concentrate on COIN. By 1987 it had increased to 3,700 personnel (a Women's Wing was formed in the same year). But the Russian aircraft had been mothballed and the air force lacked fighter-bomber capability. Old British bases from Second World War days were re-activated (for example, at Batticaloa and Sigiriya). Servicing so many aircraft, from so many different sources, particularly procuring spare parts, caused many headaches, especially as the Tiger attacks took their toll. Some aircraft were repaired in Singapore, and Canada helped with servicing the Bell chopper fleet. Like the sanctioned Rhodesians in the 1970s, who also refitted the SF 260s, the Sri Lankans proved adept in refitting for COIN purposes civilian or military trainer aircraft bought in Italy, Britain and US. Six SIAI Marchetti SF 260 turboprops were used for rocket attacks and strafing. (The LTTE shot down a number of them – for example, in September 1990 and in July 1992, when both pilots were killed.) Burma (Myanmar) helped with replacements, but in the twenty-first century the Chinese-built Nanchang PT-6 replaced the venerable SF 260s. Singapore also assisted in refitting the Bell choppers (212 and 412) as gunships and transports for commando operations. In addition, transport aircraft were utilized as bombers. The small fleet of Harbin Y-12 high-wing utility craft was equipped with bomb racks to carry up to 1,000kg of anti-personnel and fragmentation bombs. The refits were deemed successful until a Chinese Shaanxi Y-8 crashed during a bombing mission in 1992.

In the early 1990s the air force procured four Chengdu FR-7 Skybolts and two Shenyang J-5s from China. Beijing also supplied three FT-7s; because of their lack of endurance and payload, the F-7s were mainly used as trainers. Later, three F-7BS aircraft were added for ground-attack missions. Four FMA IA 58 Pucarás were acquired for ground attack. The Argentine COIN-specialist aircraft was designed for use from short rough forward airstrips, as its extensive deployment in the Falklands war proved, though it was shot down even by small-arms fire in that conflict. In Sri Lanka three of the Pucarás were brought down, two by Tiger surface-to-air missiles. The surviving Pucará was retired because of lack of spare parts. Six MiG-27s were the much more lethal replacement. The MiG-27 (codenamed Flogger-D/J by NATO) was a variable-geometry ground-attack fighter originally built in the USSR and later produced under licence in India by Hindustan Aeronautics (HAL). The Indians called it the 'Bahadur' (Valiant). Unlike the MiG-23, the MiG-27 saw comparatively little use outside Russia. All the Russian and Ukrainian MiG-27s were retired by the beginning of the twenty-first century; it remained in active service with the Indian, Kazakh and Sri Lankan forces. The Mig-27s saw extensive action bombing stratcgic targets and providing close air support in the Tiger war. In August 2000 a MiG-27 crashed near Colombo International Airport; its Ukrainian pilot did not survive. In July 2001 another MiG-27 was destroyed on the ground by the Tigers. Yet another MiG-27 crashed into the sea in June 2004. The Pucarás may have been relatively vulnerable, but perhaps the MiGs were just unlucky.

On the other hand, the Tigers – one of the very few insurgencies to possess its own air wing – were a formidable foe, on land, sea and in the air. On 24 July 2001, the day the aforementioned MiG-27 was destroyed on the ground, another twelve planes were also destroyed in a pre-dawn raid on the Katunayake air base, adjacent to the civilian International airport thirty-five kilometres from Colombo. The tally included two Kfir fighters and a Mil Mi-24 gunship, as well as military trainers and five civilian jets. The international airport was soon ringed by large anti-blast walls to protect against car bombs, and road approaches and the terminal itself were heavily guarded by immaculately dressed members of the Air Force Regiment. But the damage to national morale, let alone international tourism, had been done.

In 1993 three Mil Mi-17 aircraft augmented the helicopter transport fleet. In 1995 Mi-24 gunships – frightening flying tanks for anyone who had witnessed their lethality in Afghanistan – were acquired for close air support for the army.[28] Six years later Mi-35s were added to the helicopter fleet. Four MiG-27s were purchased from the Ukraine to compensate for the losses.

Sir Lanka shopped where it could for its aircraft. But a constant supplier of manned (and later unmanned) modern aircraft was Israel. The air combat strength had been dramatically boosted in 1996 when Israel provided seven IAI Kfirs (six C.2cs and one TC.2). How Israel produced upgraded variants of the Dassault Mirage 5 airframe is an enthralling adventure story in its own right, involving Mossad's sleight of hand in getting hold of the French designs, despite French sanctions, and then the Israeli-produced, and licensed, version of the American General Electric J79 engine. Israel Aircraft Industries then added its own avionics and sold the jets, with Washington's permission, to a number of countries, mainly in South America, but also to Sri Lanka. (Israel also leased back some of the Kfir variants to the US Navy and US Marines to act as 'adversary aircraft' – sometimes in Israeli livery; strange that Washington should simulate US v Israeli aerial combat.) The sleek Kfirs were in service in Israel from 1975 to the mid-1990s, and so were available for less advanced, or hard-pressed, air forces such as Sri Lanka's. A further nine Kfirs were handed over to Colombo by 2005.

The air force had been constantly engaged in ground-attack roles throughout the LTTE-controlled areas. By 2006 the Tigers had developed their own air force using several modified lightweight aircraft. Air-defence capability, long neglected, had to be rapidly beefed up. A radar network was set up and air-base protection boosted. Airborne interdiction was designed using fixed-wing and rotary-wing assets. From 2007 to 2009 the Tigers used their small air force to attack Colombo and several military bases with usually superficial results. The Tigers were always very clever and rapid improvisers. In October 2007 a ground attack on an air force base at Saliyapura was supported briefly by the Tigers' air wing. Eight government aircraft were destroyed and several damaged. The Sri Lankan response was the use of No. 5 Jet Squadron armed with F-7Gs to act as interceptors. A year after the Saliyapura raid, the Sri Lankan air force claimed its first air-to-air kill when it said that an F-7G had shot down a Tiger Zlin Z-143 which attempted a bombing run on a government base. The Tigers had already released pictures of their new aerial acquisitions: the Czech-built single-engine, four-seater planes modified with a mount for four bombs on the undercarriage. The Air Tigers carried out a suicide raid in the last months of the war by attacking Colombo on 20 February 2009 using two of the Czech planes. Under heavy anti-aircraft gun fire one of the Zlin Z-143s crashed into the Inland Revenue Department building in the capital and the other Tiger plane was shot down near the main air base at Katunayake.

The recent IISS *Military Balance* stated that the country had almost 150 combat-capable aircraft and 13,500 personnel, regular and reserve, whereas Sri Lankan figures put the official size as 27,400 airmen and 1,300 officers, though a number would have been stood down since the end of the Tiger insurgency. In addition, the air force, like its original RAF mentor, had an Air Force Regiment to defend bases, using infantry and light armoured units. The SLAF Regiment contained its own special forces unit for offensives as opposed to merely protecting static positions.

The air force's weapons

The IISS suggested a tally of twenty-three combat-capable fixed-wing aircraft; the Sri Lankans claimed at least ten more. These included fighters and fighter-ground-attack planes. Leading the frontline aircraft were the ten Israeli Kfir fighter-bombers of various marks, operating within the No. 10 Fighter Squadron. Despite their versatility, the Kfirs were unlucky for the air force. Although none was lost in combat, two were destroyed on the ground in 2001 and three were lost in accidents. At the end of the war, nine Kfirs were in service. In March 2011 two collided while practising for an air show. Because it was a multi-role combat aircraft, it was the premier asset, although the design was forty years old. For interceptor roles, the air force deployed eight frontline Chengdu F-7s, with six trainers in reserve. Also deployed were seven MiG-27M Floggers, with some conversion trainer back-up. China, Pakistan and the US supplied basic and advanced fixed-wing trainers.

Transport aircraft inventory was standard: two American Lockheed C-130 Hercules, the Ukrainian Antonov An-32 (five) and Chinese Harbin Y-12s and Xian MA60s. The air force lacked an effective large bomber and experimented with rolling barrel bombs out of the Y-12. It was primitive, cheap but often effective until one of the bombs went off in the Y-12, killing, *inter alia*, the only son of a senior officer. The experiment was closed down. Pakistan, however, provided more modern bombs and Israel supplied effective laser-guided weapons. The air force denied using any cluster bombs.

For maritime reconnaissance, a Cessna 421 Golden Eye and two Beechcraft 200T Super King Airs were used. Close ground surveillance was also carried out from 1996 by UAVs: Israeli Searcher Mark II and the EMIT Blue Horizon 2. The unit operating the UAVs was upgraded in 2007 to an operational squadron, but it split in 2008 to form the No. 111 and No. 112 Air Surveillance Squadrons. The provision of Israeli UAVs extended beyond the Searcher and Blue Horizon drones. The Sri Lankans tested the old Israeli Scout and then the US-Israeli jointly developed RQ-2 Pioneer. The numbers were small, but Colombo tended to be cagey about the details of its UAVs and the Israeli intelligence/procurement connection.[29] The air force ended up with two Searchers (by 2012 just one) and four Blue Horizons.

At the end of the conflict the number of surviving Russian attack helicopters, variants of the Hind, was eleven. The support helicopters were multi-national: Russian Mi-17s, and a medley of US Bell variants for transport and VIP travel. The Sri Lankan Air Force Regiment deployed defence systems and towed artillery.

As the war reached a crescendo in early 2009 the air force planned to modernize. Much of the kit was old. Negotiations were held with Moscow to get helicopters. New transports were discussed with Beijing. The interceptor role needed strengthening, hence the possibility of MiG-29s – these would replace the even older Kfirs and MiG-27s. What made air force chiefs salivate was the thought of the US F-16s, but politics and budget restraints made that unlikely. These and other projects were discussed in the specialist aviation press. But the demands for a peace dividend could stall modernization and expansion across all three services.

Air force tactics

According to a former air force commander, before 2006 'morale was very low because of the stop-start nature of the campaign'. But when the National Security Council was revitalized in 2006, he said: 'At my first meeting of the NSC I saw there was real purpose – that this thing has to be finished. Or this country is going nowhere. So the will was there.'[30]

The army and navy often fought on equal terms with the Tigers, often suffering major reversals. But the air force had air supremacy which was occasionally challenged by the five small Czech aircraft of the Air Tigers. One was shot down by the air force, the single example of air-to-air interception. Otherwise the fast jets were used to attack ground formations.

One of the main roles of the air force was to feed to the battle management centre real-time videos from UAVs and surveillance aircraft. The first UAVs were deployed in 1996, starting with the Super Scout system. In 2000 the Searcher Mark 2 was added to what became No. 111 Squadron. In 2007 the Blue Horizon was introduced to a new 112 Squadron. They were dedicated to intelligence gathering, reconnaissance at sea and land, battlefield surveillance, artillery fire adjustment and damage assessment.

They were kept flying continuously and suffered attrition through enemy fire. (The Tigers referred to them as *Wandu* when they were being polite; it meant 'beetle'. The Sinhalese called them *Kelama* – 'gossiper'.) Compared with ground fire, more crashes were caused by icing (the machines were not 100 per cent watertight) as well as gyro and engine failures. Certainly on the ground – when I visited No. 111 Squadron – the small machine looked very frail, as did the two half-size trainers. It was odd that a whole squadron should be dedicated to a single surviving machine (but the cost of replacing them in peacetime was exorbitant). The pilots had to make do with practising with small multi-coloured wooden aircraft they had built themselves. It was not a waste of time, as the Israeli machines have to be launched using a small toggle device similar to model aircraft controls before the ground station takes over when the plane is out of visual sight. The Americans could spend billions on Predators armed with Hellfire missiles in Afghanistan, but the Sri Lankans managed near miracles with their tiny budget and tiny aircraft. The petite Searcher might look like a hobbyist's dream, but it proved an effective war machine.

Attack helicopters, especially the Mi-24s, played a very active role. Access to the flying logs provided a wealth of details on the range of fighting. A summary of some of the Mi-24 crashes gives a flavour of the intense combat:

19 March 1997 — Missing in action

10 November 1997 – Missile attack

26 June 1998 – Small calibre anti-aircraft gun

23 January 2000 – Missile attack

24 May 2000 – 'Enemy fire'

19 October 2000 – 'Enemy fire'

27 November 2009 – Tail rotor failure.

Although the details of close support of ground offensives as well as more mundane tasks such as riding shotgun on the *Jetliner* navy convoy or distributing leaflets are of interest, what is especially revealing is the air force's role in 'hot' extractions of special forces. The records of No. 9 Attack Helicopter Squadron show:

2 July 2001: A long range reconnaissance patrol had been surrounded by Tigers deep inside the Vanni jungles. The Mi-24s flew a decoy mission nearby. LTTE cadres rushed to the site, allowing the SF to escape.

22 November 2001: Two Mi-24s provided top cover while a Bell 212 and a Mi-17 extracted from the Periyamadhu area four SF personnel, two of whom were severely wounded from an anti-personnel mine.

1/2 July 2007: The squadron was ordered to airlift a casualty from a team from the 3rd Special Forces Regiment forced to retreat under heavy fire. The extraction was twenty-five kilometres behind LTTE lines in the Northern Vanni region. Thickly wooded terrain and constant enemy fire made the airlift difficult, especially finding a suitable landing zone. Eventually the coordinates for a suitable site were given. Two Mi-24s got in close, with a Mi-17 standing off, while a Bell 212 managed to land. All SF men were safely extracted.

29 July 2008: three SF members under intense enemy fire needed airlifting from an area eight kilometres northwest of Mankulam. With the careful coordination of the No. 9 Squadron commander and the CO of the 3rd Special Forces Regiment, a Bell 212 was sent in but with the cover of only one Mi-24 (the standard second aircraft had developed an engine problem). Flying just above the jungle canopy, the Bell extracted the special forces men under heavy fire.

The air force, sometimes with liaison officers on the ground, worked closely with the army, but particularly special forces. Other infantry sources claimed that the air force was tardy in responding to urgent requests for air support – but that kind of complaint can be found in all wars, daily in Afghanistan in the bitter NATO fighting in Helmand.

Extractions under fire required immense skill by the young flight lieutenants in the cockpits of the Mi-24s. It would take on average forty-five minutes to reach the target area, once the tasking was complete and the co-ordinates fixed. In the extensive use of the Hinds in ground support operations the air force could augment their firepower by using the Kfirs. In the battle that prompted Eelam War IV, in July 2006, the gunships attacked positions around the Mavil Aru reservoir. Close air support required careful co-ordination to avoid blue-on-blue incidents; the Mi-24 intercepted a large group of LTTE cadres crossing a paddy-field and, according to the air force logs, 'inflicted heavy damages to the enemy'. In open terrain, the 12.7mm cannon protruding from the nose, the bombs and the S24B rockets under the stub wings could create carnage. In operations around Mavil Aru, the Mi-24s flew forty-two combat missions, logging 162 hours of flying time.

In later operations in the fighting around the Tiger capital, Kilinochchi, No. 9 Squadron deployed all its available choppers, although the constant flying was wearing out the machines. The unavailability of main rotor blades prevented flying for the initial stages of the army operation; by cannibalizing other machines, six choppers were eventually made airworthy.

The aircraft flew in formations of four to attack LTTE strongholds at night, for example hitting LTTE bunkers north of the Giant's Tank area. The air force deployed forward-looking infra red equipment (FLIR), night vision goggles and laser-guided munitions. The pilots looked enviously at the Apache's performance abroad; even the Mi-28s would have proved more capable at night. Despite the extra equipment, night operations in a Mi-24 were hazardous. In another night raid on a LTTE radar station at Nagasigvanturai, on 18 August 2008, two choppers killed twenty female LTTE cadres, 'creating disorder among the LTTE'. Sometimes the attacks were very close to army lines. A particular target of the Mi-24s was heavy earthmoving machinery which the LTTE used to erect their ubiquitous bunds. The No. 9 Squadron also hit Sea Tiger bases.

The main aim of the air force was to 'hit LTTE supplies and their leadership and break their will to fight', according to Air Chief Marshal Roshan Goonetileke, the former air commander and then Chief of Defence Staff. He reached the most senior post, despite being a Christian. He said that ethnicity or religion were not an issue in the air force. The former chopper pilot had 'a Buddhist and Tamil in my air wing when I was flying,' he said. He also insisted that the air force fought 'a very clean war', using all available technology to avoid collateral damage.[31]

Spares were often a problem, he confessed, although there were no supply problems with the Russian helicopters. (He didn't mention the delay in securing rotor blades, described in his own squadron's logs.) The biggest problem, he said, was manpads – shoulder-launched surface-to-air missiles. The first missiles struck on 28 and 29 April 1994 and brought down two aircraft. 'They were Stingers,' said the Air Marshal. 'They were coming from Afghanistan, even though the US was paying US$400,000 to buy them back [from their distribution to anti-Russian Jihadists in the 1980s]. But other terrorist groups were paying more to the Afghans.'

He said that initially LTTE ground fire caused real problems.

> We needed bigger and bigger choppers with bigger guns and we had
> to go higher and higher. Then came the missiles – the manpads, the
> SAM-7s – we were not ready for that. We were slow in getting
> equipment to respond to that threat. We had to ground the helicopters
> and that affected the army, not least with logistics.

Anti-missile systems from Israel solved many of the threats. But overall the
air force lost twenty-seven aircraft and thirty-seven pilots during the war.
Six Mi-24s were downed in combat, and two lost in crashes. Finally the
pilots got used to lower-level flying. But by the time the LTTE moved into
conventional fighting, it became hard for the Mi-24s to provide continual
ground support. The army started complaining about the diminishing air
effect. The Air Marshal explained that,

> Sometimes the Mi-24s were just 75 yards from the enemy. You know
> when the Mi-24 turns, it is very vulnerable. Some got hit. They would
> land with 60-70 bullet holes. We would patch them up and send them
> out again. The pilots were very brave. It was a tough fight.

The air force started with Bell 212s but bigger better-armed choppers with
heavier bomb loads were required. The firepower of the Mi-24s' rockets and
cannon was needed. Extra firepower was provided by the Chinese F-17s and
the Kfirs. The jets helped to bring back the balance in the government's
favour after the growing missile threat. No jets were lost in combat. The Air
Tigers were not an effective military threat, but the five Czech Zlin Z-143
light planes had a psychological impact, the Air Marshal conceded. 'They
were very small aircraft flying slowly and very low. They were flying in the
night with very small heat signatures. If I'd had a good missile I could have
shot all of them down.'

He said again that it was a tough war, especially casevacs at night. But
he conceded that the Sri Lankan government had air superiority, the most
vital ingredient of an air war. He also said that the LTTE 'were very
committed and disciplined in what they did'.

> They had Stingers and SAM-7 *Strelas*. They also had SAM-14s and
> 16s and were trying to get the SAM-18s. A low-flying helicopter
> would have found it difficult to survive an 18. We are grateful to the
> US for stopping that procurement of SAM-18s …

We flew every day – morning and night. Low. We kept up the pressure. And we had good intelligence from the UAVs and the army. It took a lot out of our pilots. They did thousands of missions. That's a lot for a small air force.

The Air Marshal paused and smiled, 'Of course the air force does not always get the due credit.'

Paramilitary forces

The Police

The police force in 2012 numbered around 85,000. During the war, the police came under the control of the Ministry of Defence; recently, however, critics have called for the police once again to become independent of the military.

The force can trace its origins to 1797. At the outbreak of the Great War, 119 police stations had been established, with a complement of 2,306. Women were first recruited in 1952. The Police Special Task Force, a specialized counter-insurgency unit, was set up in 1983. The reserve police force was abolished in 2006/7 and its personnel absorbed into the regular force. The head is known as the Inspector General of the Police and various subordinate ranks relate to control of the posts in a decentralized structure known, in police parlance, as ranges, divisions and districts.[32] During the height of the war, police stations expanded to around 2,000, many of them regular targets of the LTTE. To counter the threat to internal security the Counter Subversive Division was set up to deal with the JVP. This was replaced by the Terrorist Investigation Department to focus on the Tiger insurgency.

Domestic intelligence matters first came under the responsibility of Special Branch, set up under the Central Investigation Department (CID); the British influence was obvious in this structure. Later, the Intelligence Services Division was established. The ethnic disturbances of 1983 were seen as a failure of police intelligence and in 1984 a new National Intelligence Bureau was created. Although it was headed by a senior policeman who reported directly to the Ministry of Defence, it was a multi-service structure which combined intelligence units from army, navy and air force as well as the existing police network. After various reorganizations, the main national agency became known as the State

Intelligence Service (SIS), which was dominated by policemen. This new bureau worked closely with the two main counter-terrorism units: the Terrorist Investigation Department (TID) and the Special Task Force (STF).

Senior police officers claimed that their intelligence affairs were well co-ordinated, not least on the weekly national intelligence meetings on a Tuesday, when the other state security organs were assembled. In fact the police had many intelligence problems, beyond constant LTTE assassinations of their informers and officers posing as civilians. The police District Intelligence Bureaux had long been seen as almost retirement homes for officers completing their last posts in their own districts. According to a senior police intelligence officer, Special Branch drifted into 'a state of neglect as much as the TID'.[33] The TID and CID were often in conflict; the former was supposed to concentrate on COIN and the latter on classical police collection of evidence to be used in courts. One of the Keystone Kops episodes happened in September 2003, when the Director of Internal Intelligence (as it was called then) placed an advertisement in the print media inviting the public to visit his HQ and inspect items to be sold at an auction. Nice bit of PC transparency maybe, but also a gift for LTTE saboteurs. The fast-tracking of favourites when a new political administration came in also undermined police morale as did the advancement of so-called 'graduate probationers' – a resentment felt in many western forces. Many of these issues were resolved when the Rajapaksas took a grip of the security effort after 2005, guided by the influence of the far more proficient military intelligence officers.

Initially, police treated the insurgency as a criminal matter but various emergency laws enabled the police to deal with COIN on a more political basis, although right to the end the police tried to collect evidence for use in the clogged civilian courts. The Prevention of Terrorism Act (updated in 1982) was the useful catch-all for extensive police powers. Although the fighting was heaviest in the north and east, Colombo was the iconic target for the LTTE. Numerous Tamils lived there, especially in the northern part of the large city. The LTTE had planted a large number of long-term sleeper cells. In response the authorities developed a complex community policy system at street level as well as extensive registration for Tamils and Sinhalese. The common catchphrase — 'Not all Tamils are terrorists, but all terrorists are Tamils' — was not strictly true. Old-fashioned policing in Colombo tracked down Sinhalese underworld gangsters who were helping the LTTE for financial gain, as well as capturing on one occasion two Christian clergymen who had been forced to smuggle in suicide explosive vests, because a young relative had been kidnapped. The passion for mobile phones also played into police hands. Electronic interception or simply the capture of SIM cards unravelled a number of sleeper cells. Nevertheless, the sheer number of LTTE agents meant that they pulled off a variety of grisly spectaculars. The insurgents were often very patient. When President Premadasa was assassinated, the police later discovered that his killer had been tracking him for three years. Many of the sleepers were activated in the last stages of the war, when the LTTE was utterly desperate to retaliate against army advances.[34]

Besides using intelligence the police deployed their Special Task Force (STF) to engage in an urban SWAT role. The STF originated in a visit to Pakistan in 1983 by the then army commander. The President of Pakistan, General Zia Ul-Haq, advised the Sri Lankan, 'Your problem is that you have nothing between the army and the police.' So Colombo decided to go for the so-called 'third force' option, a policy discussed extensively in Britain and adopted in France. The Special Task Force was designed as a police special forces unit, dealing in counter-terrorism and COIN. It was always intended as a primarily police, not military, unit, but it soon assumed many paramilitary functions. The army trained the Task Force in the use of infantry weapons and jungle warfare tactics. Its initial complement was 3,000 personnel, but it grew to 10,000.

Around 100 ex-British Special Air Service personnel were also said to have provided specialist instruction under the aegis of KMS Ltd. KMS – Keenie Meenie Services (stemming from SAS slang for special operations[35]) – was one of the variously titled organizations by which the UK government could pursue useful – but deniable – covert policies. KMS soon spun off into other related or similar companies, especially if one of them were to be exposed. Training Afghan *Mujahedin* was kept under wraps, but the Iran-Contra affair disclosed sabotage operations in Nicaragua. KMS's first big job was training the Sultan of Oman's special forces. In 1983, with the UK government's approval, KMS started to train the Task Force. Press reports, especially in the LTTE media, claimed that KMS withdrew in 1987 because of Task Force indiscipline. Similar sources made comparisons between the Task Force and the notorious *Koevoet*, the brutally effective South African police special unit deployed against insurgents in South West Africa/Namibia. The Afrikaans name means 'crowbar': to prise the insurgents from the local population. Allegations were also made that South African troops were involved with Sri Lankan police training. The Sri Lankans did use *Koevoet*'s trademark Buffel, the very effective mine-proofed South African armoured vehicles. Tamil critics also claimed that the police unit also copied *Koevoet* tactics, especially the aggressive use of dogs.

In addition, the Israeli internal security organization, *Shin Beth*, was also said to have provided more continuous training. Asian intelligence organizations also contributed expertise. During the height of the fighting after 2006 the Special Task Force launched semi-independent offensives, the first being Operation DEFINITE VICTORY in January 2007. The successful commando-style raids led by the Task Force sometimes were criticized by the UN and other international bodies, especially for alleged human rights abuses, both in the field, and in the STF HQ in Colombo.

In Sri Lanka, the STF was regarded with great respect, in both police circles and by the LTTE, for different reasons. Regular policemen would move into areas 'cleared' of LTTE cadres, but behind enemy lines the STF operated very aggressively, often deploying the small group principle. Although it did not fight in the north, the STF 'made the LTTE run around in circles in the east, particularly in Batticaloa and Ampara'.[36] Using small-group penetration and surprise ambushes, the STF created the impression of omnipresence. The second commandant of STF, Lionel Karunasena, assumed an almost heroic status in some police circles; to others he was considered a dangerous maverick, especially in army High Command because he preferred lone-wolf tactics, and tended to disdain the notion of joint operations. He was perhaps the police equivalent of Orde Wingate in British army folklore. Effective but a loose cannon, he was eventually eased out of command.

Police weapons

The police normally carried rifles and pistols while on patrol during the war. The Special Task Force was typically equipped with a wide range of infantry weapons for COIN operations. The police arsenal contained the well-known brands of handguns – Glock 17, Beretta 92, Webley, and Smith and Wessons. They could fall back on H & K MP5 submachine guns as well as access to sniper rifles and a range of army assault rifles. They also deployed the HK 69 breech-loading grenade launchers for firing tear gas rounds during riot-control operations. Their vehicles were usually Hyundai patrol cars, as well as Land Rovers and Suzuki 500cc motorbikes. In the civilianization process after the war the police were disarmed. By 2011 most police officers had to hand in their infantry rifles, but kept their side-arms.

The Home Guard/Civil Defence Force

With the onset of the Tiger insurgency, villagers in mixed Tamil/Sinhalese areas began to arm themselves with shotguns provided by the government. The volunteers were dubbed the Home Guard (although, unlike the British image of 'Dad's Army' in the Second World War, these volunteers saw a lot of action). It started in 1985 with a complement of 18,000 but grew to 41,500. The force also developed a commando section of 400. Roughly 90 per cent were of farming stock, only ten per cent were graduates or local teachers. Women comprised fifteen per cent. The volunteers were paid $5 a day and 546 were killed during the conflict. Pensions, almost the same level as army remuneration, were paid to the widows/widowers. They were officially tasked with protecting rural areas including temples and schools. 'The fundamental aim was to prevent ethnic cleansing,' said the unit's commander, a former admiral.[37] The members were issued with uniforms and came under the command of local police stations. As the war intensified, they were issued with automatic rifles and basic training of two to four weeks was provided by the army. In 2006 the Home Guard was absorbed into the Department of Civil Defence, and renamed the Civil Defence Force.

The National Guard

Originally designated for guarding VIPs and prominent buildings, after 1989 it grew into a large volunteer regiment with thirty-two battalions. The IISS put the size as 15,000, but the number of battalions suggests this was another underestimate.

Other paramilitary units

Various informal pro-government militias were formed during the war, not least the Tamil fighters who broke away from the main LTTE leadership.

Sri Lankan procurement

It may appear that Sri Lanka developed a hotchpotch style of weapons acquisition. But it was a developing country with a tiny industrial base, and the government fought a very long war. Also, some countries, especially the US after 2007, refused to supply modern weapons so Colombo had to play the non-aligned game, courting Russia and China as well as the USA. Sometimes it had to deal in the black market or covertly, as in the case with some Israeli kit. Its engineers learned to patch and mend and then adapt to produce large modern naval vessels for example. The armed forces largely gave up on the UK's mentoring (and supply) role. But the defence budget (including weapons procurement) came to consume a fifth of all public spending.[38] Any criticism of Sri Lanka in this context should bear in mind that procurement in *all* advanced countries produced weapons that were often very late and very much above original estimates. Britain, Sri Lanka's original military model, has produced catastrophic procurement results (according to the UK parliament's Defence Select Committee), exemplified by the decommissioning of its only aircraft carrier (just before it was needed in the 2011 Libyan war), and the expected gap of at least a decade before two more are produced, even though only one can be deployed, and, so far, the purchase of aircraft which can operate from it is highly problematical. Meanwhile, India, Sri Lanka's big brother, deployed an aircraft carrier (the former HMS *Hermes*) while Britain could not.[39]

The main channel of defence procurement, a limited company owned wholly by the government, was Lanka Logistics Ltd. It was set up by Gotabaya Rajapaksa in early 2007. The aim was to cut out the many middlemen who had fleeced previous governments. It also cut off intelligence on new purchases from the LTTE. Lanka Logistics ran a very tight ship indeed: it had just twenty-one employees, including a single accountant and two drivers. It dealt primarily with Pakistan, China, Russia, Ukraine, Israel and sometimes Brazil. The earlier Indian deals were arranged at a political level.

Grand Strategy

The key to the strategic success of the government forces was the dynamic and 'joined-up' political leadership. Previously, for short-term political gain or a willingness to bend to international pressures, the various governments had not felt able to maintain a determined and coordinated strategy. From the beginning of 2006 President Mahinda Rajapaksa decided that his main aim would be the destruction of the Tigers. His civilian permanent secretary at the Ministry of Defence was his brother, Gotabaya Rajapaksa, who had served in the army for twenty years. This fraternal combination proved a successful civil-military interface. Many of the army commanders had served with the former Colonel Rajapaksa and found him a responsive if demanding boss. His first task was the selection of a new top brass, appointed on merit alone. Military commanders would ring the Secretary and, if he could not provide an instant answer, the brother would ring the President. This provided a loyal and rapid central command.

Sri Lankan President, Mahinda Rajapaksa.
(Author)

The Permanent
Secretary of the Ministry
of Defence, Gotabaya
Rajapaksa. (Author)

And their principal antagonist, the leader of the Tamil Tigers, Velupillai Prabhakaran. (TamilNet)

The Chief of the Defence Staff, Air Chief Marshal Roshan Goonetileke. (Author)

Commander of the Army, Lieutenant General Jagath Jayasuriya. (Author)

Chief of National
Intelligence, Major
General Kapila
Hendawitharana.
(Author)

Former head of the army, General Sarath Fonseka. (SL Ministry of Defence)

The former Indian Prime Minister, Rajiv Gandhi, assassinated by the LTTE in 1991.

The New Delhi-Colombo relationship was a key factor in the military victory: President Mahinda Rajapaksa with Manmohan Singh, the Indian Prime Minister.

An army armoured
personnel carrier on
patrol near Jaffna.
(Author)

A Chinese-built amphibious tank. (MoD)

The Mil Mi-24 was worked to death by the air force. (MoD)

The Mi-24s (codenamed Hind by NATO) would often return from operations with over fifty bullet holes in the airframe. The aircraft fitters frequently had to cannibalize their fleet to keep the squadrons flying. (Author)

Special Forces
operating from a Bell
(the U3 'Huey' in
Vietnam) helicopter.
(Author)

An IAI Searcher UAV, the sole survivor in the air force. (Author)

A pensioned-off MiG-27 (NATO codename Flogger). (Author)

A sleek Israeli-made Kfir, the frontline fighter despite its age. (Author)

The navy's fast-attack flotilla in Trincomalee harbour. (Author)

A fibreglass boat of the Sea Tigers (Author)

A Sea Tiger Pigeon ship captured by the navy, at anchor in Trincomalee harbour. (Author)

A mix of homemade, Chinese, Singaporean and Pakistani landmines laid by the Tigers just lifted by army sappers. (Author)

The rebuilt Jaffna library, a repository of Tamil culture. The LTTE blamed the army and/or police for firebombing it twice. (Author)

The LTTE waged a very successful international propaganda war. (TamilNet)

Nature intervened: the tsunami of December 2004. Over 30,000 Sri Lankans were killed; a survivor near Galle.

The Tigers attacked the most sacred Buddhist site, the Temple of the Tooth, near Kandy.

Tigers on patrol in their zone of control. (TamilNet)

Colonel Soosai, the
head of the Sea
Tigers, in a fast-
attack craft, 2003.
(TamilNet)

Police guard a bus hit by an LTTE landmine in Buttala. (Sri Lankan Police)

Small-unit deep penetration was one of the main elements of the army's successful counter-insurgency. (MoD)

The Special Forces and commandos conducted most of the long-range deep penetration raids. (MoD)

Most of the fighting depended on walking to battle; there were no paradrops and only limited use of helicopter transport. Roads were infrequent and often impassable, because of mines and monsoons. (MoD)

Indirect fire – mortars and artillery – caused the majority of fatalities on both sides. (MoD)

Heat, rain, disease, jungles and heavy loads required fitness, commitment and good logistics. (MoD)

Much of the combat in the last few months of the war revolved around fighting in and around lagoons as well as flooded reservoirs. (MoD)

Fighting around the Nandikadal Lagoon in the last few weeks of the war. (MoD)

The hijacked and then grounded Jordanian ship was used as the last Sea Tiger base. (Author)

The last few days of the Cage, hell on earth for civilians trapped inside.

Last few hours of the Cage: an infantryman offers water to a desperate civilian. (MoD)

When the guns fell silent. The author visited the Cage to see damaged cars and buses everywhere, but also – perhaps most poignantly – neatly arranged racks of rusting cycles extending for hundreds of yards. (Author)

Armour lined up for a victory parade at the end of fighting in the Cage. (MoD)

The army erected a victory monument near the site of the final battle. (Author)

Foreign critics damned the conditions in the IDP camps set up for over 300,000 civilians displaced by the last stages of the war.

The majority of IDPs were returned home within eighteen months although some had to wait for their villages to be demined. (Author)

Hearts and minds: troops engage in a Hindu ceremony near Jaffna. (Author)

Hardcore Tiger females in rehabilitation camp. (Author)

Army private shows the names of the fallen servicemen and women at the national memorial in Colombo. (Author)

US Marines re-train Sri Lankan Special Boat Squadron after the war (US Department of Defense)

Sri Lankan forces continued their UN deployment in Haiti, 2010. (US Department of Defense)

Gotabaya Rajapaksa persuaded the President to enlarge rapidly the armed forces and to equip them properly. A massive media campaign was launched to encourage possible military recruits that victory was inevitable. The army's nine divisions were increased to twenty; its forty-four brigades expanded to seventy-one and the 149 battalions increased to 284. In 2005 the army stood at 120,000; by the end of the war it had reached nearly 230,000. The navy stood at 74,000. The air force comprised 40,000. The police, including the Special Task Force, had reached almost 85,000 and Civil Defence totalled around 42,000. This was the full-time active strength, excluding wounded.[40]

According to Gotabaya Rajapaksa,

> The military never asked me for expansion. The generals didn't have to ask me. It was me who decided that, if we are going to win, we have to expand. The new battalions, the special forces etc – this was the key to victory. Nothing changed in the structural sense. The biggest change was manpower. We could approach the war from different axes. We could move whole divisions around.
>
> … A huge army does not solve all the problems of course. But we couldn't do that before – advancing on various axes with a broad line. When you do a thin-line advance the LTTE come around the back … you need troops for a broad attack.[41]

Before 2006 the army could defeat the LTTE in battle but then troops would have to be moved to counter other threats, allowing the Tigers to creep back. This was a 'whack-a-mole' strategy. The new military command decided that the enlarged army should insist on holding whatever territory it seized. The military used all its manpower to hold ground — including navy and air force personnel as well as police. This was taking combined operations to a logical conclusion. 'If we clear, we must remain,' said Gotabaya Rajapaksa. 'We just pumped in troops. We put the air force and the navy in the jungle. They could hold and allow the army to fight.'[42]

Lanka Logistics, a wholly government-owned company, was formed to acquire all the new equipment to support the strategic expansion. It was created by the Permanent Secretary. 'I wanted to stop all the corruption and cut out all the middlemen,' he insisted.[43]

The Rajapaksa government had outlined a clear strategy of military defeat of the Tigers and proceeded to increase the size, quality and equipment of the armed forces. The new government also decided that it would fight. The time for negotiations had passed. And that required political finesse. Firstly, the government had to win over its coalition partners in parliament. Domestic economic demands had to be assuaged. But much more important was the international environment. Here Indian support, or at least their turning a blind eye, was crucial. 'Unless we had won the support of the Indian government, we couldn't have won this war,' was the pithy summary of the Permanent Secretary of Defence. The US, France and the UK could exert diplomatic pressure on Sri Lanka, but only India could directly affect the military campaign.

The mechanism deployed was called the 'troika', a continuous diplomatic dialogue with the Indians. The Sri Lankan team consisted of the Secretary of Defence, another brother, Basil, and the ubiquitous *eminence grise*, Lalith Weeratunga, secretary to the President. The Indian counterparts consisted of a former national security adviser, M. K. Narayan, the then foreign secretary, Shivshankar Menon, and Vijay Singh, the defence secretary. Often the central government in India was weak, and politicians would use Sri Lanka as a lever in domestic politics, especially if they were wooing the 60 million Tamils in Tamil Nadu. During the final dramatic stages of the war the Tamil Nadu link became paramount. The troika system was a very useful means to manage Centre-versus-states politics in India. Occasionally, the troika members would meet in Colombo at a few hours' notice during the final stages of the conflict. It was this ability to satisfy Indian demands which allowed Colombo largely to ignore Western and UN criticisms at the height of the international furore over civilian deaths in early 2009.

An Indian defence expert aptly summarized the 'Rajapaksa model' of fighting COIN thus:

Political will
'Go to hell' (ignore domestic and international criticism)
But keep important neighbours in the loop
No negotiations
Control the media
No ceasefire
Complete operational freedom
Promote young and able commanders.[44]

The Rajapaksas ran an effective domestic (and familial) system of command and control as well as establishing clear and continuous lines of communication with India, as well as with allies in China and Pakistan. The successful grand strategy ultimately depended, however, on internal co-ordination of the war effort.

Command and Coordination

After independence Sri Lanka established a pattern of the prime minister (later president) assuming the role of minister of defence as well. (The prime minister also took on initially the role of foreign minister in order to centralize external policy in the Cold War years.) In 1977 the defence and foreign affairs portfolios were separated. Except for brief periods, the president has since retained the defence portfolio. In 1985, with British and Israeli advice, a Joint Operations Centre (JOC) was set up to co-ordinate the military, police and intelligence COIN ability, though it did not have the grand strategic dimensions of the later National Security Council (NSC). In 1999 the NSC was established to centralize political command and control. The Ministry of Defence assumed a large number of responsibilities, besides the armed forces. It ran the intelligence services as well as the police. In addition, its portfolio included defence training and education, as well as the national cadet corps, civil defence and veterans' affairs. The departments of immigration and emigration, and 'registration of persons' in addition to the control of dangerous drugs came under its purview. Such extensive powers provoked the criticism that Sri Lanka was a 'national security state'.

After 2005 the executive core of the political management of the war depended upon the two brothers, Gotabaya and Mahinda Rajapaksa, with the administrative support of Lalith Weeratunga, a civil service mandarin. Gotabaya handled the military side, Mahinda managed the domestic and international political issues and the wiry and diminutive Lalith operated the domestic civil service, as well as being an amanuensis to the President; Secretary Weeratunga, aged sixty-one and a yogi, was roughly the equivalent of Gus O'Donnell, the cabinet secretary during Tony Blair's later wars. O'Donnell handled the Cabinet *and* headed the civil service, before Prime Minister David Cameron separated the posts. It was not just for his initials that Gus O'Donnell was nicknamed 'God' in the Whitehall establishment.

Another Rajapaksa brother, Basil, was a special presidential adviser and an MP, later a minister of economics. The ever-loyal Lalith Weeratunga called it 'Rajapaksa Incorporated', and compared the arrangements to a successful business. 'If the directors of a company don't trust each other, then you can't run a company.'[45]

Although the government ran a very bloated Cabinet (because of the initial need to satisfy the ambitions of the coalition) military decisions were made in the National Security Council. The NSC was an administrative arrangement with no real statutory or constitutional basis. This was made up of the inner triumvirate along with the service chiefs plus intelligence and police officials as well as occasional specialists. It met every Wednesday, more often during extreme emergencies. If the President was abroad, no meeting was held. Mahinda Rajapaksa chaired, the military agenda was set by the Permanent Secretary of Defence, and the only note-taker was Lalith Weeratunga (who — despite being an iPad fan — kept the NSC notes in small neat handwriting in old-fashioned paper notebooks: the only comprehensive record of the inner war council).

The meetings, conducted in English, could last up to three or four hours. It was held in the upper floor of the official presidential residence, Temple Trees, an ornately furnished building with an odd preponderance of large fish tanks. The army commander would start, with a twenty-to-twenty-five-minute presentation, then the navy and air force chiefs would follow; finally there would be an overall intelligence briefing.

One of the central frictions of the NSC was whether the eastern or northern insurgencies should be settled first. The army wanted to finish off the war in the symbolic Tamil heartland, the Jaffna peninsula, then push south. President Rajapaksa came down firmly on ending the LTTE occupation of the eastern province. Despite the Rajapaksa brothers' dominance, views were freely expressed. Regular NSC participants told me that the President was a good listener. The differences between the army and navy commanders became frequently fractious, however. The air force commander (later chief of the defence staff) took to sitting between them. On a few occasions the President briefly lost his temper with the two rival commanders, especially the ambitious army chief, General Sarath Fonseka.

The President confided to me: 'Yes, I did lose my temper with them, briefly, but actually I used to laugh at them because they reminded me of my own children when they started squabbling.'[46] Lalith Weeratunga later glossed this with his own version: 'HE [the most common designation of the President] would say: "Don't behave like Montessori children. This is not a kindergarten. Both of you have to fight the LTTE, not each other."' (After the war ended, however, the trenchantly independent views of General Fonseka were to cause a major political upheaval. But the army-navy friction, according to other NSC members, originated in a bitter rivalry while the commanders were pupils at the same school as much as contemporary differences.)

The President would listen carefully and then reach a decision. According to Lalith Weeratunga — who developed the annoying habit of finishing his boss's sentences if the President was tired, ill or struggling for a word in English — 'He was always in command, on top of meetings. I can't think of a single meeting when he was floating and didn't know what to do, or at the mercy of the commanders. I never saw that.' Then the gist – but not the detail – of the decisions would be communicated to the Cabinet, who were also consulted if a major expenditure, such as a large arms purchase, was being mooted.

The NSC provided effective decision making and overcame numerous pressures from abroad and military reversals in the field. The President's authority – all present appreciated his determination to win, compared with previous vacillating political leaders – made him an effective chairman. But the real secret was good command of the intelligence data. The Secretary of Defence would chair on the previous Tuesday a long meeting of the intelligence services. This enabled him to present an NSC agenda – 95 per cent his work and 5 per cent the assiduous Weeratunga's – which enabled the President to be a step or two ahead of even his best-informed military and police advisors.

Intelligence

The Tuesday intelligence meetings were held in the ministry of defence HQ in Colombo. It is a nondescript practical edifice, with Spartan rundown offices even for the top brass, but adorned with a stunning view of the adjacent sweeping sandy bay. The national intelligence meetings would start at 10.30 am and continue for up to five hours. It was chaired by Gotabaya Rajapaksa. But if Weeratunga was the *eminence grise* of the NSC, the dominant organizing force in the national intelligence meetings was Major General Kapila Hendawitharana, the chief of national intelligence. The bespectacled Major General was not a physically imposing man; he blended into any background like an Asian version of John le Carré's enigmatic spy chief, George Smiley.

Usually, around twelve men attended the intelligence meetings, including Gotabaya Rajapaksa, the director of the State Intelligence Service (SIS), the naval and air force intelligence heads as well as specialists from the police, including Special Branch and CID plus from time to time experts such as the head of presidential security. (Lalith Weeratunga did not attend.) A crucial member, however, was the director of military intelligence (DMI). The DMI controlled the six intelligence regiments of the Intelligence Corps (around 2,000 strong).These meetings very rarely produced the personality clashes which enlivened the NSC.

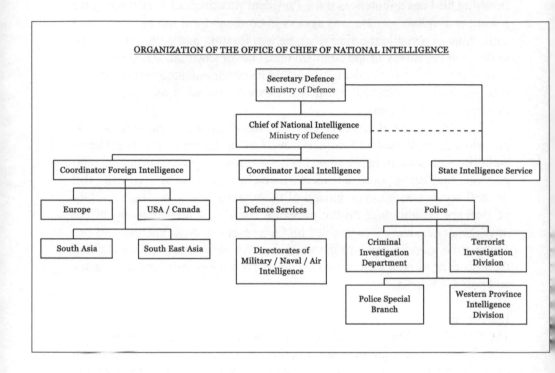

ORGANIZATION OF THE OFFICE OF CHIEF OF NATIONAL INTELLIGENCE

Hendawitharana was the keeper of all the secrets and knew where all the political skeletons were buried. Luckily for Sri Lanka, he headed all the combined intelligence services. There were few of the MI5 v MI6 v Special Branch squabbles that undermined British intelligence, nor the turf wars between the American FBI and the CIA over domestic versus international jurisdiction. The latter was the ultimate factor in not 'joining up the dots' about the numerous warnings of the 9/11 abominations. If the FBI and CIA had shared a little more information, some of the perpetrators of the al-Qaeda plot could have been apprehended *before* they flew into the Twin Towers. The Sri Lankan spy supremo had authority over domestic *and* international resources. Hendawitharana, tough but impeccably polite, had served as the director of military intelligence for six years, and for eleven years as head of counter-terrorism in the SIS. Although the Sri Lankans used high-tech surveillance methods, Hendawitharana was of the old school and he knew where everything was kept in the hard-copy 'registry'. He told me: 'I knew where everything was in the registry – everything was sent to the registry.'[47]

The SIS was the prime Sri Lankan intelligence agency. It was not controlled by the police but rather it was a military organization under the aegis of the Ministry of Defence. Again, unlike Britain and the US where intelligence is divided, and stove-piped, between the Home Office, Foreign and Commonwealth Office and Ministry of Defence in the former, and between *inter alia* the State Department, the Pentagon and Homeland Security in the latter, Sri Lanka had a streamlined system. The chief of national intelligence not only had oversight over all military and police data, but he also co-ordinated with the CIA and the Indian agencies and even, occasionally, the British. The intelligence chief reported directly to Gotabaya Rajapaksa or sometimes, when necessary, to the President, who was the commander-in-chief, as well as minister of defence. In short, in the small island the dots could be joined up.

The Sri Lankan spy boss was a man quietly suffused with a righteous anger. Many of the other top brass may well have paid formal obeisance to Rajapaksa Incorporated. While probably believing in the official mantra, they also knew they had to say it politely, and often. With the director of national intelligence, however, the fire of commitment burned deep in his psyche. He had seen so much intelligence gold turned into base metal by the fatal vacillation of previous administrations. The chief spook had served under many permanent secretaries of defence who would not even approach the head of state. He said simply: 'The key to winning the war was the brother combination. And the Secretary took a grip – the armed forces increased from 100,000 to 300,000 and he provided the wherewithal to fight.' The intelligence chief was also deeply suspicious of the failed ceasefires. 'Previously, I was asked to cut the army by half. I said "No, don't cut my legs off and expect me to run." I never changed. I never reduced the strength [during ceasefires] because I knew we had to fight … Time and time again the politicians submitted to international pressures.'

And he never underestimated the enemy's skills and determination to fight. When I asked him how he rated the LTTE compared with other insurgencies, he replied:

They were definitely one of the deadliest. They had the ground fighting troops. They had a very strong Sea Tiger wing. Their air wing spread a lot of fear. And then there was the culture of suicide among the suicide cadres. No other terrorist group in the world had all three arms.

The director of national intelligence was also prepared to talk about his successes: 'Capturing K P [the post-war Tiger chief] and interdicting the Pigeon ships [the LTTE's floating arsenals], as well as the regular interdiction of sea supply shipments. We got most of them,' he said. He also explained that hiving off a third of the LTTE cadres, under Colonel Karuna, to join the government side, was the work of national intelligence, not the politicians.

And the greatest failures?

The spy chief did admit to a major cock-up when the police arrested some of his operatives tasked with assassinating Prabhakaran in 2001 and he ended up being accused of using the team to kill the prime minister.

The war has ended, surely some more secrets can be told?

'We suffer in silence.'

Propaganda

In most wars, people believe what they want to believe. In many wars – NATO in Afghanistan or the white population in Rhodesia for example – the public likes to think its side is winning. In Sri Lanka, before 2006, most people at home and abroad believed that the Colombo government could not defeat the Tigers. The Rajapaksas launched a massive media and PR campaign to mobilize the country for war.

Television was introduced to Sri Lanka in 1981; in the following year Rupavahini became the national TV station (funded initially by the Japanese government). TV soon became immensely popular even where villagers shared a set in a communal building. It soon overtook the radio as the popular medium for news and entertainment in the three main languages. The military were quick to respond to its potential. In 1987 a docudrama based on the commandos was screened. It was called *Nohakkak Nomatha* ('Nothing is impossible' – the commando motto). Besides dramas, various government-sponsored advertising campaigns tried to lure youths into the 'nothing is impossible' army culture. They were not successful. One in mid-2002 prompted the enlistment of only 470 soldiers, whereas the target was 5,000. Shortage of manpower was one of the reasons for the government's agreement to the 2002 ceasefire.

When the Rajapaksas took over, the media campaign was put into top gear. Slick TV ads, especially appealing to the young, were produced. Also real social welfare reforms were made and money was pumped into the two main organizations catering for the disabled under the (existing) banner of 'care for those who dare'. The military reversals, especially the major defeat at Elephant Pass, and poor recruitment had created a very negative image of the soldier. According to Gotabaya Rajapaksa, 'We wanted to completely change how the people looked at the soldier; that the military was not an outsider, he is one of us – a saviour.' The senior military leaders were encouraged to talk to the media – the government controlled much of the press – because straight-talking men in smart uniforms were far more credible than political leaders banging on about military successes.

Improving pay and conditions of those serving and care for the wounded and their families were one part of the morale-boosting campaign. Feature films, ads and TV and radio jingles dominated the air waves. Some of the jingles became very popular; they were even downloaded as ring tones for mobile phones. Nothing succeeds like success, so the media campaigns continued to interact with the advances on the battlefield after 2006. The secretary of defence summed up the campaigns thus: 'We took complete control of the media culture.'[48]

The problem was the Colombo government was preaching largely to the converted. Yes, effective media campaigns could raise Sinhalese morale and boost recruitment, but it could not compete with either domestic LTTE propaganda to Tamils or, more importantly, the LTTE's skilful manipulation of the new media to ram home its messages, especially in countries with large Tamil diasporas.

Chapter 10

The Tigers

A one-man war

Sri Lanka used to have a railway system that passed through some of the most beautiful routes in the world. Trains, which first appeared in 1864, were called by the locals 'coal-eating, water-drinking, sprinting metal yaks'. In the 1950s steam began to give way to diesel locomotives. The Yal Devi, or northern line, used to run from Colombo to Jaffna and beyond. The route would pass Anuradhapura, the island's ancient capital, once teeming with monasteries, royal palaces, pleasure gardens and artificial lakes. Then the train would travel on to Kilinochchi and Elephant Pass before traversing the narrow isthmus into the Jaffna peninsula.

The rail track ran fairly close to a small coastal town on the northern edge of the peninsula, called Velvettiturai. On 26 November 1954 a male baby was born in a small hospital in Jaffna and was then taken by his parents to their home in this nearby town. The boy grew up to be the leader of the Tigers, Thiruvenkadam Velupillai Prabhakaran. The war he was to lead would destroy many things, not least the railway system. The once bustling and charming colonial railway station in Jaffna, first opened in 1902, ended up as a weedstrewn shell, occupied by just one squatter. It had been attacked by Tigers and bombed by the air force. Nevertheless, a casual foreign visitor might have wondered what had happened to the rail tracks. The answer is straightforward: over the years the steel rails were taken to build the numerous bunkers that littered the island's northern and eastern landscapes. Prabhakaran's paranoia spawned a widespread bunker mentality. The roads are now opened and the northern line is being slowly rebuilt, but it will take longer to heal the war psychosis of both Tamils and Sinhalese.

In Hindu homes the birth of a boy is treated with special celebration. Prabhakaran was the fourth and last child and was spoiled by his parents. His mother was deeply religious and his father, who worked as a district land officer in government service, was an affectionate but strict man who demanded unfailing discipline from his two sons and two daughters. The family was well respected in the town. As a boy, Prabhakaran would regularly visit a local shrine, dedicated to Shiva, the Hindu god of destruction, perhaps a portent of what was to come. The pampered child's nickname was, in retrospect, unpropitious: '*durai*' or 'young master'. It was a term used by Tamil servants to address former colonial employers, like the South African *bass*. The parents tried to keep the boy at home as much as possible; family friends of the period describe him as 'homebound'.[49] The boy was a loner, shy around girls and tended to bury himself in books and comics, in Tamil.[50]

In one of his rare later interviews Prabhakaran admitted: 'From my young days I have been a lover of books. The pocket money my parents gave me I spent on books. There was a bookshop in my village. It became a habit somehow … to buy all those valuable books there and read them.' In the 1950s many young Tamils tended to hero-worship Mahatma Gandhi, the prophet of non-violence. Prabhakaran preferred to read about Indians who had resorted to force against imperial rule. One was Bhagat Singh, a young Sikh who formed a secret society and was hanged by the British in 1931. Another hero of the young Tamil was Subhas Chandra Bose. He had helped to recruit troops from the British Indian Army who had been captured by the Japanese and to lead them – ineffectually – against the British. Prabhakaran memorized and often repeated one line from Bose. 'I shall fight for the freedom of my land until I shed the last drop of blood.' The young revolutionary also read avidly about Napoleon's exploits. Prabhakaran was also said to be impressed by the Hindu epic, the *Mahabharata,* one of the longest poems ever written. Besides being one of the finest surviving accounts of primitive war, almost exclusively fought by foot soldiers armed with bows and arrows, it tells of great battles finessed by adroit politics.

Despite his extensive reading the young Prabhakaran was not a successful student. His father worried that his poor results would prevent his getting a good government job. A part-time tutor was arranged. The tutor happened to be a Tamil nationalist. Prabhakaran reminisced later that it was the part-time teacher who 'impressed on me the need for armed struggle and persuaded me to put my trust in it'.

The Jaffna peninsula at this time could be taken for a part of southern India. Shops were full of saris and posters and magazines about Tamil film stars. Tamil music blared from the shops. Some of the schoolteachers hailed from next-door Tamil Nadu. So many Tamils looked north to their fellow Tamil speakers in India rather than to the Sinhalese chauvinists in the south in Colombo. It was in this environment that the bright – if academically unsuccessful – Prabhakaran grew up. Already Tamil nationalists were being persecuted. The intense young man developed an unwavering commitment to a single cause: independence for a Tamil homeland in Sri Lanka.

Prabhakaran saw himself a warrior in this cause. He gave up kite flying and started developing military skills. A catapult gave way to an air gun and he practised incessantly. He took up judo and karate, much to the amusement of his family who still saw him as just a shy schoolboy. He also experimented with improvised bombs made from firecrackers, although that grew more serious as he pilfered chemicals from schools and started producing Molotov cocktails.

The boy became a man and still he had a fascination with guns. But to put to one side the apparent image of a young psychopath, an embryonic Pol Pot, one of Prabhakaran's oldest and most trusted long-term friends, and later a senior Tiger, was interviewed by me. 'K P' (Kumaran Pathmanathan) insisted that the guerrilla leader had 'a soft side'.

> He was not power thirsty, but he was very self-disciplined and very committed. And he had no regrets, even after his son and daughter were killed. He was a natural leader ... but he could have achieved more through economic power ... He used to like cooking and badminton; he was not a man for indulging in women or alcohol. But he did love guns and hunting.[51]

By 1972–73 the young man's fascination for weapons, violence and Tamil separatism attracted the attention of the police, especially an earnest Tamil police inspector called T. B. Bastiampillai, who had earned a reputation for tracking down Tamil militants. The inspector called at the family home but Prabhakaran was not there. The policeman (later to be killed by the Tigers) issued a stern warning to the young man's mother, 'If I get hold of your son, I will break him into a hundred pieces.' This was colourful language from an officer known as a tough outgoing character. The next time the inspector called late at night. The stocky officer was packing two revolvers, as he always did. Prabhakaran had his clothes ready to hand and he slipped out of the house from the back and into the next-door house owned by his uncle. His shirt was torn when climbing the fence but the uncle gave him another one. Prabhakaran was then eighteen. He left his home never to return. Before he left his house he had destroyed all pictures of himself. The young radical first went to India but soon returned for the armed struggle. A Tamil version of the Scarlet Pimpernel, he was to live a life on the run for the next thirty-seven years, leading a charmed existence, escaping first the irate police and, later, divisions of avenging professional soldiers.

Origins of the LTTE

Prabhakaran's home town was also a smuggling centre as were many of the coastal villages nearby. One of the earliest fusions of militancy, criminality and smuggling came together in a well-known local fisherman, Nadaraja Thangavelu, a larger-than-life character also from Velvettiturai. The locals called these tough smugglers '*ottis*'. The young Prabhakaran sought out Thangavelu. The close-knit smuggling community, and its access to Tamil Nadu, were of obvious interest to a young revolutionary.

In 1972 Prabhakaran founded the Tamil New Tigers (TNT), one of many organizations that protested against the discrimination against Tamils. In May 1976 the TNT was renamed the Liberation Tigers of Tamil Eelam (LTTE) and known more commonly as the 'Tigers'. Many Tamil groups were absorbed into pro-government Tamil movements, but Prabhakaran was always the most hardline. He would in later years adopt the North Vietnamese model of fighting and talking, and tolerating ceasefires for tactical advantage. When the LTTE was formed, military and police intelligence estimated that thirty-seven organizations were active in Tamil militancy.[52] Most were merely a nuisance to the Sri Lankan state. Besides the LTTE, only four were of major operational and political significance:

People's Liberation Organization of Tamil Eelam (PLOTE), led by Uma Maheswaran

Tamil Eelam Liberation Organization (TELO), led by Sri Sabaratnam

Eelam People's Revolutionary Liberation Front (EPRLF), headed by K. S. Padmanabha

Eelam Revolutionary Organization of Students (EROS), led by Velupillai Balakumar

The plethora of groups, often flaunting their minor and obscure political differences, was reminiscent of the parodied Palestinian groups in Monty Python's film *The Life of Brian*. Often personality inspired the squabbles rather than politics, except that the rivalry was often deadly. For more than a decade after its foundation, the LTTE sought to incorporate or destroy rivals. For example, in January 1982, the LTTE attacked the PLOTE in Jaffna. Sometimes the personal rivalries became very personal indeed. In

May of that year there was a shootout in Pondy Bazaar in Madras between Uma Maheswaran (leader of PLOTE) and Prabhakaran himself when they both accidentally came face to face; both survived the mafia-style contest.

Ideology

Colombo was to portray Prabhakaran in many negative images, not least as a bloodthirsty ethnic warlord, and later as a messianic madman who wanted to recreate the Chola kingdom of pre-history. It was true that some Tamils wanted to be incorporated into the Tamil Nadu state and be ruled from its capital, Chennai, and not Colombo. Much (wordy) academic energy has been invested in trying to define precisely the nature of the LTTE insurgency. Numerous caste and class explanations have been offered. But the most straightforward, and compelling, rationale is ethnic separatist nationalism, based upon real and perceived long-term domination by the Sinhalese majority. The Tamils considered themselves to be the most distinct minority among other minorities such as the Muslims. The Sinhalese were a majority in the state, but acted sometimes as though they were a threatened minority. The 'majority with a minority complex' can be explained by Colombo's fear of not just the Indian superpower but also the over 60 million Tamils in Tamil Nadu, and the preponderance of Tamil speakers in the region. The Sinhalese sense of grievance and linguistic defensiveness, however, could not match Tamil suffering in the series of deadly inter-communal riots of 1958, 1961, 1974, 1977, 1979 and 1981, culminating in the horrific pogrom of 1983.

After years of discussion of federal solutions and non-violent protest, the Tigers proclaimed that an armed struggle was the only way to achieve Tamil Eelam. But that statelet would embrace 60 per cent of the coastline and nearly 30 per cent of the land mass, an arrangement which no Sinhalese political leader could accept, and hope to survive in office. It was a concession too far to a Tamil minority which numbered initially perhaps no more than 20 per cent of the population, and far less after the mass migration and fatalities caused by the four rounds of fighting.

Despite the allegation by many Buddhists that the war was primarily a religious one, the LTTE did not espouse a Hindu cause. One of the early LTTE captains was Charles Lucas Anthony, a young firebrand, who happened to be a Catholic from Trincomalee. The vaguely Marxist-Leninist tenor of what passed for LTTE political philosophy was explicitly secular. Prabhakaran himself explained that, once Tamil Eelam was achieved, his goal inside the new state would be 'revolutionary socialism and the creation of an egalitarian society'. Anton Stanislaus Balasingham, from mixed Hindu-Catholic parentage, became the chief ideologist of the LTTE. He had strong Marxist leanings. His *Towards Socialist Eelam*, published in 1979, was adopted as a manifesto by the LTTE.

Prabhakaran was no doubt charismatic, according to those who worked closely with him. And his military achievements were formidable: he built up probably the most effective and disciplined insurgent force to appear in the world since 1945. Some admirers compared him with Afghanistan's Ahmed Shah Massud (while enemies compared his ruthlessness with that of Pol Pot). The Tiger leader did approve of comparisons with Che Guevara, and some of the leadership's noms de guerre had Cuban connections. Prabhakaran even had a book written in English about Che translated into Tamil so he could read it unaided. The Tiger leader's cult of personality could be likened to Stalin's – Prabhakaran did enforce Soviet-style purges of his followers – but the military tactics were closely related to Maoist principles. The strict puritanical rules imposed on fighting cadres smacked more of North Korea, whence came much of the arms supplies. The actual rule of the LTTE in its 'liberated areas' did reveal elements of egalitarianism, especially in undermining caste (Prabhakaran was of low caste himself) and discrimination against women. The overall administration was harsh and punishments often extreme, although the LTTE – or rather its political wing, the People's Front of Liberation Tigers – explained that wartime exigencies demanded extra discipline.

Military Structure
Despite the technical separation of the political and military wings, the LTTE had one commander in chief and one president: Prabhakaran. Abroad, the organization worked diligently as a sophisticated political and propaganda system, but at home in the liberated zones the military edifice dominated. The domestic LTTE structure was as shown on the following page.

At the start of Eelam War IV in 2006, Sri Lankan military intelligence put the LTTE's land forces as 25,000.[53] This included regular and auxiliary forces used for offensive and defensive roles. By 2008, as the war intensified, the cadres increased to 30,000 partly as a result of pressganging, including forced recruitment of youths under eighteen (even though the LTTE had long agreed that it would not recruit child soldiers). With special exceptions, each family was expected to give up at least one young male or female to the war effort.

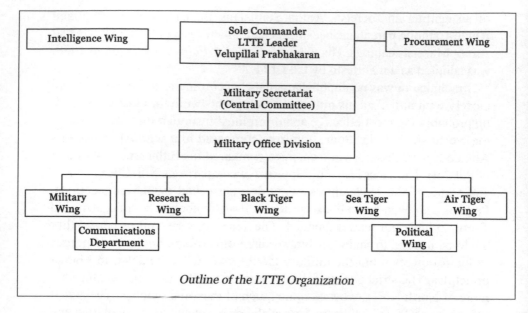

Outline of the LTTE Organization

Land forces

The vast majority of the overall fighting strength of 30,000 comprised land forces. From the 1970s a small band of militants, sometimes armed with homemade weapons, the LTTE had evolved into a very effective force capable of mixing guerrilla and conventional warfare. Two types of auxiliary forces were used.

> *Eelapadai*: volunteer home guards numbering around 5,000; usually static except in emergencies.
> *Gramapadai*: approximately 5,000 personnel deployed more actively, often in logistic roles.

The LTTE fielded advanced weaponry and specialized formations. Prominent units were:

> The Special Reconnaissance Group. Some of the most able cadres were recruited from all regiments to work in this group which acted in tandem with the Intelligence Wing.

> Snipers. They were used to limit the movements of the army during large-scale LTTE offensives, as well as for political and military assassinations in urban areas.

Assault Pioneers. These guerrillas performed critical engineering tasks.

Minelaying teams.

Tank Regiment and Anti-Tank Regiment. The main task of these units was to counter armoured vehicles. The LTTE had captured, bought or improvised (sometimes very cleverly from tractors and earth-moving machinery) a range of armoured vehicles of their own.

Equipment

Before the LTTE set up a sophisticated international arms procurement network, its weaponry was basic. First it relied on domestic sources. It made its own weapons, especially IEDs. And it captured arms from the army and police in raids on bases and police stations and from ambushes. Its first overseas supplies came from India: some older infantry weapons accompanied the training provided by Indian intelligence. The first distant forays were deals with arms suppliers connected with the conflicts in Pakistan and Afghanistan. But the arsenal grew rapidly, as money poured in from the diaspora.

The LTTE eventually fielded a wide array of equipment, including:

1 x T55 tank
12 x 130mm cannon (Type 59-1)
9 x 152mm howitzers (Type 66)
2 x 122mm guns
2 x 107mm rocket artillery
4 x 140mm mortars
150 x 120mm mortars
500 x 82/81mm mortars
350 x RPG rocket launchers
16 x SA-16 (IGLA) missiles
5 x IGLA missile launchers

Land tactics

The insurgents usually fought on home ground and so knew their terrain well. They often deployed in civilian clothes so they could blend in both for penetration and retreat. Civilian dress also improved the access to intelligence on security force activities. The cadres attacked isolated garrisons, then used their conventional forces to deny the army's capability to reinforce the besieged units. Simultaneously, on multiple fronts, the LTTE would launch guerrilla strikes on any relieving forces. On some occasions, such as the regularly contested main base at Elephant Pass, the LTTE could kill hundreds of soldiers (10 July 1991: 156 killed and 748 injured; 23 April 2000: 708 killed and 2,576 wounded). The LTTE's aim was to induce a universal fear psychosis among government troops, by unceasing wave attacks as well as suicide units, plus the efficiency of its indirect fire capability. The numerous IEDs and reluctance to take prisoners (or to accept surrenders and then massacre prisoners) also demoralized government troops. The LTTE were often highly successful in their offensives. Before the final stage of the war after 2006, the LTTE had killed 19,282 security force personnel; 82,104 were wounded; and 2,609 were missing in action. That was a very high tally for a small professional army.

Training

Basic training was given in almost every village the LTTE controlled. Refresher training was given frequently to regular cadres. Special operations training was given for long-range penetration attacks as well as suicide attacks on land and sea.

Basic training would include weapons handling, working with explosives, mapreading, communications, ambush and survival skills. More advanced training would involve intelligence gathering, encryption skills, demolition devices, forgery techniques and computer training.

Recruitment

The LTTE practised an extreme form of conscription where at least one person from each family, male or female, had to do military service. The movement did not always adhere to this policy, however. During the last stages of the war, every capable Tamil was expected to fight. Many felt coerced, but the sophisticated propaganda campaigns and endless ceremonies extolling the war prompted voluntary enlistment. In the orphanages run by the LTTE young children, often effectively brainwashed, were recruited when they reached twelve to fifteen years of age. Children were used in all capacities from infantry to intelligence roles. They were also trained in suicide missions. Women and children were less likely to undergo detailed searches at government checkpoints. When Colonel Karuna famously broke away from Prabhakaran, he defected with a large number of cadres, including – according to police sources – around 2,000 children. Women and girls were recruited into female brigades such as the Malathi

Brigade and Sothia Brigade, while some were absorbed into a female Sea Tiger Brigade. The women fought and were killed in large numbers.

Discipline

The original constitution of the LTTE laid down a code of conduct perhaps more suitable for a monastic order rather than a blueprint for a new nation. It expressly forbade love affairs and death was proscribed for disloyalty. Prabhakaran had a personal mania about cleanliness and this may have inspired his obsession with moral rules. He loathed homosexuals as much as the most rabid imam. Smoking, liquor and sex were forbidden for serving cadres, although sometimes deviations were overlooked. The guerrilla chieftain certainly expected higher standards from his inner circle. One of Prabhakaran's close security team was forced to admit to having had sex with a female cadre in the leader's entourage, after the woman was discovered to be pregnant. They confessed to committing the act while they were both on duty, an even more serious crime. Prabhakaran refused all pleas for mercy and they were both executed.

Weapon discipline was also strict. If an insurgent lost his weapon, he would never be armed again. If a cadre was careless enough to accidentally fire his or her weapon, he or she would be put on kitchen duties for a period If the shot caused an injury, he or she would be confined to camp and endure a very extended period of washing up in the kitchens or cleaning toilets.

Despite the strict code, a form of Maoist egalitarianism prevailed in the beginning of the war. No formal rank structure existed publicly. The rank would be revealed only after death in battle which would also lead to a posthumous promotion. Rank and even membership of the LTTE were denied to the many women and men classified as 'helpers', who provided secret logistic support throughout the country. Intelligence and procurement specialists also hid their affiliations and ranks. A small group specialized in assassination. This so-called 'pistol group' would not reveal any Tiger connections and were used to assassinate people but also allow LTTE deniability.

Discipline was also maintained by periodic purges of the military forces in classical Stalinesque style. They were dubbed 'counter-intelligence successes'. A friend from the beginning of the struggle and then senior comrade, Mahathaya, was one of the early victims. Sometimes LTTE counter-intelligence talked of getting rid of 'Mahathaya groups'. Colonel Karuna's defection in 2004 was prompted by the fear that the Eastern Tamil leader was next in line for a purge.

Sea Tigers
Created in 1984, the force reached around 3,000 personnel at its height; in 1991 Colonel Soosai (Thillaiyampalam Sivanesan) became the commander. The LTTE could launch a very well-equipped and highly trained maritime fighting force capable of countering the navy in semi-conventional, guerilla and suicide missions. The LTTE needed a maritime capability to ensure its extensive weapons procurement, which came by sea. It also provided a coastal penetration capability. In the early 1980s it deployed fishing boats for smuggling and gun-running. In the 1990s it started using fast boats with a selection of large outboard motors to fight in groups of five or six boats to engage the navy in wolf-pack tactics. When the navy applied similar swarm tactics, the Sea Tigers started to deploy fibreglass boats with a minimum crew, usually two, but packed with explosives. The suicide boats would also mingle with fishing boats to launch surprise attacks. In the late 1990s the LTTE started experimenting with suicide divers and semi-submersible craft. In the last years of the war the LTTE started work on building its own mini submarines. The Sea Tigers also used sea mines.

The LTTE could not use secure harbours or launching areas because of Colombo's air dominance, so the insurgents used trailers to launch and recover their boats. They would be hauled by tractors a few kilometres inland. They would remain hidden until ordered to engage in the next surprise attack. Battle attrition and interdiction of the Sri Lankan navy wore down the Tigers, despite their energetic ingenuity. In 2006 the navy had twenty-one major encounters with the Sea Tigers, while in 2008 this had been reduced to four. The last period of the war forced the Tigers to resort to desperate surprise attacks, deploying mines and frogmen with semi-submersibles.

The LTTE's main maritime assets were:

25+ cargo ships
20/30 fast-attack craft
20+ transport boats
23 suicide boats
6 locally manufactured submarines
20+ underwater/diving scooters
1 remote-controlled boat
76 fibreglass boats
115 fibreglass dinghies

The LTTE also deployed a wide array of radars, including KOEN, FURONO, JRC, JMA, TOKIMEC and Ray Marine.

The fibreglass boats consisted of four main types. The 45-knot *Thrikka*, which had four crew members and a machine gun, was also used to deploy frogmen. The 45-knot *Muraj* usually had a crew of around ten which sported three machine guns; this was used for attack and for inserting ground troops. The two-man *Idayan* was a 45-knot suicide craft designed to explode on impact. The 10-knot *Sudia* was armed with a single machine gun.

These boats were a triumph of ingenuity, often built in jungle workshops using off-the-shelf materials and constructed by a mix of unemployed artisans and engineering graduates. These homemade craft had low superstructures which maximised their stealth characteristics. As one military observer noted, 'They created out of sheer will and fibreglass a force that could operate across the spectrum of conflict.'[54]

In sea battles, some lasting hours, the Sea Tigers, especially suicide boats, sank eight major naval vessels, twenty fast-attack craft and twenty-eight inshore patrol boats, killing fifty-two officers and 348 sailors. The Sea Tigers also engaged in international sea piracy by attacking twelve merchant vessels off the coasts of Sri Lanka, including — incautiously — a Chinese trawler.

Air Tigers

Almost unparalleled among insurgencies worldwide, the LTTE also set up an air wing. The assets consisted of civilian aircraft obtained through front organizations abroad, then smuggled into Sri Lanka via the Sea Tiger cargo ships and modified for offensive purposes. Several runways were constructed in the Iranamadu, Mullaitivu and Kilinochchi areas, laid out in a conventional configuration which included hangars, clearways, navigation aids and parking areas. The pilots were trained in private flying schools in South East Asian countries. Cadres also underwent courses in aircraft maintenance and parachuting prior to the onset of the final phase of the war. The Air Tigers deployed SAM missiles, including Stingers, to shoot down or destroy by ground operations fifty-two aeroplanes, military and civilian, as well as helicopters. The LTTE air wing also launched aerial assaults in their light aircraft, hitting the international airport at Katunayake and the oil refinery at Kolonnawa. Often the air attacks did little damage, but the occasional night raids caused panic in the urban areas. Colombo was blacked out on several occasions as a precautionary measure. The international airport was also forced to close sometimes. Some international airlines cancelled flights to Colombo as a result, further undermining business confidence and tourist traffic.

The air assets comprised:

2 microlights
5 Zlin 143 light aircraft
2 helicopters
2 UAVs

The most dramatic attack of the air- and land-based Air Tigers was on 24 July 2001, when Colombo's main airports were hit. The assault on the air force base at Katunayake cost ten aircraft, including two of the frontline Kfirs. An Airbus A340 and an A330 were also destroyed at the nearby international civilian airport. Six people were killed. Fatalities were much higher in a series of SAM missile attacks on air force transport aircraft and helicopters (three sorties in 1995 killing 163 on board; one in 1996 killing thirty-nine; and an Antonov An-24 in September 1998 killing fifty-four on board). In October 2007 eight planes and choppers were destroyed at Anuradhapura air base; twenty personnel were also killed.

Black Tigers

The LTTE inspired a cult of suicide as a form of martyrdom for the cause which they described as *punitha yutham* (pure/holy war). Ordinary cadres wore a cyanide capsule around their necks to avoid, they said, rape, torture, interrogation and death if there was a possibility of capture. But the Black Tigers were different: they were highly trained martyrs tasked with special missions that would involve their self-sacrifice. Besides training similar to special forces techniques, they were accorded a high status in the LTTE organization. They would practise their missions in great detail, often training on a replica of their targets if buildings were involved. Sometimes the targets would be groups of security force personnel. On other occasions the targets could be VIP civilians, including well-known assassinations such as Rajiv Gandhi. Planning could take years and was usually meticulous, including the assassination of President Premadasa. One Black Tiger spent three years on his mission, including over two years spent embedding himself in the President's close circle. The LTTE publicly admitted that 274 male suicide bombers and 104 female suicide bombers had died in action between 5 July 1987 and 20 November 2008.

Suicide operations

Few other groups, including radical Jihadists, refined suicide tactics as effectively as the LTTE. The Tigers were unique in killing two national leaders in two different countries. Between 1987 and 2009 the LTTE carried out 123 suicide attacks on land, sea and air. Besides killing VIPs, the Tigers also destroyed religious, economic and military infrastructure. The Tigers drew some of their inspiration from the *Hezbollah* attack on the US Marines in 1983. Prabhakaran had recently introduced cyanide capsules for the cadres, declaring that 'to terminate one's life voluntarily is the highest and the noblest achievement'. The LTTE formed its first suicide unit in July 1987 which immediately went into action in Jaffna against the Sri Lankan army.

The fighting against the Indian peacekeeping force disrupted the development of the Black Tigers, or *Karum Puligal* as the LTTE called them. Pottu Amman, the head of the LTTE Intelligence Wing and mastermind behind the suicide operations, was injured and was evacuated to South India. The second phase of the war, after 1990, saw the first seaborne suicide mission. Cadres tried to ram a boat full of explosives against the naval vessel *Edithra* on 10 July off Velvettiturai, where Prabhakaran grew up. In the third round of the war, after 1995, the Black Tigers switched to iconic religious sites. They hit Dalada Maligawa, the Buddhist shrine housing the sacred tooth relic, using an explosive-laden vehicle. The first suicide attack on an economic target came on 20 October 1995 on oil installations in Colombo.

The Tigers began operations with IEDs in vehicles, then expanded to human bombs, as well as sea and air delivery. The human-bomb system underwent a series of innovations to improve the suicide jackets. The first-generation jackets were large and bulky, using gelignite and C-3 explosives. This type killed Rajiv Gandhi and President Premadasa. The second-generation jackets were smaller and filled with TNT explosives. Ball bearings and explosives were used in a ratio of 1:2 to cause maximum destruction. It meant that the suicide cadre did not have to get so close. The jackets then got smaller, and were filled with C-4 explosives. Predating the al-Qaeda underpants experiments by over a decade, the LTTE experts started designing underwear with explosive fillings, which made them harder to detect during cursory searches, especially of females, at roadblocks or during VIP protection.[55]

Youngsters competed to join the Black Tigers. Some had been indoctrinated since early childhood, others wanted to avenge real or imagined government actions against their families. A general cult of martyrdom was encouraged. The LTTE used some of the following selection criteria to short-list the many volunteers:

loyalty towards the leader
should be over fifteen
unmarried
physically fit, although sometimes a war wound or other disability might
    be acceptable
loss of a family member in the war
displaced during conflict
unemployed
anger/hostility to enemy
ability to speak Sinhala

In his annual message to his followers, Prabhakaran would make a request for volunteers to the Black Tigers. Until 2006 the overwhelming response meant that only the very best would be recruited. This selection procedure ensured that the martyrdom unit consistently outperformed other terror organizations which adopted the tactic. Selected and trained annually, LTTE cadres were allowed to delist themselves in the following year. Despite the successful annual appeal, LTTE intelligence officers regularly visited schools to identify promising Black Tigers. Orphanages (especially Sencholai and Kandaruban in the Vanni area) also provided volunteers. After 2006, because of international criticism of child recruitment, and because the orphanages were a very useful source of foreign funding, the LTTE became much more careful about recruiting children from these orphanages and other schools. All such caution was thrown to the wind in the final desperate months of the conflict.

The Black Tiger recruits typically underwent basic military training for three months. If they passed, they would undergo training on a replica of their chosen targets, plus relevant specialized skills such as riding motorbikes, driving lorries, piloting boats or handling explosives. Also basic intelligence skills, such as counter-surveillance techniques, were taught. Their leisure hours would allow them time to watch English-language adventure films, interspersed with videos of previous successful martyr missions. On completion of training, the individual or group would be given an opportunity to have a meal with Prabhakaran himself. Here the young volunteers could admire a photo gallery of previous martyrs, with their own pictures now added.

Target selection was naturally highly secret and various cells, usually unknown to each other, would prepare the ground, once the leader and head of intelligence had selected the target. The military value of the target would be assessed as well as domestic economic and political impacts, plus possible international repercussions. At least three agents would work independently on the target sites, testing for LTTE sympathizers in the locality as well as careful use of maps and satellite imagery.

An operational intelligence cell would set up a safe house and provide food, transport and security and make sure that the arms for a group or a suicide jacket were available. Typically the suicide operator or group would move into the safe house a few days before the planned execution of the mission. The cadre would leave LTTE-controlled areas with fake documents citing reasons such as seeking foreign employment, higher education, medical treatment or perhaps employment as drivers or assistants to Tamil parliamentarians or work in an NGO in government areas. The group or individual would spend a few days familiarizing themselves with the area around the safe house and the target area. In military missions often the most difficult element is extraction. With death inevitable, the Black Tigers did not face this problem.

Sea attacks were different. The head of the Sea Tigers would choose the mission after consultation with the leadership. Boats were frontloaded with explosives with a control panel and switch. Usually the boats were powered by two 250 HP engines and the two-man crew were often disabled cadres. Up to five or ten LTTE attack craft would try to isolate a naval vessel. Under maximum firepower from the main group, the suicide craft followed in the wake of the LTTE command vessel. The command craft would try to damage the hull of the enemy vessel and this is precisely the point where the suicide boat would try to strike.

Of the 123 major suicide attacks:

46 attacks were by jackets
44 by boats
23 using vehicles
2 using aircraft
8 by group attacks on land.

In these attacks, from 1987 to 2009, an estimated 432 Black Tigers died (according to Sri Lankan intelligence). Male cadres accounted for 74 per cent; the remaining 26 per cent were female Black Tigers. For almost all the group operations men were deployed; for individual missions females tended to predominate. Although in some attacks cadres as young as fifteen were used, the majority of the suicide fighters were aged twenty to thirty-five, indicating that the LTTE gave priority to mature youths who had proven physical and mental capacity.

What did these tactics achieve? Prabhakaran said, 'With perseverance and sacrifice, Tamil Eelam can be achieved in 100 years. But if we conduct Black Tiger operations, we can shorten the suffering of the people and achieve Tamil Eelam in a shorter period of time.' Certainly the series of assassinations of senior political leaders did undermine the morale of the government. The economic impact was also significant, and not just on tourism and foreign investment. The attacks on the Central Bank, the World Trade Centre, the oil storage installations in Kolonnawa and the international airport were all significant strikes. Suicide assaults on military facilities and high-ranking officers took their toll, for example the assassination of Admiral Clancy Fernando, the former commander of the navy. There were near misses on the leading architects of the war, Gotabaya Rajapaksa and General Sarath Fonseka.

Intelligence Wing

The LTTE infiltrated its agents into Colombo to establish an extensive labyrinth of cells. The agents acted as handlers for suicide cadres and would set up safe houses. Intelligence agents also managed to suborn a number of Sinhalese and Muslims serving in the armed forces and police. In addition, LTTE intelligence operatives helped plan assaults on military and police bases throughout the country. They also ran prison camps and interrogation centres for LTTE dissidents and captured security force members; few of either category survived their ordeals.

Internal administration

The LTTE's statelet never declared independence but it ran a comprehensive administration which included elaborate media and propaganda sections. It also set up a judiciary and deployed a police force. Women were encouraged to join the Tamil Eelam police. Crime rates dropped dramatically, especially in the Jaffna area, and women also felt more safe, especially when travelling alone, with the deployment of female officers. Except for law and order and finance, the LTTE's political front, the People's Front of Liberation Tigers, administered the 'liberated' zones.

At the height of its power the LTTE controlled 15,000 square kilometres, just under a quarter of the island. That was still short of the one-third of the land mass which it claimed for Eelam. The LTTE did not control, however, the entire eastern and northern provinces. It did have complete mastery in two districts, Mullaitivu and Kilinochchi, for long periods. In many other areas government garrisons or counter-offensives – except during the ceasefires – created an unstable quasi-state. Also, the public services in LTTE territory were often still provided by the Sri Lankan state. These included health, education, power, water and some food supplies. Public servants, paid and supplied by the state, contrived a variety of tacit understandings whereby they also obeyed the stringent LTTE rules. The chief of Sri Lankan intelligence aptly summarized this paradox: 'This was the only terrorist group that was fed by the government.'

International networks

The diaspora was largely made up of exiles; many had sought asylum in the West. It was ironic that the Tamil exiles' support for the Tigers heightened the violence and the government counter-violence thus creating a vicious action-reaction cycle which boosted the diaspora numbers. In some countries the Tamil community stood next to the Jewish diaspora if not in wealth perhaps in organization; it was less assimilated too. It was much smarter at playing on tender hearts in the host community while funding an insurgency back home. It outdid the Kurdish, Irish, Kashmiri and even Palestinian diaspora in this regard. Many in their host countries might regard the Tigers as terrorists, but it was hard to ignore the plight of people who felt they had to live in an alien (if more affluent) culture and perhaps suffer racial discrimination and low social status rather than submit to the indignities and humiliations in the homeland most did not want to leave.[56]

The LTTE milked the diaspora and its political allies and support groups abroad for all that it was worth in propaganda and money. The Tigers' International Secretariat established a worldwide system of weapons procurement, financial and political support and media outlets. Much of the network survived intact after the defeat of the insurgency in Sri Lanka itself. The international system was very complicated often involving criminal or ideological groups which had no Tamil members – they were often in the game for personal gain. The central Tiger overseas system was divided into two parts. One was headed by the intelligence chief, Pottu Amman. Sometimes called the Aiyanna Group, this provided the foreign enforcement. This did the 'wet ops' in the jargon: killings. It could be anything that needed muscle, from policing protection rackets in London to kidnapping a reluctant business donor in Toronto or anywhere in the various 'Little Jaffnas' that sprang up in the diaspora. The second part of the network, the so-called KP Department, formally the Office of Overseas

Purchases, as the name suggests, bought the weapons. Its coordinator, K. P. – Kumaran Pathmanathan – ran a system of legal front offices. Dirty or dangerous work was left to the hard men associated with the intelligence outfit. K. P. was a born entrepreneur. He displayed a mastery of operating in the ungoverned spaces whether on land in Africa or Asia, or in the ultimate ungoverned space, the oceans, where he floated his naval warehouses. He made so much money that his friend from schooldays, Prabhakaran, grew suspicious that he was lining his own pockets. 'I was sidelined,' K.P. told me, in sorrow rather than anger. Although he claimed that he earned only a tiny personal salary, less than a schoolteacher's, he never dipped into Tiger finds, he insisted. Eventually, Prabhakaran bought him back into the fold in the last stages of the war.

Funding came via a large number of front organizations, often registered as charities, especially in countries such as Canada and Britain which had large Tamil diasporas. Fundraising methods, legal and illegal, varied enormously. Some involved voluntary contributions; others were coerced. Sri Lankan Tamils abroad who resisted were often told that the safety of their relatives still in Sri Lanka could not be guaranteed, nor could their own return trips to the homeland be trouble free. Unofficial taxes were placed on foreign Tamil businesses, especially small outfits operating petrol stations and supermarkets. Some of the businesses were encouraged to operate rackets including credit card fraud. The funds raised were then laundered to acquire weapons.

After the LTTE was banned in the US and the EU, various front organizations were set up in fifty-four locations in thirty-two countries. The LTTE contained some brilliant propagandists who established a range of TV and radio stations, websites and printed media.

The front organizations worked assiduously on foreign politicians as well as the approximately one million Tamil exiles, notably in Europe and North America. The UK accommodated over 300,000 Tamil exiles and Canada almost 380,000. Toronto alone hosted more Tamils than any city in Sri Lanka. Political activity was intense in India, where an estimated 150,000 Tamil exiles lived. Germany, France and Australia boasted large and politically active pro-LTTE populations. Hundreds of Tamil schools were set up in the diaspora regions (350 in Europe alone), to inculcate third-generation children in the cause. Often these children were mobilized on behalf of pro-LTTE protests.

Sri Lankan intelligence calculated that around ten per cent of Tamil exiles were active radicals. They were often successful business people and highly capable of organizing vote banks in regions and cities where their numerical concentration could sway the local vote and thus secure a ready ear from politicians. In Britain the LTTE (under a political and legal guise) formed dedicated organizations to liaise with both the Labour and Conservative parties.

The Sri Lankan government faced international strictures because of criticisms of its human rights regime. For example, the US stopped all military aid in 2007. The proscription of the LTTE was much wider, however. India banned the LTTE in 1992. In October 1997 Washington listed the movement as a foreign terrorist organization; Britain took similar action in 2001. In 2005 the UN Security Council condemned the LTTE for its conscription of children. In 2005 the UK acted against some of the fronts and they were de-listed as charities. In 2006 even Canada proscribed the LTTE, as did the EU in the same year. Yet despite these international pressures, the tentacles of the LTTE's International Secretariat continued to nourish the insurgency at home.

The LTTE owned in the end a large shipping empire, run by K P. Over twenty large vessels and a considerable number of trawlers were acquired and registered under different flags. Boatyards were also bought in South East Asian countries, especially Thailand. That freewheeling country also hosted the LTTE's large weapons supply centre in Phuket. Arms were shipped under the guise of normal cargo. Among these ships were the so-called *Sea Pigeons*, floating arsenals. In the early stages of the war, the Indian and Malaysian navies were active in seizing and later destroying these vessels; in the last stage of the conflict, the Sri Lankan navy sank the cargo ships.

But for a long time the LTTE ran a very extensive and complicated procurement chain. Although most of the military hardware came from North Korea, much of the kit was East European transported via Odessa (Ukraine) and Varna (Bulgaria). The larger ships were often purchased from Japan, which used to renew its merchant fleet every ten years and sell off the older vessels at a knockdown price. An example of LTTE enterprise was the purchase of five Czech light planes. They were taken to Hamburg by land in large containers, then shipped to Singapore, then taken by sea to Indonesia. There the planes were stacked in a bonded warehouse until they were shipped to Sri Lanka.

A large illicit smuggling empire for weapons was easy to adapt for other lucrative criminal activities. Drug smuggling was one of the first variations. For example, in 1986 a former head of the LTTE International Secretariat was arrested and convicted in France for smuggling drugs into Paris. Human trafficking also brought lots of cash into the LTTE treasury. The earliest cases go back to the 1980s when 155 Tamils were smuggled into Canadian waters from West Germany and set adrift in lifeboats. Later, people smuggling centred on South East Asian nations such as Cambodia, Laos, Thailand, Indonesia, Malaysia and Singapore, which became transit points to western countries. A post-war example of the traffic in human misery was the LTTE's smuggling via the *Sun Sea* and *Ocean Lady* which travelled from South East Asia to Canada in 2010.

According to Sri Lankan intelligence estimates, the amount raised by the International Secretariat from 1993 to 2002 was $50 to $75 million annually. From 2002 to 2008 this sum increased to over $200 million per year. From this $200 million plus – some estimates put it as high as $300 million – perhaps only $8 million was used annually in Tiger-administered regions of Sri Lanka. Although the black market costs and shipments of arms were high, nonetheless, to quote *Jane's Intelligence Review*, 'the profit margin of its operating budget would likely be the envy of any multinational corporation'.[57] Many millions still remained in secret bank accounts. And the key to unlocking the money was the financial mastermind, K P, one of the reasons he was still held under house arrest in Colombo, even though he had publicly foresworn the armed struggle.[58]

LTTE's strategic achievements

Prabhakaran fashioned an organization in his own image: daring, highly committed, disciplined and ruthless. The internal propaganda matched the efficacy of the international war effort – the inhabitants of the ever-changing territories run by the LTTE were persuaded or forced into a war which lasted nearly three decades. War-weariness was apparent in the lead up to the ceasefire of 2002. LTTE bitter-enders say that the ceasefire was one of the reasons why some cadres became peace-oriented and 'soft'. Nevertheless, before the Rajapaksa-led final campaigns, the LTTE managed to increase its fighting strength, its range of weapons and its cash flow.

The cadres usually fought with immense dedication and skill. The tactical innovations on land, sea and air were highly imaginative. On land and sea the guerrillas often outfought the regular forces of the state, which had the backing – logistical and political – from powerful nations such as China. No other insurgency developed such extensive capabilities and over such a long period, relying largely on its own initiatives especially after India was alienated following the LTTE's killing of Rajiv Gandhi. And yet the LTTE was defeated. In the end, Prabhakaran's strengths were probably his major weakness. His obsession with a military solution – rather than a lasting political deal when he was at the height of his power, say in the period 2002–05 – led to a military solution neither he, nor nearly all the world's security specialists, could have predicted.

THE CLIMAX

Chapter 11

Trying 'Peace' First

Mahinda Rajapaksa won the November 2005 presidential elections in the closest margin in the country's history – partly because the LTTE had ordered its people not to vote. The new president's victory by Tiger default was to prove one of Prabhakaran's biggest strategic errors, perhaps on a par with killing Rajiv Gandhi. Low-level violence continued on both sides. The LTTE stepped up its claymore mine attacks on the military as well as clashes at sea. The LTTE blamed the government for killing its sympathizers including a well-known and widely read pro-LTTE journalist, Taraki Sivaram, who was murdered after a 'white van' abduction, allegedly a common modus operandi of the government's secret black ops. Joseph Pararajasingham, a pro-LTTE MP, was also killed. The LTTE blamed the government.

At the end of 2005 the UN Special Rapporteur, Philip Alston, during a visit to the island, commented that the ceasefire was under 'unprecedented stress'. Alston met S. P. Tamilselvam, the head of the LTTE's political wing, to urge the movement to curb its attacks. Although the new President doubted the sincerity of the LTTE's commitment to peace, Rajapaksa declared that he would try his utmost to maintain the ceasefire and even convert it into a peace settlement. He often said, 'I don't want to pass this problem on to the next generation.' The President had met Tony Blair and was utterly charmed by him.[59] The British Prime Minister spent some time explaining how the Belfast Agreement had ended the turmoil in Northern Ireland. But the pragmatic new President also knew that he had to be prepared for a resumption of full-scale war. His very first action on hearing he had squeaked home in the presidential race was to ask his brother, Gotabaya, to become Secretary of Defence. The former Colonel was on three months' leave from his IT manager's job in the law faculty of the University of Southern California to help his brother in the election and also to organize his personal security.

The new Permanent Secretary of Defence was a thin, wiry, greying man, always in motion — unlike his more placid and burly elder brother. He was a listener as well as a talker, and he had spent a long time musing on the numerous mistakes he had witnessed as a highly-decorated fighting soldier. Also, in 2002, the US Department of Defense had sent Colombo a lengthy report compiled by a US Pacific Command team. Its numerous recommendations impressed Gotabaya Rajapaksa. They included the need for a combined national security council operating a clear national strategy; before the armed services had tended to fight their own wars in their own ways. A particular point of agreement was the need to end promotions on longevity, not merit. One of the first actions of the new Secretary was to appoint his old comrade, Sarath Fonseka, as army commander, just a few days before his scheduled retirement. Fonseka was not a popular choice, not least for the serving commander who was in mid-term of his appointment (he was given an ambassadorship). Fonseka was a ruthless and effective military leader, but a number of his peers found fault with his uncompromising personality. That settled, Gotabaya Rajapaksa also determined to remedy the other fault lines outlined in the US report, not least equipment. The Americans, while praising the fighting spirit of the infantry, criticized the fact that many soldiers lacked even basics such as helmets and body armour.

Much equipment was needed for naval operations, too. The Americans had correctly identified the supply of arms by sea as the LTTE's centre of gravity (although traditional COIN theory usually would select the population, the sea in which the fish swim). The Sri Lankan forces needed better armed and bigger ships but, equally important, the equipment had to fit into a new combined arms strategy. The security forces had to be prepared for conventional full manoeuvre warfare in places such as the Vanni, but also classic counter-insurgency operations in areas of mixed support, as well as conducting counter-terrorism in urban areas, particularly Colombo. The Americans also urged the Sri Lankans to improve their night-fighting capability, especially the air force, which required upgraded avionics and guided weapons. Because Colombo had bought cheaply and where it could, too much money had been spent on resupplying a whole range of kit, instead of properly servicing a smaller array of equipment. The Americans pointed out that instead of buying MiG-27s money could have been better spent upgrading the Kfir fighters. The Pacific Command also recommended the use of cluster bombs.

The Secretary was also determined to 'remoralize' his forces. Constant military setbacks had downgraded the status of military service. He wanted to improve conditions, pay and image, not least to inspire *more* recruits to join the still all-volunteer army, but also to get *better* recruits. He turned to Dilith Jayaweera of Tri Ads. The company designed a campaign which was a trendsetter in the local PR industry, and which did boost the reputation of the military. Soon military success plus PR was to boost recruitment, thus creating a virtuous circle. The Secretary, using his own extensive IT experience in the US, also set up www.defence.lk as a rival to TamilNet; it became an alternative both domestically and internationally for news on the war. Rapid improvements were made in compensation for wounded soldiers and a range of special provisions were made for funerals of the fallen.

The Secretary was capable of administrative reform of the armed forces, but where could he go to satisfy his long shopping list of weapons? Within the first few weeks of office, the two Rajapaksa brothers flew to the Indian capital. The new President first had a one to one with the Indian Prime Minister, Manmohan Singh. The Indian leader had enjoyed a remarkable career. An Oxbridge (both Oxford and Cambridge) economist of note, as a Sikh he was the first non-Hindu to become premier. Initially untouched by the Indian disease of corruption, he famously drove a Maruti 800, the humblest of local cars. A pragmatist in foreign policy, he was keen to develop a military relationship with Israel. In short, he was a man with whom Mahinda Rajapaksa could do business. After their cordial discussion, Gotabaya was called in to join them to discuss the military situation with the Indian national security advisers.

The Indians and Sri Lankans shared detailed intelligence on the LTTE's advances, notably on new equipment such as Stinger surface-to-air missiles, as well as the small but growing Air Tiger wing. The first stage, if war resumed, would be major LTTE assaults on government positions in Jaffna and an attempt to take Trincomalee, from the LTTE's new stronghold in Sampur, just south of the harbour. After agreeing to the nature and extent of the threat, the Secretary produced his weapons' list. It did not accord precisely with the American menu, but it did include requests for ten MiG-27s, new transport planes, five Mi-24 choppers and UAVs, plus a range of infantry items such as body armour and helmets. The wish list went on: two large offshore patrol craft and an intelligence plan to coordinate logistics and surveillance patrols against LTTE vessels in the open seas. During the Rajapaksas' three-day visit to India, the LTTE helpfully launched a series of attacks on army bases and police stations. The Sri Lankans came away reasonably content: the Indians could or would not provide everything Colombo wanted, but a new security relationship had been forged which would survive intact for the rest of the decade. Nevertheless, President

Rajapaksa assured the Indians he would try to reboot the peace process — despite the evidence that the LTTE had rammed their overseas fundraising campaign into overdrive. They too had a long military shopping list.

General Fonseka complained publicly that during the ceasefire the LTTE's arsenal had become '10-15 times bigger' and expressed his frustration that the Scandinavians were not responding to the many Tiger breaches of the accord. And Gotabaya Rajapaksa met regularly with the Monitoring Mission to complain about its failure to stop the rising crescendo of LTTE assaults. As his biographer noted, tartly, 'Unsurprisingly, none of the many discussions [Gotabaya] had with the SLMM were pleasant or cordial.'[60] Erik Solheim, although promoted to a government minister in Norway, still acted as a special envoy. He was determined to save the truce. Both Rajapaksa brothers thought him rather highhanded, an over-active interventionist rather than a more passive facilitator. Solheim represented the conventional wisdom that the war could not be won militarily. In late March he told the Sri Lankan president that he thought Prabhakaran was a military genius. Mahinda Rajapaksa said, 'You think he is a jungle boy from Mullaitivu – well, I am a jungle boy from the south. We'll see what happens.' The president's brother had a similar meeting with the two leading Norwegians in the SLMM who asked whether the Secretary really thought military defeat of the LTTE was possible. They were surprised when the former Colonel responded with a resounding 'Yes'.

And yet, despite this resolution, the new government still tried hard to revive the peace talks, and not just to satisfy international public opinion. Lalith Weeratunga, the presidential secretary, a very unwarlike figure, volunteered for a secret mission to meet senior LTTE people deep in guerrilla territory. Nothing came of this unorthodox diplomacy, however. The government also hired a team from Harvard University to train all the senior officials and ministers involved with peace negotiations. Workshops were run on precise details of the ceasefire agreement and techniques for negotiation.

The Americans put pressure on the LTTE to keep to the ceasefire. Condoleezza Rice, US Secretary of State in the Bush administration, also urged the EU to exert pressure and to threaten the LTTE with proscription in Europe. The State Department formed an informal intelligence group to monitor LTTE arms procurement routes in South East Asia. In addition, the FBI set up a unit to survey LTTE activities in the US. The US ambassador to Sri Lanka also publicly warned the LTTE that if war resumed the Tigers would face a much stronger military. Washington was put in the picture as to the Rajapaksas' preparations for war, should peace fail. Solheim and the LTTE's leading negotiator, Anton Balasingham, worked together to arrange new talks in Geneva in late February 2006. The government wanted to discuss broader political issues such as the nature of LTTE devolution, but the Tiger leadership focused on specific military threats to them. The Colombo team thought that the insurgents were just going through the motions to keep the international players happy. On the second day, Balasingham asked for a postponement because he said he was feeling unwell. That was the end of the talks; the government team hardly had a chance to refer to their thick Harvard dossiers brimming with facts.

Nevertheless, the parties agreed to resume in late April. For a few weeks after the Geneva talks, violence significantly decreased. But the tempo of attacks soon picked up. The LTTE blamed third parties, not their own cadres. Then came technical disputes about whether the army should assist the LTTE with helicopter transport for meetings of its regional leaders. Next disputes were conjured up about a naval escort for LTTE bosses, which was agreed by the SLMM. Finally, the LTTE — citing the transport issues — announced they were pulling out of the Geneva talks indefinitely.

On 25 April 2006 a heavily pregnant Tamil woman obtained a pass to attend the maternity clinic at the hospital adjacent to the army HQ in Colombo. National intelligence had given specific warnings that the Rajapaksa brothers and the three service chiefs were being targeted. The President gave them bulletproof vehicles from his own car pool, while new vehicles were ordered. But, on 25 April, General Fonseka was travelling a short distance within the heavily guarded compound. He used his official thin-skinned car. It was a well-timed assassination attempt. The Black Tiger female, Anoja Kugenthirasah, set off her bomb. Although a number of military personnel were killed, the General survived with serious wounds. He was taken to Singapore for specialist surgery. The Secretary was furious, but, after a cold calculating conversation with his brother, for the first time since the long ceasefire began the air force carried out retaliatory air raids on LTTE targets in Sampur, south of Trincomalee.

Local attacks also compelled the government to close the A9 road, the main link between north and south. Violence mounted quickly thereafter. On 11 May 2006 the Sea Tigers tried to sink the *Pearl Cruiser,* a passenger ship with 710 military personnel aboard, escorted by four Dvora fast-attack craft. The Dvoras engaged the Sea Tiger suicide boats while the larger ship moved out into deeper waters. One Dvora was sunk, losing two officers and fifteen seamen. This was a major breach of the ceasefire. Shortly afterwards all the EU states banned the LTTE, with some arm-twisting from Washington. The LTTE retaliated by ordering any members of the Monitoring Mission from EU countries to withdraw from the north and east as 'they could not guarantee their safety'.

The international mediators tried once more to patch up the broken ceasefire. Talks were scheduled for Oslo in early June. Both delegations arrived, but the LTTE refused to meet the government representatives because it said some of its senior members had not been given safe passage by Colombo to attend. It was a return to the old transport issue. Even the ever-patient and sympathetic Solheim had had enough: he said that the LTTE should take direct responsibility for the breakdown of the talks.

In the same week a family of four Tamils was tortured and killed in Vankalai village in the district of Mannar. The mother and the nine-year-old daughter were allegedly raped before being killed. The TamilNet internet sites carried gory images of the attacks, creating much international controversy. The army was blamed; Colombo said it was an LTTE attack.[61] A week later two claymore mines blew up a crowded bus in Kebithigollewa, killing sixty-four Sinhalese passengers. The Rajapaksa brothers flew there immediately in a chopper. The President visited the nearby hospital where the bodies had been taken. He was visibly and genuinely affected by the sight. He went to the wards to speak to the injured. The mood of the locals around the hospital was tense and also hostile. Mahinda Rajapaksa could sense for himself that people had had enough of the war and the government's failure to protect them. Extra troops and police commandos were sent to the area to reassure the population. Retaliation raids were launched by artillery on LTTE bases in the Sampur area, as well as air strikes on targets in Kilinochchi and Mullaitivu.

War seemed inevitable now, although the government still held back. On 26 June the Tigers assassinated the third-highest-ranking army officer, Major General Parami Kulatunga, in a suicide attack just outside Colombo. On 14 August an unusual attack occurred. Most first-time visitors to Sri Lankan cities will be terrified by the kamikaze tactics of the trishaw ('tuk-tuk') drivers. The Pakistani High Commissioner's armed motor convoy was assaulted by an LTTE bomb hidden in a trishaw in the heart of Colombo. The diplomat escaped unhurt. It was assumed to be the work of Indian intelligence or the LTTE because of Pakistan's arms supplies to Colombo. The original target had been a Sri Lankan minister; the trishaw was not piloted by a suicide bomber but by a remote device, which had malfunctioned. The intended target — a minister — passed by, unaware of his lucky escape. The remote device was repaired, then along came a motorcade with a military escort. Assuming it was a government bigwig, not a foreign diplomat, the LTTE agent tried again. Although he had killed four army commandos, the diplomat's escorts, and wounded eight others, the LTTE operator was given a severe dressing down by his intelligence chief for hitting the wrong target.

Despite the rising number of breaches in a ceasefire which was now almost meaningless, most analysts still believed that a full-scale war was unlikely. A continuing low-level insurgency seemed probable, not least because the LTTE was entrenching its control in its heartland and was slowly advancing elsewhere on the island. Why risk a war, when armed peace was so profitable?

After 2009 Sri Lankan intelligence came across hard evidence proving their long-held suspicion that the LTTE had used the ceasefire as a ruse to re-arm and re-train. Prabhakaran had specifically given his regional commanders five years to get ready for the final onslaught. In conversations with me in 2011 and 2012, President Rajapaksa said that the two final straws which broke his patience were the bus massacre and the LTTE's sheer bloodyminded refusal to negotiate, especially in Geneva. The President finally gave up hope of a real peace deal. Like his predecessors he would have to find peace via war.

Then came the final tipping point between peace and war: the Mavil Aru dam dispute. On 21 July 2006 the LTTE cut the water supply to over 20,000 villagers in government-controlled areas in the Trincomalee district. The water was used by 9,510 Muslims, 8,013 Sinhalese and 4,439 Tamils living in twenty villages. It was a crucial time for their crops and without water for their fields they would go hungry. A few days later the army advanced to within 800 metres of the dam, under heavy mortar and artillery fire. Their further advance was seriously impeded not only by heavily defended bunkers and trenches but by daisy chains of IEDs and anti-personnel mines. After some heavy fighting and intervention by the SLMM, the gates were opened. The LTTE claimed they re-opened the three sluice gates for humanitarian reasons, the international monitors congratulated themselves and a handful of (local) military correspondents said the army's action had effected the changes. Whoever was wearing the white hats, the army stayed in position.

Although today the Rajapaksa clan and the top Sri Lankan commanders say the Mavil Aru incident was an immediate *casus belli*, the attack was actually an LTTE feint. The real target was Trincomalee harbour. On 1 August 2006 the newly-acquired *Jetliner* with over 1,200 military personnel on board and escorted by a dozen fast-attack craft, was ambushed by a flotilla of Sea Tigers, just as the government convoy was about to enter the harbour. The Tiger boats suddenly appeared from the southern sweep of Koddiyar Bay (the naval harbour was on the northern end of the same bay). Artillery also came in from the LTTE stronghold in Sampur. The navy, helped by Hind gunships, managed to get its precious cargo into the shelter of the harbour. The lightweight aluminium hull of the *Jetliner* would not have long resisted artillery. Shells started to rain down on the naval dockyard and the navy academy. The large LTTE guns then started to range on to the centre of the harbour mouth. This was a blockade. Without Trincomalee Jaffna could not be resupplied. This was the strategic aim – to capture or at least strangle the two main government strong-points.

The *Jetliner* had just been acquired by the ministry of defence because previous naval transports had been like cattle trucks, even without lavatories for the long slow journey up and down the coast to Jaffna. Troops had to resort to plastic bags. The new fast and comfortable *Jetliner* was a former cruise ship bought from the Indonesians less than a month before. It was still manned by a (very nervous) Indonesian crew, but with a complement of Sri Lankan officers and ratings training to sail the new asset. Without getting orders from Colombo the local naval commanders needed to save the ship. They managed to get it out of the harbour under the cover of dark and took refuge around the southern coast in Galle harbour, out of range of any LTTE artillery. There the Indonesian captain and his crew immediately jumped ship and headed for home.

The LTTE then moved to complete its stranglehold on access to the harbour. Insurgents infiltrated Muttur town on the south-west of the large bay, but a combined force of naval patrolmen, army and police managed to hold on to the area around the town's jetty. The navy across the bay in the main harbour hijacked an army multi-barrelled rocket launcher to counter the LTTE artillery. After four days of fighting the combined Sri Lankan forces managed to dislodge the LTTE from Muttur town. The LTTE also hit army camps elsewhere in the region, eventually leading to the displacement of 40,000 mainly Muslim local inhabitants. In the north, the LTTE broke through some of the outer army perimeters around Jaffna. Artillery barrages were aimed at the vital air base at Palaly. Eventually the LTTE waves were repulsed, with ninety navy and army fatalities. Fighting continued in the Jaffna peninsula until September, including a thwarted LTTE amphibious assault on Kayts Island, the original jumping-off point for the army's earlier recapture of Jaffna.

The air force carried out a strike in the rebel heartland of Mullaitivu, killing a number of Tamil girls. The LTTE claimed sixty-one dead, while the SLMM counted nineteen bodies. The Tigers said the girls were not combatants in training, as the government alleged, but innocent schoolchildren attending a course on first aid at an orphanage. The raid caused an international media furore, fanned by TamilNet. At the same time, seventeen aid workers for the French charity Action Against Hunger (ACF), were found lying face-down on the floor of their office in Muttur. They appeared to have been executed, despite wearing T-shirts emblazoned with their roles as international aid workers. The LTTE and the SLMM pointed the finger of blame at the government.

Despite the propaganda war fought in the media, the rapidly reforming Sri Lankan war machine, headed by its refashioned and effective National Security Council, had weathered its first real military threat. The sinking of the *Jetliner* would have meant perhaps over 1,000 dead soldiers from all the regions of the island. That would have demoralized the government, its supporters and, above all, the army. The events of July and August 2006 could have given Prabhakaran his long-desired independent Eelam. But the encirclement around Trincomalee was broken and Jaffna did not fall. This was a significant victory for Colombo because the fighting on various fronts in the north and east had been long planned by the LTTE leadership. Urban terror cells had simultaneously been rolled up in Colombo, where the police seized a cache of mines, grenades, pistols and assault rifles. Overall, the LTTE cadres had not shown their previous flexibility and rapid deployment skills, while the government forces co-ordinated much more efficiently. The armed forces had fought a reactive campaign against a sophisticated LTTE battle plan and, for once, had come out on top. The LTTE had clearly underestimated the Rajapaksas.

I interviewed the most senior surviving Tiger, after the end of the war, 'K P' – Kumaran Pathmanathan. He believed that some of the senior fighting cadres had aged and grown soft, living in big houses, during the long ceasefire. Prabhakaran, a genuine military innovator, had been distracted by negotiations with international leaders, as well as kept busy by courting the Tamil diaspora. Also, the administration of a statelet had distracted the leadership while the burdens of taxation, courts and permits to move around had alienated many erstwhile supporters. And war weariness and emigration had also taken their toll.

The threat to Trincomalee had not been totally removed. It could not be until the LTTE cadres were driven out of the southern area of the Koddiyar

Bay around Sampur. In late August, spearheaded by special force units operating in small groups in and between the LTTE lines, the army cleared the area around Sampur. The LTTE withdrew with 30,000 Sampur inhabitants to the south. This had long been Tiger territory; now improved tactics and invigorated soldiers had taken it back. This was the first significant change of territorial control since the ceasefire began in 2002. The defeat prompted the LTTE to warn that if the army did not cease its offensive the ceasefire would be over; the Tigers also put out feelers via back channels to the Norwegians that a return to talks might be a good idea.

On 11 October 2006 the army launched a surprise attack; it was certainly a surprise to the National Security Council in Colombo. The army pushed across the Muhamalai line, the crossing point between government and LTTE territories in the north. The LTTE turned it back in less than two hours, killing around 300 soldiers and capturing a bonanza of military hardware, including eight armoured vehicles, and four T-55 tanks. The air force had to step in to steady the old defence lines. Pictures of captured tanks and the handover of dead bodies by the LTTE to the International Committee of the Red Cross humiliated the government and Gotabaya Rajapaksa in particular. The northern debacle, after the successes in the east, brought back all the nightmares he had promised to expunge. The Secretary must have had very frank words with the army commander, Sarath Fonseka, now recovered and back in charge. The official spin was that it had been an unplanned hastily-prepared opportunistic attack and that is why it had failed. The line had been held in Jaffna but the National Security Council also drew a line in the sand with the commanders. This was to be a combined operations war and no one would be allowed to go off and wage war on his own. Those days were gone.

A few days after the Muhamalai disaster, an LTTE suicide truck bomber struck a naval convoy near Habaraba, killing 107 sailors coming home on leave. It was the deadliest suicide attack against the armed forces. Two days later, five suicide boats entered the naval base in the southern port city of Galle. The attack was repulsed: one sailor was killed, versus fifteen Black Tigers. Psychologically, however, it was a victory for the Tigers, because Galle was so far to the south and had not until then been directly involved in the war.

The ceasefire was dead in the water, but neither side was quite ready to take responsibility for an official funeral. Despite all the fighting, both sides agreed to meet again for talks in Geneva in late October. Erik Solheim dutifully explained that the international community would not recognize a military solution. Both sides haggled over the government's closure of the

A9 highway because, Colombo said, the LTTE was taxing the cars and buses to raise money for arms to fight the government. Predictably the talks failed but neither side, fearing international repercussions, officially abrogated the ceasefire.

The killing went on. Both sides claimed that the combatants were targeting more civilians. On 9 December 2006 a prominent human rights lawyer and Tamil National Alliance parliamentarian, Nadarajah Raviraj, was shot dead by two assassins on a motorbike in the heart of Colombo in broad daylight. He had supported Tamil freedom his whole life, but he had also not been afraid to criticize the LTTE, particularly just before his killing. In a template of mutual accusation the government and the LTTE blamed each other. Unusually, the government invited in the Metropolitan Police to send a forensic team from Scotland Yard, which it did. After the war ended, the Sri Lankan police claimed they had found evidence of LTTE complicity.

Three weeks later another plot to kill a prominent Sri Lankan in the centre of Colombo was enacted. Over twenty-five kilos of C-4 explosives were packed in a trishaw. It was aimed at a government motorcade, but the bomber exploded a fraction too early and hit the police outrider. The powerful bomb, much bigger than the human bomb that nearly did for Sarath Fonseka, also blasted an armoured BMW. Three of the bodyguards were killed, but the target, Gotabaya Rajapaksa, survived. His remaining escorts switched cars and the Secretary was driven straight to Temple Trees, the residence of the presidency. The picture of the two brothers hugging each other in relief was one of the rare examples of media displaying the informal side of their close relationship. The plot, the police later discovered, was long in preparation and precise in many details, but it had failed, though only just. It had been ordered and personally supervised by the LTTE's head of intelligence, Pottu Amman.

With the final failure of talks, the army was keen to finish off the job they had started in the east (although the 'north first' strategy was still popular among some army leaders, the failed breakout from the Jaffna lines silenced them for a while). The LTTE retreat from Sampur meant cadres and civilians had congregated in the Vakarai stronghold in the Batticaloa district. The army began their offensive in early December but it soon stalled, partly because of the monsoons and the presence of so many local civilian residents and recent refugees.

The government's own handling of internally displaced people was often adequate (and sometimes good after the war ended). But the LTTE was keen to work with international agencies, which the government usually perceived as being far too friendly with the insurgents. Nevertheless, Gotabaya Rajapaksa understood that co-operation with the international organizations was vital. In October 2006 the Consultative Committee on Humanitarian Assistance (CCHA) was set up. Technically it was run by the ministry of disaster management and human rights, but it was essentially a defence operation. The Committee met every two weeks in the defence ministry in order to co-ordinate relief efforts in the north and east. The group comprised major NGOs as well as senior members of the diplomatic corps, plus regular VIP attendees such as senior UN personnel. The usually effective Committee did not stop Colombo sometimes suspending NGO activity, including for a while the normally impeccably regarded *Médecin Sans Frontières*, because the government accused it of being in cahoots with the insurgents.

The delayed operation to capture the strategic town of Vakarai slogged on to the end of January 2007. The army cleared the jungles first and the towns and villages followed. Special forces and commandos played the cadres at their own game: operating in small groups, setting up ambushes and constantly disrupting the LTTE at night and during meal times. The cadres were put on the back foot and started, according to Colombo, stopping food supplies to the civilian population to once again prompt international intervention. The NGOs blamed the army for the blockade, as did the Tamil National Alliance in parliament. Even the ICRC had problems sending food in, but the organization eventually made a deal with the LTTE.

By the end of January 2007 the army declared the Vakarai operation a victory, and without the death of a single civilian, according to Colombo. In the north, however, the LTTE claimed that fifteen civilians had been killed in an air force raid on a Sea Tiger base. Colombo then pointed out that the LTTE had killed a number of Sinhalese tsunami aid workers in the Batticaloa district. The government also lambasted the Tigers for blowing up a civilian bus in Ampara, killing seventeen, including three children. The mutual recriminations could not conceal the major retreat of the LTTE in the east. Certainly, never before had the army captured such a cornucopia of small arms as well as two 152mm artillery pieces.

The army's success in Vakarai prompted a rare visit by a head of state to an active frontline position. On 3 February 2007 President Rajapaksa flew in and posed for media shots standing alongside his special forces (presumably they had no say in the government spin, despite the obvious breach of SF security). Colombo wanted to proclaim the eastern victories, which were real enough. Batticaloa district was largely cleared of LTTE, including jungle pockets. Army publicity teams were having a field day – the capture of a multi-barrelled rocket launcher was a great propaganda photo opportunity. As the LTTE retreated farther south to the Ampara area, the army gave the cadres no respite to regroup and rearm. By the end of July 2007 the army claimed that it had almost complete control in the east as it handed over security to the police (including, it said, to newly recruited Tamil policemen). For the first time in fifteen years the government could claim free access to the entire A5 highway.

The problems of demining and the IDPs were still enormous. The rows between some NGOs and the government intensified. Colombo was particularly exercised by numerous Tamils working for the UN – some were accused of using their freedom of movement to transport arms and explosives to Colombo on behalf of the LTTE. The LTTE, as ever when it was on the back foot, tried hard to manipulate international sentiment via the NGOs and UN over conditions of civilians in the new areas controlled by the government.

The LTTE was also mourning the death of its chief theoretician and negotiator, Anton Balasingham, who had died of natural causes in December 2006. His death was likely to strengthen those around Prabhakaran who believed a military solution was still possible. Despite the major setbacks in the east, the LTTE wanted to maintain the strategic initiative. It was at this time that it planted twenty-five conventional sea mines (off Nayaru) as well as attaching two very well-designed homemade limpet mines on a commercial ship (MV *Tabernacle Grace*) discovered in Trincomalee harbour. The mines were clever but not clever enough to have an anti-removal device. Military intelligence put out the line that the mines were dummies. The police were actually given replica dummy limpet mines so that they could play their role to the media with conviction. Intelligence did not want commercial shipping to be spooked, nor prompt a big rise in insurance premiums.

The failure of their mine warfare strategy made the LTTE commanders look elsewhere to compensate for the beating in the east. The Tigers were always innovative; hence their shift to an air campaign. The first Air Tiger attack on Colombo arrived on 25 March 2007. The target was primarily the Katunayake air base, causing some damage and a handful of casualties. The small Czech planes of the new Tiger air force escaped. It was an astute switch of strategy, but not a masterstroke to deflect the growing government successes. Colombo had fretted about air attack and had installed two old limited-radius air defence systems in the northern government defence lines, as well as one around Colombo. That had been an Indian response to Colombo's request, as New Delhi discouraged shopping in China. Nevertheless, the Chinese soon provided more modern systems. The government installed more AA guns especially in Colombo. They also developed blackout procedures for the capital. Hotels had to issue air-raid precaution leaflets to visitors, not a great incentive to tourism. No simple solution, however, was available to stop very small single-engine planes flying low at night and piloted by fanatics sitting on top of high explosives. With effort, the urban human bombers could be countered; so could the suicide boat swarms. To develop a small-plane swarm response by the air force, at night, was not practical, however. The international intelligence community, especially the Americans, had failed to find a straightforward technical solution to this universal threat. Most fast jet interceptors travelled too fast, nor could the helicopter gunships work as a counterbalance. The Air Tigers conducted a number of raids on military and economic targets, but their impact was usually more psychological — especially in the capital. One of the LTTE's last throws of the dice was a kamikaze raid on Colombo by two planes in February 2009; both were brought down.

A more promising alternative LTTE strategy, however, was to switch to the tried and tested urban infiltration. The intelligence services anticipated a city shock-and-awe bombing campaign. In the first four months of 2007 four bus-bomb attacks had killed over forty-five and injured 140 civilians in various parts of the country. In June alert police at a roadblock at Kotavehera found over 1,000 kilos of C-4 explosives hidden in a truck transporting coconuts. A few days later, after a tip-off from a mole deep in LTTE intelligence, the navy in Trincomalee seized a freezer truck packed with over 1,100 kilos of C-4 explosives. These two massive devices were five times the size of the bomb that caused carnage at the Central Bank in 1996. The success in the east could easily have been undermined by bombing spectaculars in the capital.

In June 2007 police rounded up nearly 400 Tamils in Colombo who were living temporarily in the city, usually in 'lodges' (cheap hostels), and took them in police-escorted buses officially to be returned to their home districts. The Secretary of Defence typically came out with a robust comment: 'Everyone knows the LTTE is infiltrating Colombo. We can't arrest 300 people and detain them. What is the best opinion? You can tell them, "You don't have any legal business in Colombo and there is a security problem in Colombo. We don't want to detain you. You go back to your homes."' As it happened, most did end up in a detention centre, in Vavuniya.

Human rights groups immediately complained of ethnic cleansing and the Supreme Court intervened. Buck-passing ensued and the President criticized the police who claimed they were protecting the resident Tamil community. But many long-term Tamils in Colombo as well as temporary residents complained of harassment by the police including searches and detention.[62] Interestingly, a case brought by a Sinhalese man stopped at a permanent roadblock led to the Chief Justice ordering the dismantlement of all permanent checkpoints as they infringed the freedom of movement. The courts also imposed restrictions on house searches, especially at night. These edicts in December 2007, just before a major offensive in the north, and inevitable retaliation by LTTE urban terrorism, rattled the intelligence services. Some permanent checkpoints were removed; they were usually replaced by what the army and police conveniently termed 'mobile units'. The Secretary had visited Israel on a number of occasions and was determined to emulate the Israeli model of very thorough roadblock searches to prevent suicide bombers entering from the West Bank. The intelligence services produced a small booklet for the armed forces listing the often ingenious methods of concealing explosives, including placing them in drained coconuts. The LTTE also used a 'suicide bra', which looked like a normal padded bra. Such a device was used to attempt to assassinate a minister, Douglas Devananda, in November 2007. It was a rare example of a human bomber caught exploding herself, filmed on a CCTV camera in the Minister's office. Watching the film, it is clear that the bra was fatal to the wearer, but the range of effect seemed limited even in a confined space.

Because the LTTE had made it difficult if not impossible for Tamils to join or stay in the police, the security forces suffered from translation problems, whether in intelligence penetration or normal police questioning. Many Tamils spoke Sinhala, but few Sinhalese knew Tamil. The government tried to rectify these obvious social and security deficiencies, for example by encouraging the recruitment of Tamil policemen once the east had been pacified. But often the screenings of Tamil suspects, especially during the June 2007 mass round-up, were rough-and-ready affairs. The intelligence services argued that their screening, in Tamil, was thorough and that Tamils were relocated only if they could not explain what they were doing in the capital. Suicide cadres routinely used the lodges as well as safe houses but how many of those expelled were hardcore LTTE was difficult to prove. The expulsions, recalling memories of the 1983 pogrom in Colombo, caused a human rights firestorm.

The LTTE may have been thwarted in some of its urban plans by such security measures but the main switch in LTTE strategy was in the north. The LTTE and the army stepped up tit-for-tat artillery barrages across the forward defence lines. The lines in the north were demarcated by an eleven-kilometre fortification through Muhamalai on the Jaffna isthmus. In the south the fortified line stretched from Mannar to Kokkuttoduval via Omanthai in the south; this line was 140 kilometres long. Inside these two lines were 6,792 square kilometres of Tiger territory. Minor incursions turned in to a big push as the army overwhelmed LTTE bases and then, on 27 December, the main insurgent stronghold at Parappakandal in Mannar district. Typically, the army commander, Major General Fonseka, predicted publicly that the army would roll up the LTTE bases in the Vanni within six months. Pressure from the National Security Council forced Fonseka to backtrack somewhat; the other military leaders believed that victory was possible later in 2008, but not in the six months following the December 2007 progress.

Propaganda intensified on both sides, though Colombo now had much more to crow about. The air force claimed that their strikes had seriously wounded Prabhakaran in one of his bunker complexes in Jayanthinagar in November. I visited some of the command bunkers;[63] they were very elaborate affairs extremely well defended and skilfully camouflaged, often comprising two reinforced concrete levels built below a normal small house (but with an emergency exit as well). Prabhakaran's quarters were very small and simple, although the accommodation for a large number of bodyguards and rings of small pillboxes emphasized the leader's passion for personal security. The command bunkers were extremely difficult to spot from the air. And Prabhakaran switched his locations regularly, sometimes daily. The injuries to the leader were largely wishful thinking, though there might have been genuine intelligence crossed wires initially because S. P. Tamilselvan, the head of the political wing, was killed in a separate air strike at the same time. The security forces were clearly working on some kind of 'decapitation' strategy. They also had a lucky strike. On 5 January 2008 the head of military intelligence, Colonel Charles (Shanmuganathan Ravishankar), was killed in an ambush, involving a claymore mine, probably the result of a deep-penetration raid by special forces. It was perhaps an ironic end for a man who had organized so many claymore attacks on his opponents, both military and civilian. The Colonel had joined the movement in 1985 and had been head of its military intelligence wing since 2004. TamilNet confirmed his death along with three lieutenants while riding in a van.[64]

Gotabaya Rajapaksa was now determined to make the final big push, without any diplomatic constraints; by late December 2007 he was urging his brother that it was time to abandon formally the ceasefire agreement. On 2 January 2008 the government did so. For over six months the escalating conflict had forced the moribund SLMM mission to abandon proper investigations of ceasefire violations. The LTTE tried a diplomatic sleight of hand. It claimed that Colombo had unilaterally abrogated the 2002 agreement, whereas the LTTE was prepared still to honour it, so the western states should remove the various bans it had placed on the organization. This cut little ice in the international community.

Government forces were now given a free rein for the major offensive. From now on, despite occasional operational setbacks, the strategic offensive was to destroy totally the LTTE within a year, six months more than the optimists in the National Security Council had hoped. It was to be one of most savage series of battles the contemporary world would witness.

Chapter 12

Eelam War IV: Towards All-Out War

From the vantage point of the victory in May 2009, it would appear that the fighting in the previous two years was part of a rapid and inevitable triumph. It was not so. To both the poor bloody infantryman on the ground and the politicians in the Cabinet military victory was far from certain in 2007, even late into 2008. The LTTE was a remarkably resilient and resourceful foe.

The Secretary summarized the final years of the war. He told me:

> Mavil Aru was the initiation. We had to start there. We could not work in the north without clearing the east before touching the Vanni. There was no lull for debate [on north versus east] or for the LTTE to consolidate. We kept pushing, without a break, one of the principles of war. It was two and a half years of continuous warfare.

That was the view from the top. In February 2012 the then army commander tried to summarize what it was like at the bottom of the chain:

> The soldiers knew we were on a winning streak. Even though some of the soldiers did not sleep in a bed for two years ... They slept under trees, in bunkers, in trenches. They did not have the luxury of a bed but still their morale was high.[65]

The army had been expanded by 100 battalions in three years, although by definition many of the units contained inexperienced troops. Between 2006 and 2009, 121,000 new troops had to be inducted, a major logistic and training exercise. But the pressure of attrition and demands of ground coverage soaked up all these men and women. The Ministry of Defence deployed navy and air force personnel as well as police and civil defence to hold the ground cleared to allow maximum use of army firepower at the front. Thousands of servicemen unable to return to active duty were deployed in administrative roles to ensure the full tally of frontline fighters. Injured men, often minus a limb, were also given intelligence surveillance roles in Colombo. The fighting forces and equipment were in place for the big push in the Vanni.[66] The terrain, however, varied enormously from thick jungle interspersed with the close-knit fronds of palmyra trees to wide open dry scrub to swampy paddy fields. Despite the rapid successes in the east, the advance in Mannar province in the Vanni, the last LTTE stronghold, was very slow.

The initial setback in the Jaffna and the difficult advance into the Mannar region played into the hands of those who still opposed a military solution. From the perspective of the post-2009 political ascendancy of Mahinda Rajapaksa it can be easy to forget how, initially, his narrow presidential win and then loose coalition probably caused him as many sleepless nights as the setbacks in the war (although he always claimed never to take his problems home with him). Grand strategy on the international front and on the battlefield would capture the headlines of Sri Lankan history, but the President had to attend to endless domestic political and economic matters. His brother, Gotabaya, would take the strain of much of the military management and another brother, Basil, worked on economic issues. The President did not always have a smooth run in the National Security Council, though his ascendancy was rarely questioned. This was not the case in his Cabinet, where he was often challenged, in particular by Mangala Samaraweera, a minister who was responsible *inter alia* for ports and civil aviation. He was accused of using his influence in the media to take constant swipes at the conduct of the war. He and his allies campaigned on the need to separate Tamils in general from the LTTE in particular as well as human rights issues. The members of the unofficial 'peace camp' emphasized, with some justice, that their views helped to prevent a repeat of the 1983 anti-Tamil pogrom in Colombo even though Tiger bombs in the city had stirred up further ethnic tensions. The Minister was sacked, partly because the Rajapaksas were determined to maintain a unified war effort, not least to shore up morale among the armed forces. Support for the coalition constantly shifted: at one stage it held a majority of just six in parliament. Sometimes the military campaign directly interacted with the intricacies of parliamentary horse-trading. The devastating Black Tiger attack on the air base at Anuradhapura on 22 October 2007 coincided with a tight budget vote. Even the support from the hardline JVP often wavered. It tended usually but not always to support the Rajapaksa coalition. During late 2007 the government could have been defeated in parliament as well as on the battlefield.

While the army was still clearing the last insurgent remnants in the east, in the Thoppigala jungles, the push on the north started. The army advanced slowly from the south into the jungle areas of the eastern Vanni. In the jungles the army was further developing its small-unit strategy. Penetration by small formations of commandos and special forces – usually of eight men – had been common in the east. Large formations on a linear advance, the previous practice, had afforded endless targets of opportunity for LTTE artillery. The target signature had to be reduced. The small unit principle was applied to the general infantry by setting up Special Infantry Operational Teams (SIOTs).[67] Unlike the SF long-distance penetrations for up to a month, the SIOTs would move forward from the lines at night and advance a kilometre or two for up to forty-eight hours, to return to be replaced by another unit from the battalion. They would try to disrupt the LTTE rear, thus allowing for a main-force advance, while also killing LTTE. The tactics cut drastically the casualties from artillery and mortar fire (60 per cent of infantry fatalities) though SIOT death rates were obviously increased. The goal was for each small unit to kill at least one insurgent per day, though that figure was often more an ideal than a reality. The army based its penetration roles consciously on the highly successful tactics of the Selous Scouts, a counter-insurgency unit within the Rhodesian forces in the 1970s.[68]

The penetration tactics worked better in dense bush but less so in open terrain, which was the case in much of the north-western theatre, to the west of the A9 highway. Much of this Tiger territory was scrub with many open patches, especially in the region dubbed 'the rice bowl'. In the last quarter of 2007 this was where much of the fighting took place. In August the coastal town and Sea Tiger base of Silavathurei was taken but three LTTE bases remained in the eighty-square-kilometre rice bowl area. The paddy fields offered little cover and what little there was was heavily mined and booby-trapped. The landscape was often scarred by the sight and pungent smell of rotting animal carcasses, testaments to the ubiquity of mines. In the monsoon rains, the conditions were miserable. The Tigers were dug in and their bunkers offered a wide and open field of fire. Facing heavy mortars with often zero cover, and widespread minefields, the army advanced sometimes only metres rather than kilometres a day. LTTE snipers enjoyed a satisfying headcount because the opposing infantry had such poor cover. The sappers often had to resort to 'Bangalore torpedoes', a local development of the

British Indian Army device invented in 1912. The Americans used a sophisticated version in Afghanistan called the APOBS (Anti-Personnel Obstacle Breaching System) and the British deployed a rocket-fired device called the Python from 2010 in Helmand. But such mine-clearance took time and was never more than 90 per cent effective. In the end, it took nine months to capture the whole Mannar region.

Despite being mired in the rice bowl, the army pushed on elsewhere and focused on preparation for the advance on eastern Vanni, the real centre of Tiger military power. The LTTE maintained its reputation for diversionary tactics, by hitting the Vavuniya air base on 9 September 2008. They also kept up their suicide bomb attacks including killing a retired general. The army's land offensive moved on. From Mannar district the army pushed into Kilinochchi district. The army rolled up remaining Sea Tiger bases on the north-west coast. Pooneryn was captured in November. In a push in the centre of Tiger territory a new front was opened to the east of A9 by capturing Mankulam and surrounding area on 17 November.

The plight of the 200,000 newly displaced people was turning into a humanitarian disaster. The LTTE had called for a ceasefire earlier in 2008, but it was met by scepticism in Colombo and abroad. Western governments and, critically, India, despite the mounting civilian tragedy, did not try to intervene formally. For Colombo, India was always the paramount component of its political strategy. The informal 'troika' meetings of Basil and Gotabaya Rajapaksa plus Lalith Weeratunga and the chief Indian security ministers and advisers had been set up in early 2006. Protocol was pushed aside and the troika members would often phone each other, even late at night, on personal mobile phones. Constantly short-circuiting political masters was highly unusual in hidebound Asian diplomacy. Even late into 2008, the Indian government, ever responsive to Tamil Nadu sensitivities, stated publicly that no military solution was possible. In private, however, a meeting of minds was evident, except sometimes on issues of Tamil devolution and local police powers. By October 2008 New Delhi stopped calling for a political solution, understanding that Colombo was committed to outright military victory. The Rajapaksa steamroller had been given a permanent green light by New Delhi ... or so it seemed.

The army still had to achieve what the Secretary had promised the Indians, a triumph in the jungles of the Vanni, where even the mighty Indian army had faltered. There were three main axes of advance in the 2008 campaigns: the slow but eventually successful western drive in Mannar through the rice bowl. Then came an advance in the centre, along the A9 from June 2008. The Madhu Church area, on the outskirts of the elephant sanctuary, had fallen in early April. The LTTE was using the famous Roman Catholic church itself, as a depot and medical centre. The army was under strict instructions to avoid deliberate offensives around cultural and religious sites. Instead, the army cut off supply routes around the church and the LTTE withdrew. The Catholic Church was grateful and soon celebrated a special Mass in the building.

The third spearhead, the drive through the eastern jungles of Mullaitivu, had begun very methodically after January 2008. The territory was thick primary forests with some open cultivated areas. Despite the canopy cover the advancing army avoided grouping to limit the effects of LTTE artillery, even though the naval blockade had somewhat diminished the insurgents' firepower. Towards the end of the war the numbers of shells, but not the accuracy, declined. Their dogged determination to fight as long and hard and close as possible did not diminish. But the four new Chinese radar artillery systems, in spite of the humidity and rains that could undermine their accuracy, proved to be very effective counter-battery weapons for the Sri Lankan army.

The fighting on the eastern flank meant overcoming large defensive complexes, especially the notorious 'One Four Base', a massive complex of connecting bunker systems in the Andankulam forest reserve. It took months to clear. Facing advances on three fronts, the LTTE was becoming more and more desperate. According to one well-sourced account of the war, the Tigers resorted to chemical weapons in the tough combat in the eastern Vanni. The army's medical services were said to have produced 50,000 improvised gas masks for the troops. Without mentioning the chemical, it was claimed that the LTTE had improvised their own mortar rounds containing persistent chemical agents. The army suffered casualties from burns, but no fatalities.[69] Such a use of unconventional weapons would have been a propaganda gift of mass proportions for Colombo and would have damned and perhaps doomed the LTTE internationally. The later government line was that Colombo's release of the information would not have stopped the Tigers, and it would have impacted on army recruitment. The LTTE countered by saying that the army's masks were proof of the *government*'s use of chemical weapons. But why the government should risk using illegal and highly controversial weapons in the last stages of a victorious campaign was not explained by LTTE apologists. In the small international intelligence community which focused on chemical weapons, some 'chatter' emerged about both sides occasionally deploying such devices (even though the government was party to the Chemical Weapons Convention). Colombo later disclosed that it had captured an improvised underground laboratory in the Vanni, which was producing toxic weapons. It is likely that LTTE technicians were experimenting with toxic industrial chemicals rather than formal chemical warfare agents. According to one of the leading independent experts on chemical and biological weapons, Gwyn Winfield, 'My best guess would be some kind of white phosphorous — the "shake and bake" the Israelis (among others) used. It is classified as a chemical weapon and will cause choking.'[70] A UN International Expert Panel could not reach a conclusion about the government's use of chemical weapons. In addition, accusations were made that both sides used thermobaric weapons. This can be bombs or rockets that use a fuel-air explosive capable of creating overpressures equal to an atomic bomb. Colombo listed several thermobaric weapons on the post-war inventory of the captured LTTE arsenal. The Russians developed and were accused of using their RPO-A rocket systems in Chechnya. Colombo was alleged to have purchased a number of these rockets via a British arms company. The Sri Lankan forces were also accused of deploying cluster bombs. Without conclusive expert international corroboration, it may be that both sides dabbled in illegal weapons, especially chemical agents, though only on a minor and occasional experimental basis, not at an effective operational level.[71]

Despite the hand-to-hand fighting in the eastern Vanni, as well as the numerous trenches and bunkers, it would be wrong to characterize the fighting as akin to First World War trench warfare, with echoes of regular mustard-gas attacks. The jungle conditions and the more mobile fighting were obvious contrasts with 1914–18. But one similarity was the LTTE's mastery of defensive earthworks, the so-called bunds. The air force pounded these fortifications and destroyed much of the earth-moving machinery. One bund stretched for over thirty kilometres. It linked Nachchikudah on the coast to the Akkarayankulam tank (reservoir) and then across the A9 to the Iranamadu tank. It was nicknamed 'the great wall of China' by the infantry. The bund was constructed in L-shaped segments, which allowed for counter-attacks even if an armoured thrust punched through one section of the wall and anti-tank ditches. The army lost 153 soldiers in breaching just one eastern section of the great wall. Another twelve-kilometre bund lay to the north-east, however. It had large sections of free-fire cleared zones in front of it. The army had to dig infiltration trenches to be able to get close to the bund for night-time attacks. Fighting against well-defended and fortified positions in the jungle in monsoon rain took a heavy toll, not least with diseases such as malaria as well as endless problems with rotting feet. The army engineers designed special containers with big driers so that the infantry could sometimes dry their clothes and boots.

The three axes of advance from the south and especially the capture of Pooneryn meant that the threats of artillery fire into Jaffna or incursions via the Jaffna lagoon were finally removed. This allowed the release of some of the 40,000 troops in the peninsula to create a pincer movement from the north. The main target of the three southern advancing task forces was the Tigers' administrative capital of Kilinochchi. Long-range patrol groups of special forces and commandos penetrated ahead of the three southern battle groups. Never before had the LTTE to fight on so many fronts, as their area of control shrank. The onslaught on Kilinochchi began on 23 November 2008. The Tigers fought long and hard for the capital they had captured more than a decade before. Casualties mounted rapidly on both sides. The army finally outflanked Kilinochchi by capturing Paranthan, to the north of the LTTE stronghold, thus separating the capital from the Tigers' Elephant Pass bases. The next day, 2 January 2009, the now indefensible capital fell to the army advance. The surviving cadres withdrew to the last bastions in the Mullaitivu jungles. Gotabaya and Mahinda Rajapaksa flew to the enemy capital to congratulate the troops. The President said it was an unparalleled victory and called for the LTTE to surrender.

Yet again domestic politics disrupted a presidential triumph. On 9 January 2009 the editor of the *Sunday Leader*, Lasantha Wickremetunga, was assassinated in a most brutal way. Two motorbike riders had forced his car to stop and the two pillion passengers got off and smashed the vehicle windows. They pushed in a steel club device once common in abattoirs; the club had a single pointed spike which was driven into the editor's brain. The death of a prominent pro-opposition journalist caused a furore. As it happened, the editor had recently made a secret rapprochement with the President, but before that Wickremetunga had long been a bitter critic of the Rajapaksas and the war. Parliamentary enemies launched into the government, blaming Sarath Fonseka for the attack. Using parliamentary privilege, opposition MPs accused the army commander of spending more time running political death squads for the Rajapaksas than fighting the LTTE. It was said he wasn't fit to run even the Salvation Army. The increasing army fatalities were lambasted, and the recent victories were underplayed. The east had been cleared in 1993 but lost again, they said. Kilinochchi had been captured in 1996, but taken back two years later.

Gotabaya Rajapaksa went into a media overdrive, especially on the government-owned ITN news channel. He praised his army commander and compared the military death tolls favourably with previous governments' campaigns. Such domestic attacks played into the hands of the international lobbies which called for an end to the war, or at least a ceasefire to ease the humanitarian situation for tens of thousands of civilians trapped in the battle zones. The government rejected calls for a ceasefire, but did offer an amnesty to surrendering rebels. The retreating LTTE fought on, with vigour, and later sent two suicide planes to hit Colombo. Even at this very late stage in the war, victory was by no means certain, either on the political or military fronts.

The drive from the north had been long in coming. On the isthmus between the large Jaffna lagoon and the Indian Ocean the two forces had dug in behind heavily fortified positions at Muhamalai. Heavy artillery barrages across the lines had substituted for any real movement. Both sides had tried hard to break this regional stalemate and had failed. The superstitious in both camps, and there were many, felt this battlefield was jinxed. Avoiding a frontal assault, and instead using small raiding parties at night, digging infiltration trenches and planting mines against the bunds, the army slowly progressed, eventually taking the first line of defence, after a week of serious combat, in late November 2008. The LTTE's second line of defence was weakened by extensive infiltration methods and constant attrition. Special forces came across the small lagoon on the army's left flank, and moved into the LTTE rear. Finally, after nearly ten years, the LTTE's rough equivalent of the Maginot Line, undermined by a flanking manoeuvre, fell in the first week of January 2009.

The army quickly moved into Elephant Pass, the site of so much carnage in the past. The insurgents abandoned the whole Jaffna peninsula to seek sanctuary in the Vanni hinterland it had controlled for nearly twenty-five years. The LTTE was now encircled and entrenched in the jungles of the Mullaitivu district. Sometimes the army advanced easily using main roads, such as the A35, meeting little opposition. At other times the retreating LTTE fought as well as the German *Wehrmacht* in 1944–45 in retreating and then counter-attacking. Pitched battles were fought in some places such as Dharmapuram. At other times precipitate flight was evident. For example, the army came across large abandoned consignments of food stocks from the World Food Programme. On 25 January, the strategically important town of Mullaitivu fell, with comparatively little fighting. Both the Sri Lankan high command and LTTE supporters waited for the expected masterstroke by Prabhakaran. Numerous courageous counter-attacks emerged at local level, but no strategic counter-offensive was conjured up by the LTTE leadership. Nevertheless, the cadres showed amazing resilience and frequently seized immediate tactical advantage through sheer grit and ingenuity. On 7–9 February, the LTTE counter-attacked in the area between Puthukkudiyiruppu and the fateful Nandikadal lagoon. The army's 59th Division took a heavy battering in three days of non-stop combat. The cadres pushed in everything, including suicide trucks packed with explosives and even motorbike suicide bombers. The 53rd Division, in reserve, had to be thrown into the battle to reinforce the army's lines.

On the coast a new task force advanced slowly along the bank of the Nandikadal lagoon from the south. Inland, the Tigers blew the walls of the Kalmadukulam tank (reservoir), flooding fifteen square kilometres. Sri Lankan infantrymen were caught in the inundation but many managed to escape by climbing trees. The cadres quickly responded by launching fishing boats to shoot a handful of the tree-hugging survivors. Ironically, the army also had access to a large number of small boats inland. As the Tigers drove civilians into an ever-diminishing zone of control, the people had tried to take their most important possessions with them. Boats had been towed and then abandoned throughout the centre of the Vanni. The army had used the boats as temporary baths, but when the Kalmadukulam dam was breached, some of these baths were returned to naval service to rescue soldiers clinging to trees or stranded in two-storey buildings.[72] The LTTE also ordered the destruction of the dam wall of the Iranamadu Tank, the largest reservoir in the north. Its breach would have caused a catastrophe. According to government intelligence sources, the cadres tasked with the mission disobeyed orders, and surrendered to the army. This was a rare case of trained insurgents refusing to conduct a major mission on moral grounds.

One of the toughest advances was by elements of the 55th Division, along the narrow sand spit from Vettelankerny to Puthumathalan. It stretched for roughly forty kilometres and was only on average a kilometre or so wide. The army had to cross various waterways – some were only twenty-five metres wide and the depth varied according to the tides. The Tigers, as ever, had built numerous sand bunds. The army used their 'Stalin organs' (the MBRLs from Pakistan) to launch a few rockets, not a full salvo, with a depressed trajectory to fire them straight into the defended bunds — sometimes at a range of 500 metres. The Sea Tigers, even at this late stage, organized around fifty boats to attempt to mount an amphibious operation to sneak around the rear of the 55th Division. The MBRLs were deployed again using full salvos of airburst rockets to scatter the Sea Tigers. That was almost the last of the Sea Tiger attacks. Not least because the major Sea Tiger base at Chalai was taken in February after a week of fierce combat. The Tigers kept fighting against all the odds, suffering and yet inflicting heavy losses. For example, in the final few kilometres of fighting along the narrow sandy spit from Puthumathalan, the army lost 459 men, with 2,499 wounded.

In 2006 the Tigers had held 15,000 square kilometres. At the height of LTTE territorial control the movement directly controlled perhaps one-fifth of the island's 2.5 million Tamils. By January 2009, approximately 330,000 civilians had been pressed into the north-eastern corner of the Vanni, about one-third the size of London. Within three months, to re-use the London analogy, the Tigers were pushed into an area not much bigger than Hampstead Heath.[73] In the last few months of the war, hundreds of thousands of civilians were herded into a shrinking battle zone: some as willing volunteers, most as human shields or cannon fodder as forced recruits. Despite the establishment of so-called 'no-fire zones', thousands were killed, by accident in crossfire, by deliberate shelling or sometimes by close-quarter atrocities. The treatment of civilians in 'the Cage' fuelled an international controversy which still rages.

Chapter 13

The Cage

The LTTE's herding of hundreds of thousands of civilians into the war zones complicated the government's military operations immensely. Colombo called the final stages of the war a 'humanitarian' effort to save civilians, although it was primarily a strategy to destroy the Tigers once and for all. In 1995 in Jaffna the LTTE had similarly insisted that civilians retreat alongside the fighting cadres. If the population had remained and the cadres fought instead an urban guerrilla war it would have made it much more difficult for the army; arm-twisting from India may have curtailed the operation. Most of the Tamil population returned so the LTTE lost the peninsula *and* its direct control of the population. The Tigers had repeated this error in the east in Sampur when it forced over 30,000 people to withdraw with them, although most of the civilians found their way later into government-controlled areas. The LTTE did the same in Mannar and the Vanni jungles. That left the clear-up operations in the army-dominated areas much easier – the surviving Tigers could be fought with far less risk of hurting civilians. Nor was there a mass exodus by boat to India, which could have fired up the usual political sensitivities in Tamil Nadu and New Delhi.

Colombo argued that the Tamil civilian population could be controlled only by LTTE terror and no doubt the vast majority of refugees accompanying the Tigers went very reluctantly. LTTE propagandists explained that the civilians were escaping army terror and chose to stay with the Tigers. The reality was also that the LTTE needed a recruitment pool as attrition had sliced into their numbers. The insurgents in addition required a large work force to erect the numerous defensive bunds. But the major factors were to limit government attacks and above all to secure international intervention. Right until the last few days of the war the LTTE leadership expected to be rescued by international pressure for a ceasefire or, in the last resort, via Indian or western warships. Meanwhile, the LTTE enforced a very tight control over their hostages, shelling, shooting or imprisoning would-be escapers. Many managed to flee to army lines, and then reached resettlement camps, however. Even there they were not safe. On 29 February 2009 a Black Tiger bomber killed twenty-three Tamils who had arrived in the Dharmapuram IDP camp.

Still the fighting raged as the cadres retreated. They used what the army called 'pedal guns', naval guns placed on trailers. The large-calibre guns, operated by foot controls, had rapid rates of fire. One of the last-ditch battles was at Iranapalai on 4–5 April. Many of the top commanders were killed, including the leadership of the female cadres. The overall regional commander, Brigadier Theepan, led from the front of his troops, and died bravely, fighting to the last. The Brigadier (real name Velayuthapillai Baheerathakumar) had been overall commander of the LTTE northern front. In this battle the Tigers lost important artillery assets, including three 130mm guns. They pulled back, fighting hard and building bunds along the narrow coastal strip they still held. There was intense fighting around the earth bund built on the edge of the Puthumathalan lagoon. The army tried to breach the bund as discreetly as possible to allow civilians to escape. The army used its SF specialists in hostage situations to lead the rescues, as well as dropping leaflets and using loudspeakers to encourage civilians to get out. Even before this bund fell over 3,000 Tamil civilians had fled by sea. Indian journalists described them as walking skeletons in rags in a state of utter shock. Meanwhile, commandos and special forces soldiers were either wading chest deep across the lagoon at night or using makeshift rafts of tree trunks, plastic mortar cases and pipes to outflank the bunds. (The makeshift arrangements were partly caused by endless friction between the army and the navy, which could have provided dinghies.) In another bund-breach escape around 33,000 people fled at night on 20 April. This was watched live in Colombo in air force headquarters. President Rajapaksa made a point of inviting western diplomats to see UAV feeds and to witness live the desperate attempts to flee. On 21 April two senior LTTE men, Daya Master and George, surrendered to advancing troops. They said they had quit because they were disgusted by the shooting of civilians trying to flee, as well as the conscription of children in their early teens.

External pressure, especially from India, had prompted the government to set up no-fire zones, from January 2009 onwards, where civilians could congregate. This played a big role in Colombo's PR campaign to persuade the world that the final stages of the war were primarily a humanitarian action. But the no-fire zones were almost as ineffective as the so-called 'safe havens' set up in the 1990s Bosnian war. The Tigers ignored them and continued to utilize mobile scoot-and-shoot artillery attacks even around the few functioning hospitals in the zones. The few UN observers in the no-fire zones communicated with Colombo to update the exact co-ordinates of the hospitals, but the government's counter-battery operations continued, according to the UN. In the last days of the war, a paradoxical situation emerged: not a shot was being fired in the whole country, except for in the no-fire zones.

The Tigers were on their last legs and the Tiger media machine went into top gear to prompt international intervention. Stories of attacks on hospitals and atrocities by the army — while ignoring the numerous civilians who were shot by Tigers for trying to escape — were generated worldwide. The UN High Commissioner for Human Rights, Navi Pillay, accused both sides of war crimes. TamilNet publicized banner headlines over articles by the American jurist and human rights activist, Francis A. Boyle, about 'a war without witnesses', 'slow-motion genocide' and Nazi-type crimes.[74]

The outside world did intervene in a number of ways. The war and worldwide economic slump were playing havoc with the government's economic position. Foreign currency reserves dropped precipitously and nobody seemed inclined to lend money to Colombo. Politicking in Washington delayed for over five months an International Monetary Fund stand-by facility of $1.9 billion. Once more the war was almost stopped in its tracks. President Rajapaksa personally spoke to Colonel Gadaffi to arrange a bilateral loan and also to friends in Teheran. Even the rumour of a big loan from an oil-rich Islamic country stabilized the Sri Lankan funding crisis. India stepped in to offer finance and thus publicized what was portrayed by Colombo as a politicization of IMF support. In July, when the war was over, Colombo got its IMF facility.

On 16 April Ban Ki Moon sent his chief of staff to broker a ceasefire. The Secretary rejected the idea and also said that a UN fact-finding mission could not enter the LTTE enclave because the army would have to cease operations to allow the team in. The US State Department called for the LTTE to stop holding civilians hostage and to surrender to a third party, if they refused to lay down their arms to the Sri Lankan forces. Colombo perceived this as a stalling operation and continued to grind down the LTTE defences. International speculation mounted that western warships could help evacuate the trapped civilians, as well as the surviving LTTE leadership around Prabhakaran.

For Colombo the most irritating intercession was by two European foreign ministers. On 29 April 2009 British Foreign Secretary, David

Miliband, and Bernard Kouchner, the French foreign minister, arrived to try to stop the bloodshed. Gotabaya Rajapaksa was blunt in his meeting with them: he said the fighting would go on until Prabhakaran was dead or captured. The Defence Secretary explained that over 200,000 civilians had been freed from LTTE captivity. The Sri Lankans found Miliband 'rude and aggressive', especially when he complained that army shelling was killing civilians. Gotabaya Rajapaksa told the British minister that he should not believe Tamil propaganda. According to the Sri Lankans present, Kouchner tried to cool tempers and calm down his more volatile British companion. If the government would not allow a ceasefire, Kouchner — a veteran of many war zones as a former human rights campaigner and co-founder of MSF — offered to travel to the besieged enclave to talk to Prabhakaran himself. The Secretary acknowledged the Frenchman's bravery but explained that, even if he managed to get through to the LTTE leader, he might be taken hostage.

The two foreign VIPs asked to see the IDPs from the Vanni fighting. They were taken to visit recently established IDP camps in Vavuniya and then flown to meet the President who was staying at a guesthouse in Embilipitiya. A table was laid out under a tree by the lake. According to my interview with Lalith Weeratunga who, as ever, was at the President's side, the meeting was not cordial.

Miliband said forcefully, 'This massacre needs to be stopped immediately.'

At this, in a rare loss of temper in public, the President replied, 'We are trying to free these people from the LTTE.'

He then accused the Labour politician of condescending behaviour towards Sri Lanka. The President said sharply, 'Do you think we are still a colony of yours?'

Again, Kouchner essayed the role of conciliator. 'We are your friends,' he said. 'We want to help.'

Still angry, President Rajapaksa replied, 'I know who my friends and enemies are.'

The fact that Kouchner had been quoted in the press, before his arrival in Sri Lanka, as suggesting that British and French warships could assist in the evacuation of civilians in the Cage, had not gone down well in Colombo. And the Sri Lankan senior people present, from the President down, whom I interviewed, all accused Miliband of undiplomatic manners. The further spin by Colombo was that the Labour politician was unduly influenced by Tamil exiles in Britain who were focusing on not only a general propaganda campaign but also in the Labour-held seats in which Tamils were concentrated. The Tamil campaigns in the UK were extensive and well-organized and Miliband admitted that he was forced to spend 60 per cent of his time on the Sri Lankan crisis. Those close to Miliband, however, said that it was genuine moral indignation, not political calculation, that inspired his robust behaviour in Sri Lanka (although Wikileaks says otherwise). It must also be said that other senior diplomats, including the Indians, found Miliband difficult to deal with.

The cornerstone of international intervention was the UN Secretary General's stated desire to visit during the death throes of the Tigers. The President played the protocol card, saying he had to be present in the country to greet the UN leader but he had to be abroad on a pre-arranged visit. By the time Ban Ki Moon managed to satisfy the Sri Lankans' somewhat convenient protocol issues, the war was over. And Prabhakaran was dead. The President, however, was still alive, though it was a close call. In February 2009 security police unravelled a very complex plot, involving an army colonel, to kill Mahinda Rajapaksa with a suicide-jacket bomb carrying fifteen kilos of explosive, the largest ever discovered by the police. That plot failed but the LTTE's last suicide bombing was at a mosque in Akuressa on 19 March 2009. Fourteen were killed and thirty-five wounded.

The Rajapaksa ruling clan could ignore the British and French and usually sidestep US pressure, but they could never ignore New Delhi. Two senior delegations from the Indian foreign ministry visited Colombo in January 2009 to stress the need to reduce casualties and to discuss post-conflict political reconciliation. The government assured the Indians of the intense care the armed forces were taking and to lay out the plans for resettlement of displaced Tamils. Also, the government discussed a post-war deal with the Tamils. In March the former rebel leader, Colonel Karuna, was sworn in as minister of national integration and reconciliation. The government explained that local elections would be held in former LTTE territory in August 2009. Those were longer-term plans.

Of pressing concern to the Indians was the establishment of no-fire zones. On 29 January, at New Delhi's request, Colombo declared a forty-eight-hour period for the LTTE to release the civilians in their control. The Indians publicly stated that 150,000 civilians were still held. The LTTE rejected the offer. The Indian government had to be seen to be busy dealing with Colombo because the central government was under concerted pressure from a range of political parties in Tamil Nadu. Unlike irritating westerners, Colombo had to be seen to invite senior Tamil Nadu leaders to visit the war zones. The ruling party in Tamil Nadu, the DMK,[75] was also a member of the almost inevitably fragile coalition government in New Delhi. The Congress Party, which led the national coalition, held a minority position in parliament and needed the DMK's sixteen seats to sustain even a temporary majority in the *Lok Sabha*. For twenty-five years, no central government politician had been able to ignore the question of Tamil separatism — in India or Sri Lanka. India had faced a long series of separatist and Maoist-style Naxalite insurgencies throughout the vast democracy. In addition, it had an unequal and troubled relationship with Nepal which was not dissimilar to Sri Lanka's. India acted as the overbearing Big Brother to the Kathmandu government during its exhausting struggle with its Maoist insurgency.[76] Indian troops were dealing with a simmering insurrection in Kashmir, as well as being permanently on guard against its perpetual enemy, Pakistan. The November 2008 Mumbai massacre had brought the two countries to the brink of war. India was also engaged in high-octane diplomacy in Afghanistan. The fact that the central government in New Delhi expended so much political capital on Sri Lanka, despite other emergencies, indicated the delicacy of the crisis.

This dancing on eggs reached a breaking point at 5 pm on 23 April 2009, when Gotabaya Rajapaksa received a call on his personal mobile phone from Shivshankar Mennon, the foreign affairs secretary.

'Gota,' he said, 'the Tamil Nadu problem is hotting up. Things are very sensitive here.'

The Secretary replied: 'OK, I'll call you back.'

Gotabaya called Mahinda Rajapaksa immediately. The President was to the point: 'Tell them to come tomorrow morning for breakfast.'

It was at such crisis points that the President sought out the sanctuary of his own shrine. On the first floor of his residence, behind a gleaming white door, next to the table where photographs of his three sons' rugby exploits stood, Mahinda Rajapaksa would take off his sandals and seek peace. Inside the middle-sized room he had collected perhaps fifty statues of the Buddha, big and small, some in precious metals. In addition, taking up a quarter of the room, a smaller pantheon of Hindu deities was arranged.[77] This was where he meditated, at least twenty minutes every day and during times of emergency. This was surely such a time. The Indians could still shatter his ambitions of ending the war in his own way.

The top-level Indian security troika flew in on a specially chartered plane that night. The next morning the key players met upstairs at Temple Trees at 9 am. The Indian High Commission had a presence, as the two troikas got down to business. The Indians spoke briefly: people in Tamil Nadu believed their brethren were being massacred. Gotabaya and Mahinda Rajapaksa listened carefully, as did the President's man, Lalith Weeratunga. The Sri Lankans tried to explain, but the Indians were not fully persuaded. The Indians needed a political token to take home.

The President said firmly, 'Even if you invade my country, I am not going to stop this. We are just a few weeks away from eliminating terrorism in this country.'

He then referred to previous Indian involvement which had led to heavy fighting in the north and 'the loss of twenty years of development'.

The Indian delegation was 'crestfallen', according to one observer in the room. 'They thought their mission had failed.' All the patient years of the secret troikas – all seemed to be damned as the main players looked like falling from their high-wire act.

Unprompted by his close advisers, the President then leaned over to the Indian national security boss and put his hand gently on his knee.

'Look, my friend, short of stopping this thing, what do you want me to do?' the President asked very quietly.

The Indian security expert replied, 'At least you can stop using heavy guns – heavy artillery. And no air strikes.'

The President agreed and the Indians were visibly relieved.

The Indians said they would accept a public promise to limit military firepower, especially the use of heavy artillery and air power. (Naval gunnery was not discussed, though it later became an LTTE propaganda issue. The navy was not supporting the army with naval guns aimed on to the land.)

The President said, 'I will get this ratified at a special National Security Council meeting on Monday.' It usually met on Wednesday, but he said he would summon an emergency session.

The Indian public statement was vague. It was issued on 24 April.

President Rajapaksa confided to his closest associates that he had recently had a premonition of Prabhakaran's imminent death. The two main antagonists had never met – nor would they.

The LTTE kept fighting on their surviving two-kilometre front. It was a heroic and hopeless last-ditch defiance which LTTE sympathizers might compare with the Spartan-led Battle of Thermopylae in 480BC. The difference was that the Greeks triumphed after this local defeat, thanks to their gods they believed. The Pope, well placed literally, had expressed his concerns from a visit to the Holy Land. The Vatican was the only major organization to oppose the execution of Saddam Hussein, so what of Prabhakaran? The LTTE leader was likely to wait in vain for international – or divine – intercession. Only India could save him now. The Sri Lankan army, with a massive advantage now in numbers, could constantly recycle fresh troops and so maintain a twenty-four-hour battle tempo. The Tigers had never faced a version of their own unceasing wave strategy.

The events alongside the Nandikadal Lagoon were being studied frantically and in minute detail in Tamil Nadu. The central government could no longer restrain the Tamil politicians there. On 27 April, three days after the lacklustre official communiqué, the chief minister of Tamil Nadu, Muthuvel Karunanidhi, called for an immediate ceasefire. He said he would fast unto death if his call was not heeded. The chief minister was eighty-five, although in rude health because of his yoga regime and perhaps because of a series of marriages to younger women. Karunanidhi was not a man who could be ignored. He had proved a self-publicist of genius during his long career as a film-maker, writer and social reformer. He was also closely connected to a range of media outlets. More important were his political connections as head of the DMK party and leader of the Dravidian movement, plus control of a small but pivotal group of MPs in the national parliament; he had also been in the Tamil Nadu assembly since 1957. And he had long been associated with the LTTE. Although he had condemned the assassination of Rajiv Gandhi, Karunanidhi regularly and publically called Prabhakaran a 'friend'. Further, the regional phase of the national elections was due in mid-May in Tamil Nadu. The chief minister had timed his dramatic protest perfectly to maximize embarrassment to the government in New Delhi ... and the Rajapaksas in Colombo.

Against this dangerous background the Sri Lankan National Security Council met to discuss whether the Indian request to limit firepower could be finessed. The Indian High Commissioner, Alok Prasad, was pacing outside in Lalith Weeratunga's sparse but comfortable office. Under such circumstances the Sri Lankans unsurprisingly agreed. They would still hammer out a Tiger *Götterdämmerung* but with smaller-calibre infantry weapons. From Weeratunga's office Prasad read the NSC memo over the phone to the external affairs ministry in New Delhi, which was in turn rushed to the fasting chief minister of Tamil Nadu. This was nail-biting stuff for the Sri Lankan government on the edge of a historic military victory. It became even more cliff-edge because Prabhakaran issued a statement that Karunanidhi was a hero of the Tamil people. It was intercepted by Sri Lankan intelligence, however, before the chief minister declared he would give up his fast. Otherwise the LTTE message might have prompted him to extend his (short) hunger strike.[78]

The joint Indian-Sri Lankan statement of 27 April read:

> The government of Sri Lanka has announced that combat operations had reached their conclusion and that the Sri Lankan security forces have been instructed to end the use of heavy calibre guns, combat aircraft and aerial weapons which could cause civilian casualties. Sri Lankan forces will now confine their attempts to rescue the civilians who remain and give topmost priority to saving them.

This form of words provided top cover for the armed forces to finish the decades of war. After the army had breached the big Puthamathalan bund on 20 April, tens of thousands of civilians had fled by land or sea, although perhaps 20,000 civilians were still trapped in the tiny enclave defended by diehard Tigers fighting behind makeshift bunds. Still taking heavy casualties, the 58th Division continued to advance southwards to capture the beach and the grounded MV *Farah 111*, a Jordanian ship that had been hijacked in December 2006 and then run aground on the beach between Puthumathalan and Vellamullivaikkal. The ruined 175-metre hulk looked like a set for an apocalyptic film. It had been used as a training base for the Sea Tigers, and then became the very last Sea Tiger operations centre. The navy had set up a cordon around this area to prevent ships getting in, not out. A rescue mission still was possible. K P, the logistics mastermind behind the international network, was speaking to those around Prabhakaran and urging him to escape while he still could. K P promised on a number of occasions that he could break the naval blockade and rescue his boss. Prabhakaran never took calls himself, presumably because he correctly assumed the government's military intelligence was monitoring his communications particularly closely in the last desperate stages.

Earlier in the year K P talked to Charles Anthony, the leader's son, and said, 'I can plan your exit – very safely.'

A stubborn reply came back: 'We can fight. Just send us some more weapons.'

K P had hatched a plan involving a helicopter, flown by the usual suspects, Ukrainian mercenary pilots. A little unconvincingly, he later claimed that he had trouble raising the money from his colleagues in Scandinavia. K P, who had been Prabhakaran's equivalent of best man at his wedding, had tried on a number of previous occasions to persuade the

LTTE leader to get his wife and the two younger children out of the Vanni. He had arranged educational places in a cast-iron alias in a safe western country. Prabhakaran had told K P he would be a hypocrite if he did not expect his own children to stay and join the movement.

K P tried again in the final days of the siege, but he was told no. The Tiger leaders still expected a *deus ex machina* to save them or, once again, perhaps they indulged in military over-confidence, expecting to be able to break out into the interior.

Whether an armed LTTE rescue was now possible was a moot point. Thermal cameras on the patrolling strike craft were checking in detail the movements at night on the beach. On 9 May 2009 the Sea Tigers did attempt to break the blockade. Two suicide boats penetrated the first line of containment, Arrow boats. The Dvoras further out engaged the suicide craft with their 30mm Bushmaster guns sinking one and killing the crew of the second Black Tiger boat. Military intelligence wondered whether this was a test run for a Prabhakaran escape by sea and tightened the noose.

The army had taken the western side of the Nadikadal lagoon and then the infantry were moving from north and south in a pincer movement along the eastern spit side of the lagoon. The fourth and then the final and smaller fifth no-fire zone was contained in this narrow strip between lagoon and sea. The army said it did not use heavy artillery, in line with the Indian agreement, though the LTTE claimed it did. The government forces were not using air power nor, they said, heavy-calibre guns because so many civilians were tightly packed into the few square kilometres of LTTE territory. The 58th Division, moving southwards along the Indian Ocean beach, finally linked up with the 59th Division on 16 May. This was the first time in twenty-five years that Colombo controlled *all* the island's coastline. No escape or relief by sea was now possible. All that remained was an inland chunk of earth, a mangled mass of defences with desperate cadres and perhaps 20,000 to 30,000 civilians. National intelligence knew that Prabhakaran was bottled up there, but they did not know his exact position or the size of his personal bodyguard.

Hemmed in north and south by the army and to east by the heavily patrolled sea, the only way out was across the five-kilometre-wide lagoon. The army worried about infiltration across their extended lines and also a possible major breakout – probably across the lagoon. Small formations of Tigers still survived in the hinterland, with weapons and food supplies, for a breakout group to link up with. Multiple army counter-penetration lines were set up. Civilians were also trying to break out, some wading and swimming across the lagoon. The army was ordered to accept civilians only in the day, after a group of men, at night and claiming to be civilians, turned out to be armed LTTE infiltrators. Some infiltrators dressed in army uniforms did manage to escape. Occasional forays by LTTE small boats crossed the lagoon to test the defence perimeters. It appeared as though the long-expected breakout was about to erupt on 17 May. Boats crossed with Black Tigers and blew up two army bunkers, killing all the infantry inside. Around 120 Tigers then penetrated the breach only to be caught between two 12.7mm gun emplacements. They were all killed. The numbers on their dog tags indicated they were some of the senior cadres. In the last days of the encirclement, most cadres fought hard, some surrendered and others took their cyanide capsules or occasionally blew themselves up.

On the same night, 17 May, it was reported that Prabhakaran and Pottu Amman, with escorts, had broken through the line held by the 53rd Division and had then commandeered an army ambulance. The vehicle was halted by heavy gunfire and an RPG. It was initially thought that the two LTTE leaders had been shot and then burned to death in the flaming vehicle. When this proved later to be false information, the army commander, Sarath Fonseka, just back from a visit to an arms manufacturer in China, intervened furiously to say that the Tiger chieftain could not be allowed to escape. Prabhakaran was rumoured to have a number of doubles so the top brass were in a frenzy to locate the real Tiger leader. They were also embarrassed that the leader's alleged death in the ambulance had been leaked to the media. His (premature) death was even announced in the Indian parliament on 18 May. The great survivor was still alive, but cornered.

The infantry searched through the debris of tents, vehicles, fox holes, dead and wounded civilians and cadres. The scene was like some devil's picnic whipped up in a hurricane. At dawn on 19 May a SIOT patrol from the 4th Vijayaba battalion explored the last patch of unexplored land – a belt of mangroves, 800 metres long and twenty metres wide, right on the edge of the lagoon. Around twenty to thirty weapons were heard firing from the mangroves as the troops engaged a small group of visible LTTE men nearby. Two more eight-man special infantry teams were sent into the mangrove swamp. Three men were captured and they soon admitted that Prabhakaran was hiding there with around thirty bodyguards. The army poured fire into the swamp until return fire ceased. Prabhakaran's warm body was soon found by a SIOT team leader. A faint white stubble on his chin indicated that he had not had time to shave that morning, despite his meticulous morning ablution rituals. After all, he was being chased by perhaps 100,000 armed men. His corpse was carried aloft on the shoulders of the 4th Vijayaba soldiers and then inspected by senior officers. His ID had the number 001 on it, and his uniform pocket held a waterproof container of diabetic medicine. Former LTTE leaders in Colombo, including Colonel Karuna, were flown in to identify the body. DNA testing with comparative samples from his two dead sons was rapidly completed just to make sure.

At 9.30 am on 19 May 2009 President Rajapaksa gave an address to the nation to announce the defeat of the LTTE. The honour of announcing, a few hours later, the definite confirmation of the LTTE leader's death was given to General Fonseka. He had been reluctant to make the statement but the Defence Secretary insisted that it was the President's express wish. Soon afterwards the gory pictures of the dead rebel leader were displayed on Sri Lankan TV.

The main photograph, showing a close-up of Prabhakaran with a gunshot wound to the forehead, was flashed around the world. The official line was that he had suffered one wound which looked suspiciously like a single deliberate close-up execution shot to the head. (The death of his younger son, Balachandran, was also said by LTTE media to have been a deliberate close-up head shot, although pictures do not show a visible head wound.) The army explanation was that Prabhakaran's head wound was caused because the leader and his men had been neck deep in water and the SIOT had fired at the bobbing heads in the morning gloom. I closely interviewed the army colonel who took charge of the body and who was tasked with examining it before the final disposal. It was the first time he had been allowed to talk about this event and the Colonel confirmed that there were also three wounds around the rib cage, probably caused by an army rifle. This would tally with the explanation that the army had sprayed shots into the thick mangrove swamp, which I also visited.

It took a week for the LTTE media network abroad to acknowledge his death. Like Osama bin Laden, no martyr's grave was allowed. His body was cremated and his ashes widely and secretly scattered. Prabhakaran's wife and daughter probably perished in the final stages of the Cage. His elder son, Charles Anthony, also died in the final battle. The leader's parents, who were in their seventies, were found later in a displaced persons camp, and the government gave very public assurances they would not be interrogated or harmed in any way.

The government's security forces had won a unique victory in defeating a domestic insurgency by military means. The war, however, was not over. The physical destruction of the LTTE was to provoke an international storm and result in a propaganda war that has continued for years after the death of Prabhakaran and his military organization. The Tiger international network, particularly its media wing, was left almost completely intact. Also, the local Tamils who supported the LTTE had to be reconciled and brought into the political process. Hundreds of thousands of people had to be resettled in their former homes, after a complex process of screening and demining. In addition, the economic as well as the social costs of the conflict had to be addressed. A lot of fat ladies still had to sing ...

AFTER THE SHOOTING WAR

Chapter 14

The Long Propaganda War

Prabhakaran had hoped for a final get-out-of-jail-free card via the so-called 'CNN effect'. Saddam Hussein had adopted the same flawed strategy in the 1991 Gulf war. The power of CNN, and later Al-Jazeera, especially the visuals of dead and dying civilians, sometimes can influence western politicians if there is a policy vacuum. The sight of Kurds fleeing in the snow in northern Iraq did influence John Major, then Britain's prime minister, to draw up a hasty no-fly zone. But Saddam's sometimes staged pictures of bombed civilians did not deter the Pentagon in the next Gulf war. A nation determined on a clear strategy is likely to manipulate media not be manipulated by it. Usually, TV pictures do not persuade stubborn or determined leaders.[79] Nevertheless, the LTTE leaders were confident that they would be rescued first, by international intervention, led by India, and then finally by a last-minute exit courtesy of British, French or American warships. Prabhakaran also expected the world to restrain the Sri Lankan army. Hence the massive propaganda campaign displaying the suffering of the Tamils enclosed in the Cage. Prabhakaran lost his bet and was killed. The death throes of the LTTE led to endless political debate, however, about how many civilians were trapped, how many were injured or killed, and how – by LTTE fire or government fire? And how many civilians were deliberately killed by both sides? The number and nature of civilian casualties – as distinct from LTTE cadres killed – has never been fully answered. Accusations of war crimes still swirl around the events of the Nandikadal lagoon.

It made no tactical – let alone moral – sense for the army to kill civilians, whereas the LTTE had an obvious and cynical strategy of using civilian deaths to win their propaganda battles and to deter the military advance. On the other hand, the restrictions placed on the media and UN observers did imply that Colombo had something to hide.

The number of civilians killed in the Cage has been endlessly debated. The government insisted that the maximum figure was 3,000 which is unconvincing considering the massive amount of firepower deployed by both sides. Critics such as Gordon Weiss, in his revealing book entitled *The Cage*, suggested from 10,000 to 40,000, a very broad estimated figure used in a series of damning documentaries by Britain's Channel Four News. This contradicts the much lower figures offered by the UN and the Red Cross. Some independent Indian journalists suggested the figure of civilians killed in the January-May period was around 18,000 to 25,000. Government experts spent a lot of time analyzing the statistics, from extensive interviews with IDPs, including working out how many were in the area in the first place. They have, with some justification, picked apart the extrapolations of some outside organizations. Colombo often cited the extravagant figures of five Tamil doctors working in the last hospitals in the Cage, who later admitted that they had been forced to fabricate figures by the LTTE.

The use and positioning of the no-fire zones has also been contested. Weiss wrote about two main zones, while the government – under Indian pressure – unilaterally declared five such zones. Weiss condemned the army for firing artillery into the zones, and killing civilians, even when the co-ordinates of UN facilities and hospitals were provided. On the other hand, there was ample evidence of the Tigers firing from these zones, especially near hospitals. Weiss argued that no more than 1,500 hard-core Tiger fighters had survived in the Cage and that many of the other cadres in the siege were pressganged children or completely novice guerrillas. This may have been true, but if they were carrying arms they were legal or justifiable targets. Further, Weiss accused the government of a 'blunderbuss use of artillery' yet he also described in some detail how many ordinary infantry soldiers risked their lives to help Tamils escaping from the LTTE. Weiss wrote, 'Frontline soldiers gave their own rations to the terrified civilians who fully expected to be brutalized by the victorious Sinhalese troops.' Weiss summarized the final predicament thus:

> during the first five months of 2009 roughly 160,000 soldiers, sailors and airmen faced off against a core force of perhaps 2,000 to 5,000 Tiger fighters, seeded amidst a civilian population of some 330,000. The sixteen-week siege led to the deaths of between 10,000 and 40,000 people. If the Sri Lankan example is compared with Gaza and the figures extrapolated to make the point, the comparable death toll in the Palestinian population would have been between 50,000 and 200,000 people killed.[80]

Given these odds and the fact that the Tiger leadership was trapped by the tight land and sea blockade, Weiss asked whether there was a less costly alternative to the 'wholesale bombardment' undertaken by the armed forces. The obvious government answer would be that if an effective last-minute humanitarian ceasefire had somehow been magicked up, the LTTE leaders would have done anything to escape and then resuscitate their campaign, from exile if necessary. Colombo was determined to end the military threat once and for all.

Some evacuations did occur, for example, several seaborne removals by the ICRC of 18,000 sick and wounded from the beaches of the final no-fire zone. So perhaps more could have been done, but probably the kamikaze air attacks on Colombo were more indicative of LTTE thinking rather than saving Tamil civilians. Colombo could also be bloody-minded. According to Weiss, it rejected the attempts by Sweden to intercede, when it simply refused entry to the country for Carl Bildt, the respected former prime minister.

The government officially rejected the notion that it was using heavy weapons in the Cage. Weiss insisted that the government used 'air sorties, artillery and multi-barrel rockets' against the very final 'minor Stalingrad' defence in a cluster of a dozen sturdy houses built by international organizations following the 2004 tsunami. But even if their use were conceded by the government, its UAV and sophisticated Chinese counter-battery technology would have been precise and not a 'blunderbuss' to silence surviving Tiger heavy artillery. General Fonseka talked about conducting 'the world's largest hostage rescue operation'. The Secretary, always a fan of the Israeli military style, believed that Sri Lanka could emulate the virtually bloodless rescue at Uganda's Entebbe airport in 1976.

Frontline Sri Lankan soldiers did a great deal to assist civilians, many of whom may never have met Sinhalese before and who had been brainwashed to believe that they would all be killed or raped immediately. Civilians, once screened for arms and Tiger connections, were taken to resettlement camps. The government refused UN and Red Cross aid initially, but eventually the numbers were so large that Colombo accepted assistance. While most Tiger leaders fought to the end, a number of senior civilian leaders, including Nadesan and Pulidevan, were said to have sought to surrender using a satellite phone. With the aid of international mediators and Tamil National Alliance parliamentarians, they arranged a white-flag surrender for dawn on 18 May. A dozen men and women went forward at the pre-arranged spot to meet army officers. According to Weiss, the army started shooting them in cold blood. Nadesan's wife, a Sinhalese, shouted to the army in her native tongue, 'He is trying to surrender and you are shooting him.'

Ironically, the controversy of the aborted white-flag surrender deal was to be taken up by General Sarath Fonseka in his ill-fated political campaign to oust his former commander in chief. Fonseka was one of the most interesting characters in this whole saga. He joined the peace-time army in 1970, aged twenty. His personal bravery was frequently recognized by gallantry awards. Alongside his fellow colonel, and later his nemesis, Gotabaya Rajapaksa, he relieved the siege of Jaffna fort in 1993. At the Defence Secretary's request he became army commander in December 2005 and supervised the crushing of the LTTE on land. He gained a reputation for not only ruthless action against the LTTE but also as a stern disciplinarian in his own force. He was loved and feared by his men in equal measure. One well-known example is the popular phrase used by infantrymen, 'Better Jonny than Fonny'. Fonny was the commander's nickname; 'Jonny' was the common slang for a landmine. It meant that it was better to go forward and risk death by mines rather than incurring the wrath of the commander for not advancing. His military skills were not always matched by inter-personal ones: 'Fonny' was a difficult man to deal with, and he tended to nurse grudges. His long-running spat with his old school-friend, Wasantha Karannagoda, later to become the naval commander, was a running sore in the National Security Council. The navy commander was responsible for a number of innovations, including the blue-water strategy to destroy the Tiger Pigeon ships. But both men disagreed on matters of strategy and even basic army-navy co-ordination suffered as a result. The army's failure or refusal to use naval small-boat support in the final tough fighting in the lagoons was one example.

Fonseka also upset some of his erstwhile military supporters. At the very last stage of the war he changed command positions – those who had commanded their units at the front for years since 2006 felt they had been deprived of leading their men in the final days of victory. Fonseka replaced them with officers favoured by himself. Even before the end of the war, the head of National Intelligence, Kapila Hendawitharana, had privately warned the President that he believed Fonseka was dangerous, and that he might even organize a coup to replace the Rajapaksas. Initially Fonseka was apparently appeased by the government – he became the first serving officer to hold a four-star rank and then he was made chief of defence staff. He regarded the latter, rightly, as a demotion, because he could no longer directly influence the army. Even while still in uniform, according to the Rajapaksa version of events, Fonseka criticized some of the human rights conduct in the Cage, including the white-flag incident. Fonseka claimed ignorance of the LTTE safe-passage deal, and then blamed Gotabaya Rajapaksa for ordering the shooting.[81] The Secretary denied the accusation and later told me that a Fonseka coup, although rumoured by the General's political enemies, could not have happened. 'The President did not have to fear a coup because I was there. He was President and the defence minister – the next step was me. That was quite different from [the coup attempt of] 1962.'

Matters came to a head when Fonseka announced he was standing as the main rival to Mahinda Rajapaksa in the 2010 presidential campaign. Although the former general claimed he was standing as a non-party politician he became the common candidate for a strange mix of opposition parties, including the United National Party and the JVP.[82] Even the opposition Tamil National Alliance (TNA) reluctantly accepted as a frontman the person widely regarded as the hammer of the Tigers. Recognizing the bizarre contradiction, the TNA party leader said: 'In this case, it's better the devil we don't know.' Old school friends – schools were often the cement of professional and political alliances – begged Fonseka to reconsider, knowing that the Rajapaksa clan would regard the much-decorated officer's political move as the ultimate betrayal. One of the former school friends involved said simply, 'He was a great soldier but it went to his head.' He was even offered a choice of top ambassadorships, including Washington. Fonseka refused, believing that his alliance with the opposition parties and his undoubted popular appeal as the man who won the war would bring him a political victory to crown his military triumph. Like Winston Churchill in the 1945 general election he was proved wrong. In one of the most vitriolic elections in the country's history he lost – badly. In January 2010 Mahinda Rajapaksa won the presidential campaign by a big margin, although Fonseka rejected the outcome. In April 2010 Rajapaksa's ruling coalition also won a landslide victory in the parliamentary polls.[83] The same parliament later voted for a constitutional amendment allowing the President to seek an unlimited number of terms. The Rajapaksa clan had put itself in an unassailable position.

Then Fonseka's enemies moved in. No Buddhist compassion was allowed between the former allies. Fonseka complained stridently about vote-rigging, and said, 'There is no democracy. This government is behaving like murderers.' He added that the Rajapaksas had planned to assassinate him. The President's allies retaliated by revealing allegations of a detailed Fonseka plot to kill Mahinda Rajapaksa and his wife, Shiranthi.

Fonseka was convicted of civil offences (corruption in relation to arms purchases) and military law infringements (spreading negative rumours about the army while still in uniform). Sentenced to three years in prison, he was released in May 2012. Many in the country regarded him as a political prisoner and believed that the charges were trumped up. The disintegration of the winning 2009 'dream team' was a boon to the surviving LTTE international propaganda machine. The LTTE was for a time in denial, even suggesting that their leader had survived. The diaspora activists split over whether to continue the armed struggle or opt for a peaceful political route. Some of the millions of US dollars in the LTTE treasury were trousered by disillusioned Eelam supporters. Some formed a parliament and government in exile and continued to campaign, increasing effectively, as the Sri Lankan government was spotlighted by international human rights campaigners.

Celebrities such as Desmond Tutu, Jimmy Carter and Kofi Annan said that the persecution and disappearance of Sri Lankan human rights activists, journalists and political opponents was 'truly terrifying'. Tutu talked of the 'deafening global silence'. The rights of the defeated Tamils in the north and east were being ignored, claimed the international critics, especially as new army bases and Sinhalese-speaking settlements were strategically placed throughout the former Tiger lands. Weiss wrote of 'ethnic cleansing of the Israeli rather than the Yugoslav variety, but without the inquisitive eyes of an exterior world blind to Sri Lankan machinations'.[84] He added that Colombo's flawed democracy had become an oligarchic dynasty, galvanized by a Sinhalese supremacist creed and Buddhist fundamentalism. The EU had warned that it would suspend the country's preferential trade status over the alleged abuse of human rights. In April 2011 the UN issued a report condemning both sides in the civil war for atrocities against civilians and called for an international investigation into possible war crimes.

After the elation of winning their long war, against terrorism in its perspective, the newly re-elected Rajapaksa government was genuinely taken aback by the international condemnation and was especially sensitive to attempts to downgrade the country's role in the Commonwealth. The President had started his career as a human rights lawyer, in both Sri Lanka and abroad. Hence his early support for Palestinian rights, despite his government's later dalliance with the Israeli military. He ended up having to defend his human rights records personally at the UN and with other Commonwealth leaders. The President would frequently complain to his confidantes that, instead of focusing on internal economic development, international abuse from the diaspora and UN criticisms took up most of his time. The government was particularly incensed by the series of highly damning Channel Four News reports in London which were picked up elsewhere in the media, especially in Commonwealth countries such as Australia and Canada.

The government did the obvious things. It hired an expensive PR company, Bell Pottinger, to improve its image in the West. That backfired when the intimate nature of the deal was publicized in British national newspapers. Colombo also tried to set its own house in order. On the first anniversary of the victory over the Tigers the government announced the establishment of the Lessons Learnt and Reconciliation Commission (LLRC). It was set up partly because of internal pressures, but also as a result of consistent engagement by the UN Secretary General. Amidst the media brouhaha, what was actually happening on the ground, especially to the Tamil civilians who had survived the Cage? After so much war, what was being done to grow the peace?

Chapter 15

Building Peace

Mopping up the remaining armed cadres was very swift after the drama at Nandikadal Lagoon. Very small groups fought on in isolated areas of jungle for less than a month. Despite their fanaticism, the Tigers did not emulate the Japanese hold-outs after their 1945 defeat. Thereafter, according to Colombo, not a single significant military incident had occurred, which was very rare indeed after such a long and bloody conflict. The Allies expected much activity from German 'werewolves' after May 1945, but little armed resistance materialized. Unlike the loose franchise nature of al-Qaeda, The LTTE was very centralized and highly disciplined. Once its leadership was almost totally destroyed some Tamils reluctantly changed authority figures, which explained why in the north disgruntled Tamils tended to turn to the army for resolution of their complaints and disputes. Previous indoctrination can sometimes help in coping with a new order. The absence of post-war terrorism could also be explained by the vigilance of the very large security presence in the 'cleared areas' and in Colombo.

The Tiger international infrastructure survived abroad, though it fractured into competing claims about who would succeed Prabhakaran and whether the armed struggle finally should be dropped. K P, based in Kuala Lumpur, claimed the crown, but he was challenged by the hard men who wanted to fight on. On 5 August 2009 he was lifted from Malaysia and taken briefly to Bangkok by a Sri Lankan intelligence team. He was handcuffed and hooded for the flight and so expected the worst when he was dropped late at night on 6 August at the private house in Colombo of Gotabaya Rajapaksa, his arch enemy. In the entrance hall of the Defence Secretary's heavily fortified home stood a small Buddhist shrine and K P calmed his fears. He said to himself, 'This is a religious man; he will not kill me.' After some initial awkwardness, both men reminisced amiably about the war for two hours in English, before K P was placed later under comfortable house arrest. His main intelligence handler, though he grew to like the Tiger leader over the next two years, could not get K P to share his secrets about the missing millions he had stashed away.[85]

The social and economic costs of rebuilding were immense. Some estimates put the total fatalities of the war as up to 100,000: men, women, children, soldiers, cadres and civilians. This estimate included over 27,000 Tigers and 23,327 government soldiers and policemen killed since 1981. The number of Indian military fatalities was 1,155. In the last stage of fighting, in Eelam War IV, 5,224 security personnel – including 190 officers – were killed. Tigers killed were around 22,000 and 9,000 captured. The number of civilians killed in the last five months of the war is of course disputed. According to government figures, between 1983 and the war's end in 2009, the LTTE had engineered 200 major attacks on civilian targets, resulting in just over 4,000 civilians killed. Now Sri Lankans could catch buses and trains without fear of bombs. It had been standard practice for husbands and wives to travel separately in case of an attack so at least one survivor could take care of the children. Throughout the country, but especially in Colombo, ordinary people relished being able to travel as a family. That was an immediate peace dividend. Economic costs of the war vary, but one Sri Lankan estimate suggested $4.2 billion.[86] This appears rather low. Another more authoritative local banking source suggested that the government spent 4 per cent of GDP on defence from 2006–09, around $5.5 billion.[87] Western defence experts postulated a much higher figure, up to 20 per cent of government expenditure.[88]

When I asked the Secretary about the war costs, he was cagey about details.

'Britain was still paying off its Second World War Debts for over fifty years, how long will it take you to pay off yours?'

Gotabaya Rajapaksa laughed defensively and said, 'A long time.'

The biggest immediate problem of peace was the refugee crisis. A 'Presidential Task Force' was set up to co-ordinate but the army did most of the heavy lifting, along with international organizations. The last stage of fighting produced over 300,000 displaced persons. Many were placed in the Vavuniya district. According to Colombo's critics they were held against their will, often in poor conditions. The government responded, with justification, that it had to weed out combatants from innocent civilians and that many could not be returned to their villages because of the numerous mines, many planted randomly by the Tigers. Colombo promised that the vast bulk of civilians among 300,000 from the Vanni fighting, as well as 70,000 others from earlier battles, would be returned to their places of origin within 180 days. Amazingly, the government almost kept its promise. By the end of 2011 only a few thousand civilians were still in camps and so-called 'welfare villages', and many of these came from Mullaitivu district which was the most heavily mined. Compared with most other refugee camps in Asia and Africa which became permanent sites of misery, Colombo's military resettlement programme was perhaps as efficient as its final warfighting performance.

This assessment is based on my visits to IDP camps for civilians and rehabilitation centres for ex-combatants. A prison near Galle for LTTE hard-core soldiers awaiting civilian trial was also visited. (Sri Lanka has no capital punishment, but life sentences are not as fleeting as in the UK. The Boossa prison was meant for short-term political cases; no smoking, no alcohol and no TV were allowed, a sure recipe for riots in any British prison.) Tamil leaders called for a general amnesty for Tiger prisoners of war, but the police were holding just under 1,500 remaining combatants in early 2012. (Sixteen Sri Lankan military personnel were put on trial in courts martial or civilian courts for a range of offences, from rape to murder, from 2005–10. Whether this low figure is a comment on military discipline and human rights training or lax enforcement is an open question.) I also visited active de-mining operations. These locations were sometimes selected by me, occasionally at very short notice, to avoid straying into stage-managed Potemkin set-ups.

The complex switch from warfighting to humanitarian operations is a familiar problem for advanced NATO forces; it is far less practised in the armies of developing countries. A rapid and brief re-orientation programme was enforced in the army, with some soldiers questioning why they had to spend so much time on civilian reconstruction after they had been trained to fight. The army faced a massive demand for temporary refugee housing, initially tents, and then all the accompanying health and sanitation needs. Colombo did turn to NGOs including the ICRC to help with the massive problems of re-uniting families.

The army separated 11,664 combatants from the mass of IDPs after screening. Of these 594 were child combatants, 2,033 were females and 9,037 were males. They were placed in twenty-four centres where they underwent a series of programmes including 'spiritual' (according to their respective religions), educational and vocational elements. Around 70 per cent of the ex-combatants were reintegrated into their original communities within one and a half years. Special Branch officers were instructed, however, to keep an eye on all the ex-fighters sent into their areas. With help from UNICEF, the army paid special attention to the children, assisting around half who wanted to continue with their schooling. Of the child soldiers, 231 were girls. Some were transferred to a leading Tamil school in Colombo and others went to a technical college in Vavuniya. I interviewed a few of the young hardcore female Tigers – the army would say 'brainwashed' cadres. Some complained of boredom with their vocational course, in this case training in clothing manufacture, but not of any ill-treatment. The numerous injured cadres were given extensive medical care including wheelchairs and prosthetic limbs. Many of the Tigers had lost their legal and educational papers; help was given to replace them, as well as a range of assistance in getting back into civilian life. The army also began a construction programme to build small freestanding homes in areas such as Jaffna. The families seemed more than pleased with their brand new housing when I visited some of them, although the presence of the military and translation issues may not have presented perfect interview conditions.

For the vast majority of non-combatant inmates of the IDP camps, the initial reception was haphazard because of the sheer numbers, although the army did try to comply with international rules of allowing female soldiers only to deal with women and children. After initial screening by army medics, the injured were sent to civilian hospitals around the country; emergency cases were often moved by helicopter. Besides basic shelter, health facilities, food and water, many of the traumatized refugees were understandably keen to be reunited with their families. With the help of the ICRC, the army reunited 35,000 IDPs with their families in six weeks. Temporary religious centres, *kovils* (temples), mosques and churches were set up in the camps. Educational and vocational training was provided; resettlement allowances and agricultural subsidies were granted to enable a swift return to their villages where de-mining had been completed. Clothing and numerous other basic personal items were provided from well-supported charity appeals from across the country, Tamil and Sinhalese alike. Commercial companies also assisted in the reconstruction. The Bank of Ceylon, for example, set up small banks in the north and east to encourage returnees to open accounts. Traditionally, many low-caste Tamil women wore their wealth in jewellery or kept cash about their person. A senior banker wryly admitted that he been involved in 'serious laundering of money', in the literal sense, saying that many notes were actually cleaned and ironed before being put into new accounts. Gradually the locals realized that the banks were safe, especially when they received income paid into their accounts from relatives overseas. As a part of the return to civilian life, the government recruited 5,000 Tamil youths for training as police officers in the former LTTE zones.

Nonetheless, despite what is called CIMIC in the jargon – military aid to the civilian population – some officers admitted that, in the Tamil heartland of Jaffna, many locals regarded the Sri Lankan army as an occupying force. 'All the LTTE leaders came from Jaffna and they had an anti-south mentality,' one very senior officer told me while staying in Jaffna. 'Today, there is not just anger but a feeling of being defeated.' That anger could be re-ignited especially as the army was still busy recovering numerous arm caches from the war. House-building and banks were all very well. Even dramatic gestures by the soldiers such as providing large-scale blood donations (because of local Tamil inhibitions about providing blood for different caste groups) may not pass muster. Interestingly, perhaps because of their regimented background, resettled ex-combatants and other former LTTE supporters tended to bring complaints and personal disputes to the army, not police or civil authorities. They showed a confidence in the army to give a decisive and probably fair decision.

Politics aside, many businessmen in the Jaffna region welcomed the chance to get on with making money. Their attitude was pragmatic. One said: 'The LTTE extorted money from us, now the government does the same, but they call it tax.'

UN experts took a very different view of the government's humanitarian efforts. In the influential March 2011 Report it listed a number of serious allegations, while also castigating the LTTE.[89] In the Cage, it condemned the shelling of civilians in the no-fire zones, after the government had indicated it would no longer use heavy weapons. The Report particularly criticized the army's shelling of the UN 'hub' and food distribution systems. It accused the government of 'systematically' shelling hospitals, despite the fact that their locations were well-known to the army. After the war was over it said the survivors were placed in camps with 'terrible conditions'. Some LTTE suspects were 'summarily executed' and tortured; some of the women may have been raped. The government was also accused of human rights violations against the media and critics of the Rajapaksas. Further, the UN experts described the Lessons Learnt and Reconciliation Commission as effectively toothless and biased. It was 'deeply flawed, and does not meet international standards for an effective accountability mechanism'.

The Report was hardly a clean bill of health for Colombo. The government could dismiss the UN experts as outsiders, but reports by the

University Teachers for Human Rights (Jaffna) provided a series of harrowing eyewitness accounts from the inside. In particular, its December 2009 special report outlined examples of LTTE atrocities, for example brainwashed child soldiers casually shooting civilians escaping the Cage, but also the maltreatment of Tamils in the IDP camps, especially the bullying and extortion rackets.[90] The government spent a great deal of time on rhetorical refutation of the claims, but insufficient time on implementing substantive reforms. Without that, the human rights campaigns were likely to continue, both at home and abroad.

The government, however, insisted that it was doing a great deal of practical work to repair the damage caused by war. One of the most dangerous and painstaking challenges was inevitably the clearance of an estimated 1.6 million landmines. The army began in the heavily contested 'rice bowl' area of Mannar district. Within a few weeks in thirty-nine square kilometres over 7,000 LTTE anti-personnel mines were lifted and 1,500 other unexploded devices were made safe. This immediately led to a boost in the country's rice production. Kilinochchi, which had the highest population density, was the next priority. At the time of writing, around 1.2 million mines remained. This partly explained why approximately 5,000 IDPs still lingered in the camps – they were waiting for the 1,500 sappers engaged in demining to complete their work, largely in their Mullaitivu home villages. The process was slow because half of the anti-personnel mines were homemade by the Tigers (the rest came from Singapore, China and Pakistan). Almost no maps of the minefields existed, and around 10 per cent were booby-trapped to prevent de-activation. The casualty rate, in lost hands at the very least, had been very high among army engineers.[91]

The armed forces were retained at their wartime strength, although not replacing natural wastage. Before he switched to politics, General Fonseka suggested controversially that the army should be boosted to 350,000. A part of the reason was initial security concerns, to maintain ground coverage; then the army became involved in a massive post-war infrastructure reconstruction effort. The sappers were naturally happy to build things, especially bridges, but some of the regular infantry complained about being deployed as labourers on new roads.

In August 2011 Colombo said it would remove the state of emergency laws which had been in place for forty years. The government, however, needed to provide more tangible peace dividends for a population weary of war. As well as encouraging Tamils to take part in the district, presidential and parliamentary elections, it was important for them to share in economic as well as political reconciliation attempts. The north and the east had to be regenerated. Nationally, the economic future looked bright. The 7–8 per cent growth rate was the envy of a western world mired in endless recession. The country had suffered from war-induced austerity for too long, now it was going for growth in the form of massive public works. Inflation and unemployment were relatively low. Besides reviving tourism Colombo also wanted to encourage private foreign investment in a country which had a very high literacy rate and a good educational system with a large number of English-speakers. IT companies were particularly encouraged.

Not all was rosy, however. The country was beset by strikes in 2011–12. The military's influence in the new boom in construction allowed for extensive patronage and, some businessmen complained, widespread corruption. Colombo's political commentators made obvious comparisons with Pakistan, especially the alleged militarization of politics. And the root cause of the war had not disappeared completely. Local Tamil leaders complained of oppressive army rule in the north. The Tamil National Alliance, which won sixteen seats in the 2010 national parliamentary elections, swept local elections in the north, leaving the President's party in the dust. But Sri Lanka's politics, no matter how acrid, were surely better than a (highly unlikely) return to war.

There may, however, be positive dimensions to the maintenance of a large peacetime military force and even an expansion of intelligence and counter-terrorism forces. It was no accident that the country had not suffered a single incident of Tiger violence since the end of the war. Moreover, global terrorism – unrelated to Tamil irredentism – had increased, not least cyber-threats. Some security experts regarded Colombo's military approach to civilian reconstruction, despite the corruption, as a model for other post-bellum countries. Sacking almost the whole Iraqi army in 2003 was, for example, one of the main causes of the resulting carnage. As one American development expert observed:

> By resisting international pressure to down-size its military, Sri Lanka has avoided the potential threat of having tens of thousands of weapons-trained and battle-hardened troops being reintegrated into the hum-drum routines of civilian life where the purchasing power of their military pensions would diminish with inflation.[92]

President Rajapaksa was a clan politician in the way the Kennedys and Bushes were in the US. He was also reputed to be as keen on consulting astrologers as Nancy Reagan was. Certainly, the older generation of Sinhalese took their horoscopes very seriously. They now believed their stars were in the ascendant. The LTTE network, despite its capacity for effective international protests, was likely to decline in influence so long as Tamils on the island believed they were getting a better deal. The immense and unnecessary tragedy of the civil war would never be forgotten, by both sides, but economic prosperity, if shared fairly, could be a part of the healing process. Optimists about Sri Lanka might recall the Buddhist saying, 'What the caterpillar calls the end of the world, the master calls a butterfly.'

Chapter 16

Conclusions

The government won a military victory against all the odds and despite the predictions of military experts throughout the world. How? It was not simply the application of ruthless new tactics or a determination to sidestep or ignore foreign criticism. The LTTE's defeat was the result of cumulative internal and external forces. And, as in all wars, luck played a part. Prabhakaran was almost caught on a number of occasions. Without his cutthroat charisma, a protracted insurgency might not have crystallized around the deep-seated grievances. Gotabaya and Mahinda Rajapaksa could easily have gone the way of Rajiv Gandhi. The *Jetliner* ship could have been destroyed and thus sunk the government's war effort. Both sides made many mistakes. The art of war can often be a passive craft – not interrupting your enemy when he is making these mistakes, as Napoleon might put it. Nevertheless, an assessment can be made about which side actively and correctly did what and when, in order to win the war.

The Rajapaksas fought fire with fire. Adapting Mao, they showed they had the political will to win. They demonstrated a determined leadership absent in previous administrations. The war was effectively co-ordinated at the top in the National Security Council and — buffeted by traditional inter-service rivalry — the co-operation often worked at the lower levels, especially in combined operations. The military leaders were usually well chosen and the senior political leadership did not interfere often in operational matters. Unlike, say, Mrs Thatcher in the Falklands war, there was little evidence of 'long screwdriver' political tinkering. This was achieved by the personal influence of the Secretary both in his dealings with his brothers and his own personal relationship with the senior commanders. The military was run by Gotabaya Rajapaksa, leaving his brother, Mahinda, to deal with the politics. Firstly, internally: the President worked hard to keep Cabinet, parliament and people behind the war effort. Secondly, internationally: the government thwarted intervention from the West at crucial moments, while keeping India on side via the troika arrangement, as well as staying on good terms with India's traditional enemies, China and Pakistan. Skilfully playing off the rivalry between India and Pakistan, Colombo secured generous arms deals from both. And by playing to China's strategy of 'a string of pearls' in the Indian Ocean – a port-building plan to encircle India – secured not only Beijing's finance for a major southern port in the Rajapaksa clan's home area, Hambantota, but also won China's support in the UN Security Council, the one body that might have stamped out the army's winning offensive. The government's arms supplies were rarely seriously interrupted, while the international naval blockades kept out many of the Tigers' weapons, the latter often thanks to Indian intelligence. Diplomatic firewalls were erected, especially during the international furore created by the Cage. Colombo kept a very tight rein on the media, notably foreign correspondents. Domestic media often barked, but the watchdogs were rarely allowed to bite. Colombo waged a successful domestic media campaign to ensure a constant supply of military recruits as well as persuading the majority of Sinhalese that the war could be won and was worth winning despite the high costs of urban terror, battlefield casualties and economic pressures. This was the strategic framework for victory. At the operational and tactical levels, the army and navy often 'out-Tigered' the Tigers by using small-unit infantry penetration and developing their own wolfpacks to 'out-swarm' the Sea Tigers.

The Tigers fought a brilliant insurgency, but they lost. Why? The LTTE did not have a contiguous border sanctuary area, often described as a prerequisite in previous Asian wars, most obviously Vietnam. India, however, was for long an effective sanctuary, just a few kilometres across the Palk Strait. The Tigers trained in India and received top cover from New Delhi for a long time. That all ended with the assassination of Rajiv Gandhi. Before 9/11 the Tigers' astute international propaganda persuaded many western politicians that they were freedom fighters resisting a cruel autocracy. The clever media campaigns galvanized the support of the large and often prosperous Tamil diaspora which in turn was politically influential in countries such as Canada and the UK. States such as Norway were also important at many stages of the war, in intervening to support the LTTE. The international Tiger network was highly effective in organizing not only political and media backing but also providing an arsenal of modern weapons. Tamils were often highly educated and proved not just good propagandists abroad but innovative technicians in domestic weapons' adaption and production. The LTTE was well-organized and highly disciplined, often fanatical, in combat. Their creed of martyrdom made it difficult for a professional volunteer army to combat. And, unusually, the Sri Lankan government provided many of the administrative needs, including food and medicine, for the population in most areas of Tiger control for most periods of the war.

Before the dam closure at Mavil Aru, the Tigers did appear almost invincible. (Some of the Tiger bosses, not in earshot of Prabhakaran, joked that whoever ordered the closing of the sluice gates should never again be allowed even to switch off a tap.) The verdict of international experts that Colombo's war was unwinnable seemed justified. Up to this time, if Prabhakaran had decided to accept a loose federal or devolved deal he would probably have achieved his independent Tamil Eelam in the end. Yet, as with the two-state solution in Palestine/Israel, the longer the war the more elusive a political settlement became. In this sense Prabhakaran's absolutist determination was both a bane and a blessing. His fanatical zeal inspired a long insurgency, but it also blinded him to cashing in his winnings when he had the chance. Instead, he lost it all, and the people he tried to protect were subjected to a grotesque war and total defeat.

Initially, the LTTE leader did capitalize on his natural advantages, especially the almost knee-jerk protective instinct of Tamil Nadu politicians. But that was foolishly thrown away with the assassination of Rajiv Gandhi. Prabhakaran's almost Stalin-like cult of personality meant that he faced little opposition within his inner coterie, which largely consisted of long-term allies and friends, many from his schooldays and youth. K P was an example. When he offered independent advice to Prabhakaran, he was effectively demoted for a while. The leader's utter ruthlessness led to the removal of rival, often more moderate, Tamil leaders. Some of his military commanders counselled a return to hit-and-run guerrilla warfare, instead of trying to outfight a superior conventional foe in static warfare. If the LTTE had been true to its Maoist roots, it could have revolutionized its battle plan, adding elusiveness to its traditional resilience. It could have worn down the government in a true protracted war. But it appears that Prabhakaran's military vanity got the better of him. He thought he could hold on to all his territorial gains but 'he failed to recognize that his enemy had metamorphosed in both mind and body'.[93]

He made political errors, for example, telling Tamils to abstain from voting in the presidential campaign which allowed Mahinda Rajapaksa a narrow victory by default. Nor did Prabhakaran keep up with the tectonic shifts in world politics after 9/11 and all the anti-terrorist sentiments that tilted in Colombo's favour.

Prabhakaran's acolytes likened him to a 'sun god' and he came to believe them. And, like all dictators, he did not appoint a successor. There was no one left to challenge him after the defection of Colonel Karuna in 2004. His ruthless waging of war meant that the original one-person-per-family recruitment policy was replaced by pressganging on a massive level, especially in early 2009. Many of his originally devout followers, appalled by his cruelty, especially the use of forced labour and child soldiers, as well as suicide tactics, fled abroad or into government-controlled areas. Hence his need to corral Tamils into ever smaller zones of control as the army advanced. Like most absolutist leaders he stayed in power too long. He could not separate his original ideals of an egalitarian socialist Eelam from his own personal ambitions. And no one around him could gainsay him. His skills at organization and insurgency, which were undoubted, led him to great success by 2005. He should have done a deal, with Indian help. But he continued to believe in a military victory, and so overestimated his own resources and underestimated his new rivals, the Rajapaksas. In sum, his early military achievements blinded him to the possibility of a real political deal.[94]

Intervention, not least by UN forces, tends to prolong wars which military victory might curtail. Africa affords many examples. The definitive defeat of an insurgency by indigenous government forces is rare, however. Sri Lanka was an ethnic civil war as well as an insurgency fought in a mix of classic guerrilla tactics plus a semi-conventional mobile war and also urban terror campaigns. This was an astute adaption of Maoist strategies. The LTTE fought and talked and expected to win, as the North Vietnamese did. Without getting involved in a semantic discussion about the precise nature of the conflict, the utility of examining how the government won should be apparent to all those who study wars and how they end. The main lesson is obvious: the government applied some Maoist tenets against the insurgents – displaying will, space and time. The Rajapaksa team certainly displayed will, took space incrementally from the LTTE and fought, in the Sri Lankan context, a protracted war: a steamroller to squash the rebels. In many respects the government beat the Tigers at their own game.

Can the lessons be applied elsewhere? Both insurgents and counter-insurgent forces can usefully study the lessons of the main combatants. The LTTE had already pioneered suicide tactics copied elsewhere, especially their development of explosive vests. Al-Qaeda's fascination with airline bombings pre-dated the Tigers' deployment of their small air wing in kamikaze strikes. The Tigers' sea tactics were certainly innovative, however, and may inspire future examples of a small-boat threat to the major naval powers. Iran is an obvious example. Possible copycat developments of the combatants' *modus operandi* could fill an entire volume, but what this book has examined is a state's use of force against indigenous rebels fighting on their own soil. The US and its allies have fought recent counter-insurgency and counter-terrorism wars, most notably in Afghanistan and Iraq. Despite impressive technical developments, these wars were never winnable in any conventional sense, because the western forces were not fighting on their own turf. The French tried to argue that Algeria was French soil, but lost their savage war. The British Army, with more territorial justification, fought the most enduring insurgency in Europe, in Ulster. It ended in a peace agreement after three decades. South Africa's apartheid regime, nuclear armed and with the best army in Africa, did a deal in the end and engaged in a peace and reconciliation process, which has been copied elsewhere in Africa.

Sri Lanka never had its Belfast Agreement, the Northern Irish model. If a more pragmatic LTTE leadership had done a deal in, say, 2004–05, would it have evolved into a peaceful, prosperous and democratic two-state solution or would Tamil Eelam have become another North-South Sudan at worst or a divided Cyprus at best? Or, with much goodwill, maybe even a second Quebec or, who knows, another Scotland? Yet why should the Sinhalese majority have taken that risk once the final stage of the war was being waged so successfully? One well-known Indian journalist, a close observer of Sri Lanka, told me: 'Neither Tamils nor Sinhalese understand what democracy means. They both tend to go for the big man in politics.' Perhaps they will both have to learn democratic values if the peace-through-military-victory process is going to work in the long term. It is true that the martial triumph was impressive in purely military terms, as well as the rapid resettlement of the IDPs. And yet the moral issues remain. Peace can often be harder than war. And any government that permanently discriminates against a large minority of its own citizens condemns itself to permanent instability. In the first years of the island's independence, the majority did not treat the minority equally. Educational, employment and linguistic discrimination was bound to store up anger – and result in conflict and emigration. As a result of both the Tamil population had been reduced from around nearly 20 per cent to less than 10 per cent. For the peace to succeed and for Sri Lanka to live up to its own branding – 'the emerging wonder of Asia' – the government has to do even better than the flawed South African truth and reconciliation process. It has to embrace fully its Tamil population with magnanimity and equality. It may take generations for the diaspora to leave behind the dream of Tamil Eelam, however. How long that process takes depends upon the goodwill of the Sinhalese majority. Despite the ancient myths of warrior kings, and post-colonial strife, for some of the island's colourful history, it was a successful melting pot of ethnic and religious groups. It may be so again.

Select Bibliography

Much of this book is based on lengthy interviews and discussions with many of the key players in the drama. But I have listed some of the more accessible texts for English-speaking readers. The most immediately useful and up-to-date are C.A. Chandraprema's book (details below) which is a pro-government account with excellent access, and Gordon Weiss's book which is a well-written outsider's version and critical of the Sri Lankan government.

Balasuriya, Mahinda, *The Rise and Fall of the LTTE* (Asian Network on Conflict Research, Colombo, 2011).

Bandarange, Asoka, *The Separatist Conflict in Sri Lanka* (Vijatha Yapa Publications, Colombo, 2009).

Business Today (Colombo), 'Defeating Terrorism', July 2011.

Chandraprema, C. A., *Gōta's War: The Crushing of Tamil Tiger Terrorism in Sri Lanka* (Ranjan Wijeratne Foundation, Colombo, 2012).

Das, Gautam and M. K. Gupta-Ray, *Sri Lanka Misadventure: India's Military Peace-Keeping Campaign 1987-1990* (Vijitha Yapa Publications, Colombo, no date).

de Mel, Neloufer, *Militarizing Sri Lanka: Popular Culture, Memory and Narrative in the Armed Conflict* (Sage, New Delhi, 2007).

The Economist, 'My Brothers' Keepers', 11 February 2012.

Fish, Tim, 'Sri Lanka learns to counter Sea Tigers' swarm tactics,' *Jane's Navy International,* March 2009.

Gooneratne, John, *A Decade of Confrontation: Sri Lanka and India in the 1980s* (Stamford Lake, Pannipitiya, 2000).

——, *Negotiating with the Tigers (LTTE) 2002-2005* (Stamford Lake, Pannipitiya, 2007).

Gunaratne, Merril, *Cop in the Crossfire* (2011, probably self-published in Sri Lanka).

Holt, John Clifford, (Ed.) *The Sri Lanka Reader: History, Culture, Politics* (Duke University Press, Durham, 2011).

Human Rights Watch Report, *Funding the 'Final War': Intimidation and Extortion in the Tamil Diaspora* (HRW, New York, 2006).

Povlock, Paul A., 'Guerrilla War at Sea: The Sri Lankan Civil War', *Small Wars Journal*, 9 September 2011.

Rupesinghe, Kumar (Ed.) *Negotiating Peace in Sri Lanka,* Vol. One (Foundation for Co-existence, Colombo, 2006).

Shashikumar, V. K., 'Lessons from the War in Sri Lanka', Indian *Defence Review,* 3 October 2009.

Singh, Ajit Kumar, 'Endgame in Sri Lanka', *Faultlines*, January 2011.

Smith, Neil A., 'Understanding Sri Lanka's Defeat of the Tamil Tigers', *JFQ*, Issue 59, 4th Quarter, 2010.

Solnes, Jon Oskar, *A Powderkeg in Paradise: Lost Opportunity for Peace in Sri Lanka,* (Konark, Delhi, 2010).

Solomon, John, and B. C. Tan, 'Feeding the Tiger – How Sri Lankan Insurgents Fund their War', *Jane's Intelligence Review*, 1 August 2007.

Swamy, M. R. Narayan, *Inside an Elusive Mind: Prabhakaran* (Vijitha Yapa, Colombo, 2008).

——, *Tigers of Lanka* (Vijitha Yapa, Colombo, 2008).

United Nations, *Report of the Secretary-General's Panel of Experts on Accountability in Sri Lanka*, 31 March 2011.

University Teachers for Human Rights (Sri Lanka), *Let Them Speak: Truth About Sri Lanka's Victims of War*, Special report No. 34, 13 December 2009.

Weiss, Gordon, *The Cage: The Fight for Sri Lanka and the Last Days of the Tamil Tigers* (Bodley Head, London, 2011).

Wijewardana, Don, *How the LTTE Lost the Eelam War* (Stamford Lake, Pannipitiya, 2010).

Notes

1. See Latheef Farook, *Nobody's People: The Forgotten Plight of Sri Lanka's Muslims* (South Asia News Agency, Colombo, 2009).
2. For a brief but thoughtful analysis, see A. Jeyaratnam Wilson, 'The Militarisation of Tamil Youth' in John Clifford Holt, (Ed.) *The Sri Lanka Reader: History, Culture, Politics* (Duke University Press, Durham, 2011).
3. Gordon Weiss, *The Cage: The Fight for Sri Lanka and the Last Days of the Tamil Tigers*, (Bodley Head, London, 2011) p.57.
4. Some of the following military experts' quotes are extracted from a very useful summary of the intervention: Gautam Das and M. K. Gupta-Ray, *Sri Lanka Misadventure: India's Military Peace-Keeping Campaign 1987–1990* (Vijitha Yapa Publications, Colombo, no date).
5. Norman Dixon, *On the Psychology of Military Incompetence,* various editions, originally published in 1976.
6. *Sri Lanka Misadventure,* op. cit., p.17.
7. Ibid., p.305.
8. For a forensic analysis of the LTTE conspiracy, see D. R. Kaarthikeyan and Radhavinod Raju, *The Rajiv Gandhi Assassination: The Investigation* (New Dawn Press, Slough, 2004).
9. For an excellent summary of the ground fighting, see C. A. Chandraprema, *Gōta's War: The Crushing of Tamil Tiger Terrorism in Sri Lanka* (Ranjan Wijeratne Foundation, Colombo, 2012). The detail of the Mankulam fighting can be found on pp.92–4.
10. Ibid., p.196
11. Ibid., p. 203.
12. http://www.icrc.org/eng/resources/documents/misc/57jmas.htm
13. For a critical Sri Lankan view of Norwegian intervention, see Asoka Bandarange, *The Separatist Conflict in Sri Lanka* (Vijatha Yapa Publications, Colombo, 2009).
14. See, for example, Jon Oskar Solnes, *A Powderkeg in Paradise: Lost Opportunity for Peace in Sri Lanka,* (Konark, Delhi, 2010).
15. For a useful summary of the Peace Secretariat (formally the Secretariat for Coordinating the Peace Process), see John Gooneratne, *Negotiating with the Tigers (LTTE) 2002–2005* (Stamford Lake, Pannipitiya, 2007).

16. Cited in Ajit Kumar Singh, 'Endgame in Sri Lanka', *Faultlines*, January 2011.

17. The Minister was known for his combative humour. When Shane Warne justified Australia's decision to not play in Colombo during the 1996 Cricket World Cup because of the terrorist threat by saying that he could be targeted by a drive-in bomber while he was shopping, Kadirgamar is reported to have said, 'Shopping is for sissies'. A storm of macho protest ensued in Australia. When asked on Australian TV whether the Minister had ever played cricket, he said he had played before Warne was born, and without helmets and thigh guards, on matting wickets that were full of holes and stones, and he said he had had his share of broken bones to show for it. The Australian Foreign Minister was drawn into the fray and the two diplomats, old friends, decided to cool things down. When the whole episode was over, the Sri Lankan Minister sent a bouquet of flowers to his Australian counterpart. The message read, 'Flowers are also for sissies'.

18. *The Military Balance, 2011* (IISS, London, 2011).

19. The author was an occasional instructor for WRAC officers and soon learned that the Corps detested the acronym when it was pronounced 'rack', usually eliciting the standard response: '"Racks" are what you screw on top of car roofs, *Sir.* We are the Women's Royal Army Corps, *Sir.*'

20. The IISS figure is also 62.

21. Author's interview with army commander, February 2012.

22. Cited in 'Defeating Terrorism', *Business Today* (Colombo), July 2011, p.54.

23. Author's interview with the former SF commander, Brigadier Nirmal Dharmaratne, February 2012. This extremely effective officer had been a defence attaché in London, but was refused permission to visit the SAS in Hereford. Even the British SAS could have learned something about jungle warfare from him. Generally, the British, especially the intelligence services, were sniffy about co-operating with their Commonwealth allies in Colombo.

24. David Kilcullen, 'Overview of Counter-Terrorism' in 'Defeating Terrorism', *Business Today,* (Colombo) July 2011, pp.41–3.

25. Author's interviews in Trincomalee with fast-attack boat captains, November 2011.

26. The author interviewed the navy commander and director of operations, Naval HQ, February 2012. See also Tim Fish, 'Sri Lanka learns to counter Sea Tigers' swarm tactics,' *Jane's Navy International,* March 2009.

27. For those interested in the history of aviation, the air force museum in Colombo is well worth a visit. It is well laid out.

28. The author had been on the receiving end of the Russian Hind Mi-24s during a major Soviet offensive east of Kabul during the summer of 1984. He was travelling with the *Mujahedin.*

29. Especially since President Mahinda Rajapaksa had embraced the Palestinian cause from the early 1970s.

30. The air force quotes in this section derive from a long interview with the Chief of Defence Staff, Air Chief Marshal Roshan Goonetileke, the former air force head, February 2012.

31. Ibid.

32. Ranks relate as follows: Range — Deputy Inspector of General of Police (DIG); Division — Senior Superintendent of Police (SSP); District – Assistant Superintendent of Police (ASP).

33. For a leaden but useful insight, see the account written by a senior police intelligence specialist: Merril Gunaratne, *Cop in the Crossfire* (2011, probably self-published in Sri Lanka).

34. Interviews with senior officers in Police HQ, Colombo, February 2012, *inter alia* with C. N. Wakishta, Director of the TID, and Anura Senanayake, Director of the Colombo Crimes Division.

35. The phrase 'Keenie Meenie' has various explanations. For example, it has been claimed the name comes from Swahili for the movement of a snake through grass.

36. Gunaratne, *Cop in the Crossfire,* op. cit., p.50.

37. Author's interview with Rear Admiral Sarath Weerasekara, MP, February 2012.

38. See, for example, 'My Brothers' Keepers', the *Economist*, 11 February 2012. The magazine estimated that the defence budget (including procurement) would 'top $2 billion'.

39. The author worked (briefly) in the UK's former Defence Procurement Agency. In 2000 it employed around 6,000 people at its HQ in Abbey Wood, outside Bristol. In the author's opinion half that number should have been sacked and the pay of the remaining 50 per cent should have been doubled, and so would have the results.

40. Figures supplied by Gotabaya Rajapaksa, author's interview, February 2012.

41. Ibid.

42. Ibid.

43. Ibid.

44. V. K. Shashikumar, 'Lessons from the War in Sri Lanka', Indian *Defence Review,* 3 October 2009.

45. Author's interview with Lalith Weeratunga, November 2011.

46. Author's interview with President Mahinda Rajapaksa, February 2012.

47. Series of interviews/discussions with the author, 2011/2012.

48. Author's interview, February 2012. For an alternative view of popular culture and the war, see Neloufer de Mel, *Militarizing Sri Lanka: Popular Culture, Memory and Narrative in the Armed Conflict* (Sage, New Delhi, 2007).

49. For an effective analysis of his early years see M. R. Narayan Swamy, *Inside an Elusive Mind: Prabhakaran* (Vijitha Yapa, Colombo, 2008). See also his *Tigers of Lanka* (Vijitha Yapa, Colombo, 2008).

50. There are some interesting parallels with another young boy who also had a sense of his own destiny, who also happened to be a shy and pampered bookworm: see the author's *Mugabe's War Machine* (Pen and Sword, Barnsley, 2011).

51. Author's interview with 'KP', Colombo, September 2011.

52. A useful summary of the war from the perspective of police intelligence can be found in Mahinda Balasuriya, *The Rise and Fall of the LTTE* (Asian Network on Conflict Research, Colombo, 2011). Balasuriya was an Inspector General of Police, who led the Special Task Force and police intelligence.

53. Much of the following data on equipment and numbers comes from government intelligence papers accessed by the author and interviews with various senior intelligence officers. Where other sources disagree, I list them.

54. Paul A. Povlock, 'Guerrilla War at Sea: The Sri Lankan Civil War', *Small Wars Journal*, 9 September 2011.

55. I am indebted to Lieutenant Colonel T. S. Sallay, of Military Intelligence, for the technical information.

56. For a good summary of the diaspora, see Rohan Gunaratna, 'The Impact of the Mobilized Tamil Diaspora on the Protracted Conflict in Sri Lanka' in Kumar Rupesinghe (Ed.) *Negotiating Peace in Sri Lanka,* Vol. One (Foundation for Co-existence, Colombo, 2006).

57. John Solomon and B. C. Tan, 'Feeding the Tiger – How Sri Lankan Insurgents Fund their War', *Jane's Intelligence Review*, 1 August 2007.

58. Various interviews with senior intelligence officials, 2011–12, especially with the officer charged with monitoring the international network, Lieutenant Colonel T. S. Sallay. The Colonel, a highly impressive operative, was also charged with 'handling' K P – an interesting intellectual match.

59. President's conversation with the author, February 2012.

60. C. A. Chandraprema, *Gōta's War: The Crushing of Tamil Tiger*

Terrorism in Sri Lanka (Ranjan Wijeratne Foundation, Colombo, 2012) p.297.

61. For a contemporary and balanced account of this massacre, see: http://www.asianews.it/index.php?l=en&art=6425

62. http://news.bbc.co.uk/1/hi/world/south_asia/6732961.stm

63. After the defeat of the Tigers. The major underground bunker visited was in Puthukudiiripu.

64. http://www.tamilnet.com/art.html?catid=13&artid=24197#

65. Author's interviews with Gotabaya Rajapaksa and separately with the army commander, Lieutenant General Jagath Jayasuriya, February 2012.

66. The Vanni included the districts of Mullaitivu, Vavuniya, Mannar and Kilinochchi. The area is dissected by the A9 highway.

67. Special Infantry Operations Teams (SIOT) by definition did the SIOT training – Special Infantry Operational Training, mentioned earlier.

68. For a full discussion of the role of the Selous Scouts, see Paul Moorcraft and Peter McLaughlin, *The Rhodesian War: A Military History* (Pen and Sword, Barnsley, 2011).

69. Chandraprema, *Gōta's War,* op. cit., p.423. This is an excellent military history but on this point the author appears to be too closely tied to his government intelligence sources.

70. Correspondence with the author, June 2012.

71. http://www.idsa.in/cbwmagazine/ChemicalWeaponsinSriLanka_gulbin

72. Chandraprema, *Gōta's War,* op. cit., p.447.

73. I am indebted to Gordon Weiss for the London analogy. See Gordon Weiss, *The Cage: The Fight for Sri Lanka and the Last days of the Tamil Tigers* (Bodley Head, London, 2011) p.96.

74. Francis A. Boyle, *The Tamil Genocide in Sri Lanka: The Global Failure to Protect Tamil Rights under International Law* (Tamils Against Genocide, Glen Echo, Maryland, 2010).

75. *Dravida Munnethra Kazagam.*

76. For a comparison, see Paul Moorcraft, 'Revolution in Nepal: Can the Nepalese Army Prevent a Maoist Victory?', *RUSI Journal*, October 2006, Vol. 151, No.5, pp.44–50.

77. On one occasion the President invited me into the room alone, perhaps as a mark of hospitality or respect. Other guests remained outside. Luckily, I remembered to take off my shoes in time. Inside we discussed his spiritual views, briefly, and I mentioned that I had just written a novel partly about reincarnation. From this and other conversations, I came away convinced of the sincerity of his religious beliefs.

78. The details of the troika meetings and those with Miliband and Kouchner are based largely upon author's interviews with the President, Gotabaya Rajapaksa and Lalith Weeratunga, as well as senior intelligence officers.

79. For a detailed study of this debate, see Paul Moorcraft and Phil Taylor, *Shooting the Messenger: The Politics of War Reporting,* (Biteback, London, 2011).

80. Weiss, op.cit., p.194.

81. See also, Alex Spillius and Emanuel Stoakes, 'Sri Lanka's leaders ordered killing of surrendering Tamils, says general', the *Daily Telegraph* (UK), 9 September 2011.

82. Fonseka led the National Democratic Front.

83. The Tamil National Alliance won 14 seats.

84. Weiss, op. cit., p.255.

85. Based on interviews with both K P and Gotabaya Rajapaksa as well as the intelligence handler.

86. Figures in Don Wijewardana, *How the LTTE Lost the Eelam War* (Stamford Lake, Pannipitiya, 2010) p.16.

87. Ajith Nivad Cabral, the governor of the Central Bank, in July 2011.

88. *The Economist* , 'My Brothers' Keepers', 11 February 2012.

89. United Nations, *Report of the Secretary-General's Panel of Experts on Accountability in Sri Lanka*, 31 March 2011.

90. University Teachers for Human Rights (Sri Lanka), *Let Them Speak: Truth About Sri Lanka's Victims of War*, Special report No. 34, 13 December 2009.

91. The author spent some time with the de-mining teams working on lifting and defusing the LTTE mines, about as big as a large soup can, in Kumarapuram, August 2011.

92. Simon Harris, 'Sri Lanka: an unsung model for post-conflict security', the *Daily News* (Colombo), 22 February 2012.

93. Weiss, op. cit., p.245.

94. For a useful summary, albeit a pro-government version, of the balance of power between the two main combatants, see Wijewardana, op. cit.

Index